SCIENCE AND INTERNATIONAL AFFAIRS SERIES
Melvyn B. Nathanson, Editor

READINGS IN
COMPARATIVE
CRIMINOLOGY

Edited by Louise I. Shelley

SOUTHERN ILLINOIS UNIVERSITY PRESS
Carbondale and Edwardsville

To Donald and Hester

CONTENTS

Contents

FIGURES

TABLES

xi

Tables

ACKNOWLEDGMENTS

The impetus for this collection was a course I taught on comparative criminology in the spring of 1978. In preparing the reading list for the class, I discovered that there was no book available that addressed the breadth or the many analytical levels of comparative criminology. As a result, I started to compile a set of readings that would reflect the range of subjects suitable for comparative analysis and the most valuable research findings on the relationships among crime, criminal justice, and society.

I gathered together over 75 articles by scholars from different countries on such diverse subjects as homicide, juvenile delinquency, and crime in developing, developed, and socialist societies. The staff of the National Criminal Justice Reference Service, Paul C. Friday, and my teaching assistant, Janet Paull, provided invaluable help in recommending and locating articles.

I owe my first seminar class on comparative criminology my sincere appreciation because their critical comments and focused enthusiasm assisted me in selecting the readings for this collection. I also appreciate the encouragement of my dean, Richard Myren, to pursue the publication of this collection of readings.

I would also like to thank Ted Ferdinand for his suggestions; Dave Farraday for his help with the biographical section; my mother for her editing assistance; Ann Critzer, Joanne Flynn, and Helen Neve for their excellent secretarial help; and the American University Library staff.

LOUISE I. SHELLEY

Washington, D.C.
May, 1980

BIOGRAPHICAL NOTES

PALMER ANDERSON was an inmate of juvenile and adult institutions for a total of 14 years. Following his release, he conducted sociological research at institutions for adult and juvenile offenders, served as a college instructor in a prison educational program, and taught at Humboldt State College in California.

DANE ARCHER is an associate professor of sociology at the University of California, Santa Cruz. He has assembled the 110-nation comparative crime data file from which he has done analyses of the effects of war, unemployment, law, and policy changes on patterns of criminality. His article "Violent Acts and Violent Times" (with Rosemary Gartner) received the Gordon Allport Intergroup Relations Prize.

MARGARET K. BACON is presently a professor of anthropology at Livingston College of Rutgers University in New Brunswick, New Jersey. After receiving her master's and doctorate degrees in psychology from Brown University, she taught at Brown and at Yale University Medical School. She has published extensively on her cross-cultural studies of alcohol consumption and alcoholism.

HERBERT BARRY III is presently a professor in the department of anthropology and in the School of Pharmacy of the University of Pittsburgh. After completing his master's and doctorate degrees in psychology at Yale University, he taught at Yale and the University of Connecticut. His research and publications have centered on cross-cultural studies of the effects of drugs and alcohol. In addition to his numerous publications, Dr. Barry is the managing editor of *Psychopharmacology*.

JOHN CASPARIS is presently an associate professor and director of undergraduate studies in sociology at the State University of New York in Binghamton. He attended the University of North Carolina as an undergraduate and received his Ph.D. from Brown University. He has received awards from the Ford Foundation, the SUNY Foundation, and the Canada Council. His forthcoming book, *Swiss Society and the Youth-Culture*, with Edmund Vaz, represents a continuation of the research included in this collection.

Biographical Notes

IRVIN L. CHILD is presently a professor of psychology at Yale. He taught at Harvard after receiving his Ph.D. in psychology from Yale University. He has served as chairman of numerous professional social science organizations including the presidency of the International Association for Empirical Aesthetics. He has published numerous articles and books on esthetics, personality, and socialization.

EUGENE DOLESCHAL is the director of the Information Center on Crime and Delinquency of the National Council on Crime and Delinquency in Hackensack, New Jersey. He received a bachelor's degree from Benedictine College in Kansas and a master's from Columbia. Associated with the information center since its inception, Eugene Doleschal is responsible for *Criminal Justice Abstracts*. He has authored numerous monographs, literature reviews and articles on criminal justice.

PAUL C. FRIDAY is an associate professor of sociology and director of the Criminal Justice Program at Western Michigan University. He received his doctorate in sociology from the University of Wisconsin. Dr. Friday is currently the president of the Deviance and Social Control Section of the International Sociological Association. He is the author of numerous articles on comparative criminology and corrections as well as the coeditor of *Youth Crime and Juvenile Justice*.

ROSEMARY GARTNER is presently employed at the Institute for Research on Poverty at the University of Wisconsin where she is doing research on a large-scale study of illegal behavior by the 600 largest corporations as well as a study of how an employment program affects the crime rates of ex-offenders. She is continuing her research on homicide with Dane Archer.

TED ROBERT GURR is the Payson S. Wild Professor of Political Science and chairman of the department at Northwestern University. Since 1964, his research has focused on civil conflict and public order, and in 1968–69 he was co-director of the History Task Force of the National Commission on the Causes and Prevention of Violence. For this commission T. R. Gurr and Hugh D. Graham published the report *Violence in America: Historical and Comparative Perspectives*. His 1970 book, *Why Men Rebel*, received the American Political Science Association's award for the year's best political science book. He is also the author of approximately a dozen other articles and books.

JERALD HAGE is the chairman of the Division of Behavioral and Social Science at the University of Maryland. After receiving his Ph.D. in sociology from Columbia University in 1963, he taught at the University of Wisconsin as well as conducting research at La Maison de Science de L'Homme in Paris. He has published numerous articles and five books including *Techniques and Problems of Theory Construction in Sociology* and *Social Change in Complex Organizations*.

Biographical Notes

MARIA LOS is a research fellow at the faculty of Law, University of Sheffield, England. She received her master's and doctorate degrees from the University of Warsaw. Maria Los has studied and lectured in the United States on a Ford Foundation grant and in Europe. Her articles and books, written in several languages, encompass a wide field of sociological thought, from sociotechnics to the sociology of law.

WOLF MIDDENDORF is currently a judge of the traffic court of Freiburg, West Germany, as well as a professor of criminal psychology at the University of Freiburg. He is also a lecturer on criminology at the State Police School and a member of the Max-Planck Institute, in charge of historical and traffic criminology. Wolf Middendorf has authored approximately 20 books and numerous articles in criminology.

LOUISE I. SHELLEY is an assistant professor in the School of Justice, American University. She has her master's in criminology and her Ph.D. in sociology from the University of Pennsylvania. Louise Shelley studied at the law faculty of Moscow State University while on IREX and Fulbright-Hays fellowships. She is the author of several articles on problems of Soviet criminality.

RITA J. SIMON is the director of the Law and Society Program and professor of Law and Communications Research at the University of Illinois. Since gaining her Ph.D. from the University of Chicago, she has written extensively on law and sociology. Dr. Simon is presently the editor of the *American Sociological Review*. Among her publications are *The Jury and the Defense of Insanity* and *Women in Crime and the Criminal Justice System*.

JACKSON TOBY received his master's degree and doctorate from Harvard University. Since 1951, he has taught at Rutgers University in New Brunswick, New Jersey, where he is a professor of sociology. He served as consultant for the Ford Foundation's Youth Development Program and on the President's Commission on Law Enforcement and the Administration of Justice. Jackson Toby has conducted research on adolescent delinquency in the United States, Sweden, Japan, and other countries. His publications include many articles and two books, *Social Problems in America* and *Contemporary Sociology*.

EDMUND W. VAZ teaches at the University of Waterloo in Canada. He received his bachelor's and master's degrees from McGill University and a doctorate in sociology from Indiana University in 1965. He has conducted research in Europe, the United States, and Canada; and his articles have appeared in various scholarly journals. Among his books are *Aspects of Deviance* and *Crime and Delinquency in Canada*, coauthored with Abdul Lodhi.

HOWARD ZEHR, an associate professor of humanities and history, also serves as codirector of the Social Science and Law Project at Talladega College, Alabama. He holds a doctorate from Rutgers University in modern European history. His research in Germany and France culminated in the publication of *Crime and Development in Modern Society: Patterns of Criminality in Nineteenth Century Germany and France*. Howard Zehr is currently on leave from Talladega and is working as the director of the House of Simon, a halfway house for prisoners in Elkhart, Indiana.

INTRODUCTION

LOUISE I. SHELLEY

Crime has existed nearly universally throughout all of recorded history. No major society has been exempt from the problem and no major culture has been able to eliminate criminality. The search for explanations of its universality and tenacity makes crime an ideal candidate for comparative analysis. The pervasiveness of this social problem suggests that crime is inextricably connected with the society in which it exists and that no aspect of society can be ignored in probing the phenomenon of crime. In the words of a distinguished criminologist, "crime is not merely an individual act; it is also a reflection of rapidly changing contextual conditions. Each crime has therefore to be seen in the setting of its own time." [1]

For crime to be understood in terms of the social forces that shape it, it must be studied comparatively. Only comparative criminology can explain the impact of different political, social, and economic conditions on the levels and forms of criminality. Research in one society and one time period cannot hope to explain all aspects of crime, which is itself a barometer of the changing social order.

Comparative criminology is the historical and cross-cultural study of crime and criminal justice. It analyzes the dynamics of criminality and the social response to criminality in different regions and cultures of one country and across countries and historical periods. Comparative criminology studies crime as a social phenomenon determined by the legal norms and customs of each society. It allows research at numerous analytical levels ranging from the individual offense and offender to overall crime trends and criminal justice systems. As comparative criminology elucidates the relationships between crime and society, it will be answering some of the larger questions about the nature of social order.

Comparative criminology can address the issues of the relationship between social, political, and economic conditions and crime by determining if certain explanations of criminal behavior are unique to a particular society or have more universal applicability.[2] The conclusions of this research serve the needs of both theoreticians who seek to develop explanations of criminality and policymakers who desire improved crime prevention and criminal justice.

While sociologists since the time of Durkheim have recognized the desirability and utility of comparative analysis, the criminological community has been slower to acknowledge this need. Even though the insights it provides into the nature of crime and its relationship to society should be central to any studies of criminality, comparative criminology is rarely taught in the criminological justice community and criminologists worldwide have been slow to understand the centrality of comparative studies. As a result, the subject has only risen to academic visibility since World War II.

Before World War II world criminology was dominated by the European school, which employed medical-biological, psychological, and legalistic approaches to crime. Human traits and individual responsibility dominated research as criminologists analyzed the individual offender rather than the criminogenic aspects of society. This focus on the criminal required little contact with the larger world beyond the laboratory, hospital, or library. Furthermore, research using biological, psychological, and legal methodologies was conducted primarily within one society and one time period with little attention paid to the crime patterns of other societies in various epochs of history.

With the emergence of the American sociological school of crime in the prewar period, criminological research shifted from its previous emphasis on the criminal to a new emphasis on the contribution of the social and political order of society to criminality.

As the American sociological school gained increasing international recognition and the testability of its theories was recognized, interest in comparative criminology developed significantly.[3] The new interest in the international applicability of criminological theory, combined with the increased mobility of scholars after World War II, has resulted in the emergence of comparative criminology in the past 25 years.

At present comparative criminology is based primarily on a social explanation of crime. If criminology were still based on a biological or mechanistic explanation of criminality, as it was in much of Europe prior to World War I, there would be no need for historical and cross-cultural research that compares the experiences of different cultures and societies. Instead, the study of criminality would be restricted to a purely physical examination of groups of offenders of different social, ethnic, and religious backgrounds. The majority of criminologists, however, now accept the assumption that crime is inherent in the structure of society and that crime patterns and changes in criminality can be ascribed largely to social, political, and economic conditions of society. As a result, the central theme of comparative criminology becomes the comparison and evaluation of the effects of different social conditions on the form and extent of criminality and the structure of the criminal justice system used to address the problem.

While this important theme is present in almost all studies included in this collection, such a broad focus has not been representative of much recent research. The comparative criminological research that has appeared in recent decades has in many cases been narrowly conceived. It has not used the historical and cross-cultural method to study the relationship between crime and society but has instead focused on small-scale problems. These research studies have compared different theoretical approaches to crime, have provided simple descriptions of the crime phenomenon, and have conducted replication studies of primarily American theories in different societies.[4]

These limited studies should not dominate comparative criminological research. Instead of focusing on analyses done in one country or tests of theories based on the limited experience of a single society, researchers should make comparisons across societies and historical periods. Such broadly based studies are more likely to answer the central question of criminology: What is the relationship between crime and social forces?

Comparative criminology, based on the crime experiences of different cultures and historical periods, transcends the one-dimensional explanations of criminality rooted in the unique characteristics of an individual society or a particular time period. It allows explanations of criminality not solely in terms of the individual offender and the community but in terms of the society that formed the offender, caused the behavior, and conditioned the institutional response to it. Furthermore, crime is inextricably linked to the society in which it exists, explanations will provide insight into the society as a whole.

Scholars engaged in comparative criminology have a difficult task. They are required to integrate knowledge from different disciplines, historical periods, and cultures. The rewards of this effort are significant as the results of this research will expand our knowledge of the phenomenon of crime and the conditions that underlie criminal behavior.

RESEARCH METHODS

The need for comparative criminology has been recognized, but the means to accomplish its ambitious objectives are still not firmly established. No cohesive methodology for field research or theory construction has been delineated despite recent attempts by scholars to determine the appropriate parameters and problems. Consequently, the methodology of this developing field has integrated techniques from other disciplines and is characterized by a wide-ranging approach seeking to gain from the experience of others and to incorporate that experience. The methodological problems associated with this discipline have been sufficient to discourage many from attempting research in this area.

Comparative criminologists, motivated by the desire to explore the multidimensional question of the relationship of crime to society, have been forced to pursue an interdisciplinary perspective. They must draw on the extensive comparative experience of scholars in related fields, discussed in this section, and apply their research methods to the study of crime in different societies and time periods.

Comparative criminology incorporates the research perspectives of historians, legal scholars, and social scientists in all disciplines. The articles included in this collection were written by scholars trained as lawyers, sociologists, psychologists, anthropologists, and historians. Their different training results in the application of different techniques and insights into the problem of crime, thereby facilitating the search for more universal explanations of criminality than have heretofore been developed.

> Comparative methodology may be classified into three categories with definite advantages and disadvantages: comparative case studies, comparative analysis of statistical and archival data, and original comparative studies employing standardized (usually survey) methods. The selection of any of these approaches has depended upon the researchers, general goals and particular local conditions.[5]

The broad range of research techniques used by the contributors to this collection represents the variety of methods that can be applied to comparative criminological research. The Vaz and Casparis study of middle-class delinquency in Canada and Switzerland is based on a controlled research study administered by questionnaire to youths in both societies. Los and Anderson conducted and analyzed observational research on American and Polish prison life. Jackson Toby, in his study of affluence and adolescent crime, drew heavily on interviews with youthful offenders in Japan, Switzerland, and Israel. Zehr, Gurr, and Middendorf relied on historical and archival materials of both criminal statistics and criminal cases. The only study that analyzes contemporary crime figures from numerous countries is the United Nations survey. Other studies included in the collection apply the research methods used by sociologists to integrate theory based on quantitative studies of other researchers. The Hage and Friday article on youth crime in postindustrial society and Simon's article on women and crime are representative of this sociological research synthesis.

Each of the techniques used by the scholars has inherent problems that are frequently compounded by the introduction of different societies and cultures into the analytical framework. Sample sizes may be too small; individuals interviewed may be unrepresentative of the population under examination; cultural bias may be reflected in already recorded data; and the researcher analyzing secondary sources must contend with both analytical and statistical bias in the published research.

Despite the inherent problems in the application of the research methods cited to comparative analysis, the insight and knowledge of the criminologists pertaining to the society, period, and criminological problem under study may help overcome some of the inherent research biases. As a result, the methods used by the scholars whose papers are included in this collection can help assess whether certain crime and criminal justice patterns are universal or are attributable to the characteristics of individual societies. By incorporating the analytical components of the different disciplines, analysts of criminality can examine the phenomenon in the broadest possible terms. The studies included in this book have examined crime in different societies and time periods as influenced by political and legal structure, level and type of economic development, social and religious institutions, and national and ethnic characteristics. Such secondary variables as per capita income, social class, education, unemployment, health, longevity and birth rate, child raising, and socialization patterns have also been considered in these complex analyses. All of these variables have been shown to have an effect on criminality in at least one society that has been studied, while others have been shown to have nearly universal effects on the forms and kinds of criminality manifested.

Introduction

RESEARCH PROBLEMS

The problems of comparative criminology extend beyond those of selecting the appropriate research technique and analyzing the research findings without significant cultural bias. Criminological research executed in a comparative context also requires increased complexity in research design. While the research variables and methods of comparative criminology do not differ significantly from those of ordinary criminology, research designs must incorporate the added dimensions of different historical periods and cultures.

The added complexity places scholars in a serious dilemma. They can engage in meaningful research only with a full understanding of the societies they are studying. This requirement limits the number of countries in which they can conduct research with any level of sophistication and prescribes the range of scholarship possible for an individual comparative criminologist.

The dilemma of comparative criminologists is compounded by the requirement that research be conducted in terms of the multiple social forces that may have an impact on crime. The complexity of the relationship between crime and society precludes the possibility of simple offender and offense comparisons without attention to these forces. Thus, comparative criminological research, if it is to produce meaningful results, must use the researchers' intimate knowledge of the cultures and countries being studied in order to select the numerous societal variables to be incorporated into the analysis. The close interrelationships among these variables reduce the possibility of deriving clear-cut relationships between crime and the social, political, and economic structure of society. A reduction in the number of societal variables incorporated into a research design is, however, undesirable because the intentional or inadvertent omission of important characteristics of a particular society from a research study may jeopardize the ultimate value of the findings. Thus, scholars engaged in comparative criminological research must have both in-depth knowledge of the countries (or eras) they are studying and the ability to work with numerous societal variables simultaneously. These two demands are formidable, but essential to research of high quality.

These increased research demands combined with general statistical and definitional problems place substantial barriers before those intent upon engaging in comparative criminological research. Their research problems can be summarized in the following way:

Introduction

There are two general classes of problems faced by social scientists engaged in cross-national research. The first may be considered a straightforward extension of domestic methodological difficulties; the other, conditions peculiar to conducting research in a foreign country. Both problems must be dealt with before the question of whether such research is a realistic goal or fanciful illusion can be answered.[6]

When scholars move outside their own society, their research problems are intensified as they encounter problems in establishing their credibility and finding acceptance as well as lack of access to crucial materials.[7] The cross-cultural problems are particularly acute in the case of research on crime where findings rarely reflect favorably on the host country.[8] Because their research findings are unwelcome in countries that are sensitive to questions of internal order, comparative criminologists are frequently limited to the study of available crime data or to study in countries that make themselves accessible to foreign scholars. Scholars producing research on these atypical countries that frequently have less serious crime problems and/or more open political systems must be aware that their research findings may not be fully representative of international crime patterns or criminal justice systems.

The profound understanding of crime and criminal justice that can be obtained from the comparative study of criminality helps overcome many of the theoretical and methodological opponents of this perspective. Moreover, criminologists interested in comparative research often find ways of compensating for some of the serious research impediments they encounter. The writings of some of the scholars included in this collection demonstrate that there are several feasible methods of overcoming the problems of limited research access, uncertain data requirements, and research bias—all of which scholars frequently encounter when engaged in research in an alien society.

One way to overcome inherent research problems is to have research conducted jointly by scholars from different societies. Two articles in this collection—the one by Vaz and Casparis and the other by Los and Anderson—represent this form of collaborative research. Together Vaz and Casparis decided on necessary data elements and then formulated questionnaires used in their study of Swiss and Canadian youth. Each used his own national experience to produce the data analysis. Los and Anderson compared their previous observations of American and Polish prisons to establish similarities and differences in inmate culture and status. Sustained access to a Polish prison would be almost impossible for a foreign researcher to obtain, but the coupling of a foreign and a Polish scientist made their cross-cultural comparison on prison society feasible.

The work of other researchers included in this collection demonstrates other means of dealing with the problems of cultural bias and impediments to data collection that are so prominent in cross-cultural research. Researchers can confine their observations to historical material, as Zehr does in his article on crime in France and Germany; or they can analyze secondary sources written by reputable scholars familiar with the crime problems of their own countries. My article on urbanization in the U.S.S.R. and the Doleschal study of European criminology are representative of this second approach. Scholars can also employ researchers from other countries as did Gurr in his historical and cross-cultural study of the development of crime and criminal justice in three cities.

Scholars engaged in research studies based on historical, archival, and secondary data have different problems from those who collect their own statistics. Researchers using secondary materials must be careful to appraise accurately the work of those who have done the original field research and to understand the methodological and interpretative problems that might be incorporated into their data. In interpreting research results, these scholars must also be careful not to impose their personal biases and values upon the research conclusions.

There are certain problems that confront all researchers who are engaged in comparative criminological research whether they are collecting their own data or analyzing those of others. These problems concern the definitions of criminal offenses, the comparability of research findings, and the availability and accuracy of statistics.

The major data problems encountered by statistical researchers are definitional, administrative, and perceptive. No two societies or historical periods define crime in exactly the same way or single out the same forms of behavior as criminal. Legal definitions of crime are determined by the mores of society, and as its social values change, so do the acts characterized as criminal and the ways in which they are described under the law. The accuracy of crime reports and the stage in the judicial process at which they are collected and analyzed affect the level of criminality observed in a particular society. The societal perception of the seriousness of different offenses varies among different countries; thus, while the same phenomenon may be observed in many different socie-

Introduction

ties, its appearance may have a different significance depending on the degree of dangerousness the society attributes to the particular offense.[9]

Problems of comparability of data are further increased by the general administrative problems associated with the collection, compilation, and dissemination of statistics. Variations exist in the administrative efficiency of the police, the degree of centralization,[10] the comprehensiveness of crime statistics, and the means by which crime reports are made available to the public and criminal justice professionals.

The variation in the availability and reliability of statistics is well illustrated by contrasting the Nordic countries and the U.S.S.R. The small, relatively homogeneous countries of Scandinavia with their sophisticated criminal justice systems have particularly fine techniques for collecting and reporting statistics; whereas the large, complex, and highly secretive Soviet Union collects decentralized crime statistics that are not available to the public and are accessible only to a few highly trusted professionals.

The poor quality and lack of comparability among available crime statistics suggest that scholars should collect their own data. As was previously mentioned, scholars are, however, often forced to limit their efforts to officially collected crime statistics because many countries have prohibited or would prohibit researchers from obtaining primary statistics by means of field research.

Even when researchers have data available, they are confronted by the problem of comparability of research findings. Scholars should be careful not to compare apples and oranges, but to allow for societal variations that will be reflected in criminal statistics. Societal variations that may affect the comparability of data are the size, density, and homogeneity of the population; the sophistication of the criminal justice system; and the legal definitions of criminal acts. Only if scholars consider that all crime statistics may not be measuring the same phenomenon will it be possible for them to formulate significant results.

While the availability of internationally comparable and reliable data is desirable, several studies included in this collection demonstrate that good research providing explanations of criminality can be developed without comprehensive criminal statistics. The studies by Friday and Hage and by Jackson Toby explain juvenile delinquency in terms of the social and economic order using limited criminological data and emphasizing general social indicators instead. The Simon article on the female criminal and my article on Soviet urbanization in a comparative context also demonstrate the ability to develop sound explanations of criminality without access to extensive data. While their research conclusions might have been further enhanced if data had been available, the absence of data did not preclude serious analysis and the formulation of valuable tentative conclusions.

Few scholars have the opportunity to collect extensive crime data in foreign countries and even more rarely do they have access to reliable international crime statistics. Two notable exceptions to this generalization are included in this collection. The research by Bacon, Child, and Barry on correlates of crime in preliterate societies and the first United Nations crime survey are both based on rarely available research data. The analysis made in these studies can be used to corroborate the more speculative findings made in research where data were not as readily available.

The serious methodological problems present in comparative criminal justice research are compensated for by the insight it provides into the relationship among crime, criminal justice, and society.

THE SUBJECT OF COMPARATIVE CRIMINOLOGY

The articles included in this collection of readings provide a broad survey of the methods and the problems associated with comparative criminological research as well as a range of subjects for comparative analysis. The historical and cross-cultural comparisons included span all levels of analytical complexity from the most simple offense comparisons to complex studies of crime trends for several offenses across different countries and historical periods.

The studies included represent the full range of research objectives. While certain studies work at the broadest level of comparative criminology and attempt to establish and verify theories that explain international variations in criminality and determine universally applicable explanations of crime, other articles focus instead on comparisons of judicial and penal practice and on criminological research. All of these areas exemplify comparative criminology, and all of these levels and forms of analysis are needed to develop general explanations of crime and the societal response to criminality.

No overall explanation of criminality emerges from the articles included in the collection. Instead each one contributes to an understanding of the relationship between crime and society. Together they reveal the broad range of topics that are necessary to provide insight into the two focal problems of comparative criminology: the effect that society and its criminal justice systems have on crime and the impact that crime has on society.

The book is divided in terms of the research subject rather than research methodology in order to demonstrate the range of subjects and analytical levels that are suitable for comparative analysis. There are two sections. In the first, comparisons are made in terms of one variable: age, sex, or a single offense. In the second, crime and criminal justice are analyzed in terms of several variables: crime trends for several offenses, crime patterns in relationship to stage and form of economic development, or the societal response to crime. Examples are provided of different levels of analysis within each category.

The articles included in the first section are representative of analysis done in terms of one dependent variable. Two types of offender comparisons are included, comparisons in terms of age and of sex. Offender comparisons in terms of economic position, social position, and nationality, while feasible, have not been the subject of much research; therefore, no representative sample of this research is included.

Comparative research in terms of sex has only recently been developed. In the past most criminological research has focused on the crimes of male offenders, and very little attention has been paid to the criminality of women. The recently published research on the crimes of women has generally been comparative and has analyzed the form and extent of their criminality in relationship to that of men. So far, the research has already demonstrated that comparative criminology is the most desirable method of studying female criminality. In the research on sexual differences, the comparative approach has begun to explain the impact of economic and social conditions on criminality.

Simon's article on women and crime is representative of the sophisticated comparative research presently conducted on sexual differences in criminality. While her article addresses female criminality in the United States, she makes historical and cross-cultural comparisons to reach her conclusions concerning the impact that the new active economic role of American women will have on their increased participation in property crime.

The recent interest in female criminality is insignificant when compared to the sustained research efforts that have been devoted to understanding cultural differences in juvenile delinquency. A disproportionate amount of comparative criminological research has been devoted to the patterns and causes of youth crime. The extent of international research on the youthful offender may be partly explained by the influence of American criminological theory with its pronounced emphasis on juvenile delinquency and by the greater availability of funds for the study of youthful offenders.

The three essays included here on juvenile delinquency are chosen from a large group of relevant studies as representative of the most significant attempts to explain the interaction of juvenile delinquency and social forces in terms of economic development, familial and peer influences, and the impact of social and religious institutions. The Friday and Hage and the Toby studies on juvenile delinquency in modern affluent societies and the Vaz and Casparis study of middle-class delinquency demonstrate consistently that in modern affluent society, youth crime develops to the greatest extent when familial control is relinquished to peers. Although comparative juvenile delinquency theory and research have greatly advanced the understanding of the relationship between society and youthful criminal behavior, comparative research has failed to study the impact of the criminal justice system on juvenile delinquents; and the result is an absence of knowledge about the comparative value of different measures to control juvenile delinquency.

The second form of analysis made in terms of one variable is analysis by offense. Homicide is most frequently chosen as the subject of such studies because of its universality, the international similarities in definition, and the general cross-cultural agreement on the severity of the offense. The study of homicide chosen for this collection is just one of many studies that examine this offense in relationship to war or to the administration of justice and in terms of national and regional variations in the frequency and character of homicide.

The Gartner and Archer article on homicide in 110 nations is one of a series of articles that they have written using extensive international criminological data to examine the relationship between homicide rates and different forms of social change. In this article they analyze urban homicide data for a diverse body of nations and compare the usefulness of homicide data with that of data on other offenses as an indicator of national crime trends. The authors conclude that, although homicide is the best indicator, other offenses can also be used for analytical purposes. Homicide rates, according to Archer and Gartner, are determined not by a city's size but by the level of urbanization of that particular community relative to the surrounding areas. Urbanization is, therefore, a relative not an absolute phenomenon.

Introduction

In the second part of the book crime is analyzed in terms of several variables under three distinct headings. In the first, crime trends are discussed in relationship to historical and social developments; the second section analyzes crime in relationship to different forms and levels of economic development; and the third consists of three quite different forms of societal response to crime. The articles included in this last section represent the societal response in terms of the criminal justice and legislative system, means used to confine crime (the correctional system), and the types of research done in different societies to understand the problem of crime.

The two essays included in the section on crime trends are among the very few pieces written to explain historical crime trends cross-culturally. Gurr examines the development of crime in three cities, while Zehr performs a similar analysis for two entire countries. Both choose to study roughly comparable historical periods and examine the impact of industrialization, urbanization, rapid social change, and the criminal justice system on levels and forms of criminal behavior.

Gurr's study of three cities in different countries has been more fully documented in several books he has written on the subject.[11] All of his works record a significant decrease in threatening social behavior in the second half of the nineteenth century and the early part of the twentieth century, followed by a rise in the crime rate in the period following World War II. Although he draws no dramatic conclusions from these observations, he comments that actual changes in patterns of criminal behavior occurred independently of changes in the methods, structure, and practice of crime recording in the criminal justice system. Gurr also comments that his results were applicable to the rest of English society outside London and that data from France corroborate his general findings. Zehr who has done a comparative study of Germany and France in the period from 1830 to 1913 develops results that conflict with Gurr and with other definitive statements on the relationship between social forces and crime. His main statistical conclusion is that crime rates rose on the whole in the nineteenth century, an increase that continues into the first part of the twentieth century. He concludes from his study of violent and property crime that urbanization and urban growth do not necessarily result in crime. The rise in observed crime should be ascribed not to a breakdown in the social structure but to the modernization of criminal behavior that transpired as a result of the transition from rural to urban society. Zehr concludes that increasing crime was a response to the conflicts and pressures of modern urban life.

Introduction

The first article in the next section on crime and economic development discusses urbanization and crime in the Soviet Union in a comparative context. In it I find that in the Soviet Union, as in many other societies, urbanization is directly correlated with higher levels of crime. In the U.S.S.R., however, unlike other developed societies, crime is not concentrated in the most urban areas. This is a direct result of the controls on population mobility that displace but do not reduce the problem of crime. These controls, not found in the United States or other developed countries where there is free movement of the population within the nation's boundaries, result in a different geographical distribution of criminality.

The United Nations crime survey that follows is the first comprehensive study of world crime patterns, incorporating crime statistics from over 60 nations representing all continents. The range of participating countries permits crime analysis both in terms of the level of economic development and regional distribution. In developed countries, criminologists attribute the recent rise in crime to social and economic developments, while, in developing countries, criminologists cite social and economic inequality, lack of opportunity, and poor and uneven planning among the many complex factors contributing to the recent increases in criminality. Significant differences in crime patterns are found between societies that are already urbanized and those that are undergoing urbanization. Independent of variations in crime patterns, there is general consensus among the countries participating in the crime survey that crime is a threat to the social order and a serious deterrent to the realization of larger social objectives.

The study of cross-cultural correlates of crime, by three psychologists, that comes next is one of the few studies to examine the types of crime and the impact of society on crime in preliterate societies lacking formal measures of criminality. The analysis suggests that certain social attributes are correlated with criminality. For example, a high degree of differentiation of social status is correlated with a high degree of theft, while a high frequency of personal crime is associated with a general societal attitude of distrust. The study succeeds in isolating social and familial influences on criminality from those of the economic and political order.

The preceding essays in part two of the book analyze crime in relationship to numerous social variables and conclude that crime is a social phenomenon that results from the interaction of forces on the larger societal level and the more intimate familial and personal level. These essays demonstrate that social, economic, and political conditions have an impact on criminality but that the exact nature of their effect has yet to be described.

The next set of articles analyzes the societal reaction to crime in terms of treatment of the offender and the study of criminality. The Middendorf essay on the case of August Sangret discusses the impact that legislative changes and judicial procedure have had on the treatment of certain forms of criminal behavior. Middendorf discusses the relationship of the evidence presented at the murder trial to the sentence awarded to Sangret. The author concludes that if the trial had occurred during a later period when the definition of criminal insanity was established and universally accepted, the consequence of the trial would have been different.

The Los and Anderson article compares prison cultures in Polish and American prisons and demonstrates that the same method of treating offenders, incarceration, produces very different results in the two societies. In the Polish inmate culture, the status of offenders is fixed early in their career of institutional confinement, while in American prisons, institutional roles are not as rigidly determined by previous periods of incarceration. The implications of this research are that administrators in Poland and the United States must assume different institutional management policies as a result of the different structures of inmate life in these two countries.

The final essay examines the academic response to the problems of crime, through criminological research recently conducted in Europe. Its analysis demonstrates that the use of the comparative method is almost entirely absent from European criminological research and that their present studies continue to focus as much on the individual offender as on the impact of social forces on criminality. Few exceptions to this pattern were found to include in this collection.

The articles in this last section show that crime has elicited a similar response in many societies. While criminal justice systems and crime research exist internationally, historical and cultural differences produce variations in both the administration and the study of justice. Middendorf discusses historical changes in judicial policy in one society, and Los and Anderson demonstrate that externally similar criminal justice institutions may differ internally as a result of national characteristics. These essays lead to the conclusion that, like crime itself, the institutions that have arisen to study and control crime reflect the social conditions in which they exist.

Introduction

The articles included in this collection demonstrate that crime is a phenomenon common to both preliterate and highly developed societies and that social forces shape the extent and form of the observed criminality and criminal justice systems. They show that crime and the societal reaction to criminality must be examined in terms of economic, political, and social conditions. The discipline of comparative criminology has not, however, advanced to the degree that it can explain or predict the relative impact of these different social forces on crime. Further explanation and elucidation of the relationship among society, crime, and criminal justice institutions are the future agenda of comparative criminology. The parameters of the discipline have been illustrated by the articles in this book; future research must more clearly define and develop its theories.

PART ONE

OFFENDER AND OFFENSE COMPARISON

Comparison by Sex

I

American Women and Crime

RITA J. SIMON

EDITOR'S COMMENT: *The trends in female criminality and victimization that Rita Simon noted through the beginnings of the 1970s have been continued during the rest of the decade. In 1974, women were responsible for 24 percent of type I offenses (criminal homicide, robbery, aggravated assault, burglary, larcency/theft, auto theft) while by 1975 their share had risen to 25 percent. Their contribution to serious property offenses increased even more than their commission rates for violent criminality. Female commission rates in the mid-1970s continued to increase dramatically for arson, forgery and counterfeiting, fraud, and offenses against children and family. However, the earlier rise in female embezzlement seems to have declined after having reached a peak of 35 percent of all cases of embezzlement in 1974.*

Simon's conclusions concerning the nature of female criminality remain valid. The crimes of women are still confined primarily to larcency, embezzlement, fraud, and forgery. Though women contribute increasingly to several categories of violent crime, they are still responsible for only a small share of homicides and assaults.

On the occasion of the Hamlyn Lectures at Sheffield University, in 1963, Lady Barbara Wooton observed:

> It is perhaps rather curious that no serious attempt has yet been made to explain the remarkable facts of the sex ratio in detected criminality;

for the scale of the sex differential far outranks all the other traits (except that of age in the case of indictable offenses) which have been supposed to distinguish the delinquent from the nondelinquent population. It seems to be one of those facts which escape notice by virtue of its very conspicuousness. It is surely, to say the least, very odd that half the population should be apparently immune to the criminogenic factors which lead to the downfall of so significant a proportion of the other half. Equally odd is it, too, that although the criminological experience of different countries varies considerably, nevertheless the sex differential remains.[1]

Much has happened in the dozen or so years since Lady Wooton made these remarks. The main thrust of this article will be to describe those changes, to explain why they have occurred, and to make some prognoses about their implications for the future.

The topic, women and crime, is currently enjoying a wave of interest unknown at any previous time. Interest in the female offender is, I believe, a specific manifestation of the increased general interest and attention that women have been receiving since the latter part of the 1960s. Women themselves have been largely responsible for their increased notoriety. Having organized into a visible and vocal social movement, whose objectives are the attainment of greater freedom and more responsibility, they have also succeeded in drawing attention to themselves. One of the consequences of this attention has been to question and to research many aspects of women's roles that have hitherto been of little interest or concern to social scientists, clinicians, and law enforcement officials.

The movement for woman's liberation has changed a lot of things about women's reality; and it has been at least partially responsible for changes in women's behavior vis-à-vis criminal activities, as well as scholars' perceptions of the types of women who are likely to engage in crime. In 1966, Rose Giallombardo characterized the image of the woman offender as follows: "Women who commit criminal offenses tend to be regarded as erring and misguided creatures who need protection and help rather than as dangerous criminals from whom members of society should be protected."[2] How similar that sounds to the observations of the Gluecks, who wrote, in 1934: "The women are themselves on the whole a sorry lot. The major problem involved in the delinquency and criminality of our girls is their lack of control of their sexual impulses."[3] How strange these observations sound when one notes that in 1970, 4 of the FBI's 10 most wanted fugitives were women. Daniel Green, writing a few months ago in the *National Observer*, commented:

Before the advent of militant feminism, female radicals were little more than groupies in the amorphous conglomeration of revolutionary and anti-war groups that came to be known collectively in the '60s as The Movement. Like camp followers of old, they functioned principally as cooks, flunkies, and sex objects. Sexual equality came to the Movement in the gas-polluted streets of Chicago during the '68 Democratic Convention. Enraged by the tactics of Mayor Daley's police, Middle American daughters raised for gentler things shrieked obscenities and hurled rocks as ferociously as veteran street fighters. From then on, guerrilla women were dominant figures in the splintered Movement, particularly the defiantly militant Weatherman faction, which they purged of "macho sexism" and renamed the Weather Underground.[4]

What role has the woman's liberation movement played in changing both the image of the female offender and the types of criminal activities that she is likely to commit? The rhetoric of the woman's movement has emphasized similarity between the sexes. Kate Millett, for example, argues that all of the significant behavioral differences between the sexes are those that have been developed by culture, environment, and sexist training.[5] Others in the movement have emphasized that women are no more moral, conforming, or law-abiding than men. They have urged their sisters to neither bask in feelings of superiority nor entrap themselves into wearing masks of morality and goodness.

In their contacts with law enforcement officials, women in the movement are prepared to trade preferential and paternalistic treatment for due process in civil and criminal procedures. Movement lawyers have claimed that women defendants pay for judges' beliefs that it is more in man's nature to commit crimes than it is in woman's. Thus they argue that when a judge is convinced that the woman before him has committed a crime, he is more likely to overreact and punish her, not only for the specific offense, but also for transgressing against his expectations of womanly behavior.

The existence of such statutes as the "indeterminate sentence" for woman, or the sanctioning of a procedure whereby only convicted male defendants have their minimum sentences determined by a judge at an open hearing and in the presence of counsel, while the woman's minimum sentence is decided by a parole board in a closed session in which she is not represented by counsel, are cited as evidence of the unfair, punitive treatment that is accorded to women in the court.[6]

The position that some supporters of the Equal Rights Amendment (ERA) have taken vis-à-vis prisons also illustrates the willingness of the woman's movement to accept the responsibilities of equality. The movement recognizes that the stereotypes that are held of women in the larger society provide some advantages to female inmates. For example, physically, penal institutions for women are usually more attractive and more pleasant than the security-oriented institutions for men. The institutions tend to be located in more pastoral settings; and they are not as likely to have the gun towers, the concrete walls, and the barbed wire that so often characterize institutions for men. Women inmates usually have more privacy than men. They tend to have single rooms; they may wear street clothes rather than prison uniforms; they may decorate their rooms with such things as bedspreads and curtains, that are provided by the prison. Toilet and shower facilities also reflect a greater concern for women's privacy. Advocates of ERA have written that they would eliminate these differentials by subjecting both men and women to the same physical surroundings in sexually integrated institutions. "Ideally, the equalization would be up to the level presently enjoyed by the women. But, if a State faces an economic roadblock to equalizing up, the ERA would tolerate equalization down to a lower, more economically feasible level."[7]

One of the major goals of the contemporary woman's movement is equal opportunities with men for positions and jobs that carry prestige and authority. While the objectives of the woman's movement of the 1920s were to get women out of their homes and into factories and offices, today success is more likely to be measured by the proportion of women in managerial and professional position, by the proportion of women who have completed college and university, and by the absence of lower salary scales for women who hold the same types of jobs as men.

A review of census data indicates that the gap between men and women who occupy management and professional positions is as great today as it was 25 years ago. In 1948, for example, 29 percent of the women employed in white-collar positions occupied professional and managerial slots; in 1971 the percentage was 33. Among men, in 1948, the proportion of white-collar positions represented in the managerial and professional subcategories was 61 percent; in 1971 it was 70 percent. Between 1950 and 1970, the proportion of women who graduated from college increased by 70 percent; but as of 1971 there were still almost six men for every four women who completed four years of college. On the matter of income, the annual earnings of women between 1956 and 1970 decreased in comparison to those of men (1956:

women—$3,619, men—$5,716; 1970: women—$4,794, men—$8,845).

Notable changes have occurred, however, in the proportion of married women employed on a full-time basis between 1950 and 1970—a shift from 24.8 percent to 41.1 percent—and especially among married women with children of school age (6–17 years), where there has been an increase from 28.3 percent to 49.2 percent.

There is still much to be done before the woman's movement can claim success in achieving equality between men and women in jobs involving occupational prestige and high incomes. But the increase in the proportion of women who hold full-time jobs, the consciousness that the movement's rhetoric has succeeded in raising, along with the changes that have occurred in women's legal rights in such areas as personal property, abortion, and divorce laws, have all contributed to altering women's overall status as well as increasing opportunities and propensities that women have for committing crimes. What changes have already occurred in the area of crime will be described in some detail in the following pages.

WOMEN AS CRIMINALS

Table 1 describes the proportion of women who have been arrested for all crimes, for all serious crimes, and for serious violent and property crimes from 1932 to 1972.[8] The average rates of change in the proportion of women arrested between 1953 and 1972, between 1958 and 1972, and between 1967 and 1972 are also shown here. The last period is particularly crucial because we would expect that during this period the rate of change would be marked by the greatest increase.

The average increase in the proportion of women arrested for serious crimes is greater than the average increase in the proportion of women arrested for all crimes. The data also show that the average rate of increase was greatest in the period from 1967 to 1972—0.52 for all crimes and 0.84 for serious offenses. Note also that from 1961 onward the percentage of women arrested for serious crimes was greater than the percentage of women arrested for all offenses.

The popular impression that in recent years women have been committing crimes of violence at a much higher rate than they have in the past is disputed by the statistics in table 1. In fact, the increase in the proportion of arrests of women for serious crimes is due almost wholly to the increase in property offenses. Indeed, the percentage of women arrested for crimes of violence shows neither an upward nor a down-

Table 1

PERCENTAGE OF FEMALES ARRESTED FOR ALL CRIMES, FOR ALL
SERIOUS CRIMES, AND FOR SERIOUS VIOLENT AND PROPERTY CRIMES:
1932–1972

Year*	All Crimes	Serious Crimes†	Violent Crimes	Property Crimes
1932	7.4	5.8	6.5	5.3
1933	7.2	5.9	7.1	5.2
—	—	—	—	—
1935	6.9	6.0	7.3	5.3
1936	7.3	6.4	8.0	5.7
—	—	—	—	—
1938	6.8	5.4	7.0	4.6
—	—	—	—	—
1942	12.0	8.9	9.8	8.3
1943	16.1	10.1	10.5	9.9
—	—	—	—	—
1946	10.7	7.7	7.7	7.7
1947	10.3	8.0	8.3	7.8
—	—	—	—	—
1949	9.9	8.0	9.9	7.3
1950	9.6	8.1	9.4	7.2
—	—	—	—	—
1953	10.8	9.4	11.9	8.5
1954	10.9	8.9	11.6	8.2
1955	11.0	9.1	12.0	8.4
1956	10.9	9.0	13.5	8.0
1957	10.6	9.3	13.1	8.5
1958	10.6	9.7	11.9	9.3
1959	10.7	10.5	12.7	10.0
1960	11.0	10.9	11.8	10.8
1961	11.3	11.5	11.6	11.4
1962	11.5	12.4	11.5	12.6
1963	11.7	12.7	11.6	12.9

* Not all of the years between 1933 and 1953 are included; but the periods of the Depression, the Second World War, and the immediate postwar years are included in the sample. Between 1933 and 1953, the data reported in tables 1–3 are based on fingerprint records received from local law enforcement officials throughout the United States. They are limited to arrests for violations of state laws and local ordinances. But not all persons arrested are fingerprinted. Beginning in 1953, the system was changed, and the figures from 1953 through 1972 describe all arrests in cities with a population of more than 2,500. While recognizing that the sources for the pre-1953 data are different than those collected later, I think that for purposes of comparison—for example, male versus female arrests—they are worth presenting.

† Serious crimes, according to the U C R published by the FBI, are criminal homicide (murder, nonnegligent manslaughter, and manslaughter by negligence), forcible rape, robbery, aggravated assault, burglary, larceny, and auto theft. We have omitted forcible rape from our calculations because women are never charged with such an offense.

SOURCE: *Uniform Crime Reports* (Washington, D.C.: U.S. Department of Justice, Federal Bureau of Investigation).

1964	11.9	13.5	11.6	13.9
1965	12.1	14.4	11.4	14.9
1966	12.3	14.8	11.3	15.6
1967	12.7	15.0	10.8	16.0
1968	13.1	15.0	10.3	16.1
1969	13.8	16.6	10.6	17.9
1970	14.6	18.0	10.5	19.7
1971	15.0	18.3	10.9	20.1
1972	15.3	19.3	11.0	21.4
Average rate of change (per year) 1953–72	+0.23	+0.52	−0.05	+0.68
Average rate of change 1958–72	+0.35	+0.68	−0.07	+0.86
Average rate of change 1967–72	+0.52	+0.84	+0.04	+1.07

ward trend. The news item that, in 1970, four out of the FBI's most wanted fugitives were women must be juxtaposed against those statistics, which tell quite a different story.

The percentages for property offenses, however, show that big changes have occurred. In 1932, about 1 in every 19 persons arrested was a woman. In 1972, 1 in 4.7 persons arrested was a woman. Not only has there been a consistent increase in the percentage of women who have been arrested for property offenses, but also the biggest increases have occurred in the period beginning in 1967. This last finding is most congruent with our major hypothesis—that women's participation in selective crimes will increase as their employment opportunities expand and as their interests, desires, and definitions of self shift from a more traditional to a more liberated view. The crimes that are considered most salient for this hypothesis are various types of property, financial, and white-collar offenses.

Table 2 describes the percentage of female and male arrests, for serious crimes and for serious property and violent offenses within the total male and female arrests for all crimes.

In 1953, 1 out of 12.8 female arrests was for serious crimes as opposed to 1 out of slightly less than 10.9 male arrests. But two decades later, more women were arrested for serious offenses (about 1 out of 4) than were males (about 1 out of 5). The average rate of change among the women was greater during each of the three periods than it was for

Table 2

FEMALES AND MALES ARRESTED FOR CRIMES OF VIOLENCE AND
PROPERTY AND FOR SERIOUS CRIMES COMBINED, AS PERCENTAGES OF
ALL ARRESTS IN THEIR RESPECTIVE SEX COHORTS: 1953–1972

Year	Violent Crimes		Property Crimes		Serious Crimes	
	Females	Males	Females	Males	Females	Males
1953	2.2	2.0	5.6	7.2	7.8	9.2
1954	2.2	2.1	6.0	8.2	8.2	10.3
1955	2.3	2.1	6.2	8.3	8.5	10.4
1956	2.3	1.9	5.9	8.4	8.2	10.3
1957	2.2	1.8	7.1	9.0	9.3	10.8
1958	2.1	1.9	7.8	9.0	9.9	10.9
1959	2.3	1.9	8.3	8.9	10.6	10.8
1960	2.5	2.4	9.9	10.2	12.4	12.6
1961	2.5	2.4	10.9	10.8	13.4	13.2
1962	2.4	2.4	12.2	10.9	14.6	13.3
1963	2.5	2.4	13.4	12.0	15.9	14.4
1964	2.6	2.6	15.4	13.0	18.0	15.6
1965	2.6	2.7	16.3	12.8	18.9	15.5
1966	2.8	3.0	17.3	13.1	20.1	16.1
1967	2.8	3.2	18.0	13.7	20.8	16.9
1968	2.5	3.5	18.2	14.3	20.7	17.8
1969	2.6	3.6	19.6	14.3	22.2	17.9
1970	2.5	3.6	21.3	14.8	23.8	18.4
1971	2.7	3.2	21.5	15.3	24.2	19.2
1972	2.9	4.4	22.3	14.8	25.2	19.2
Average rate of change, 1953–72	+0.04	+0.13	+0.88	+0.40	+0.92	+0.53
Average rate of change, 1958–72	+0.06	+0.18	+1.04	+0.41	+1.11	+0.59
Average rate of change, 1967–72	+0.02	+0.24	+0.82	+0.22	+0.90	+0.46

NOTE: When the data are examined in this way, only the years in which all
arrests have been recorded are included

SOURCE: *Uniform Crime Reports* (Washington, D.C.: U.S. Department of
Justice, Federal Bureau of Investigation).

the men. But the time span from 1967 to 1972 does not show a greater
increase when compared with time periods that extend farther back. The
percentage increase of men who have been arrested for violent offenses
over the two decades is almost four times the percentage increase for
women. For property offenses, it is the percentage increase for women

who have been arrested that is three times the percentage increase for men.

Studying women's participation in the specific offense categories that are included in the index of serious offenses from 1932 to 1972 (type I offenses), it is possible to note that among all six offenses, only one shows a marked increase over time. After 1960, the proportion of women who have been charged with larceny or theft in any given year is much greater than is the proportion in any of the other offense categories, property as well as violent. It is interesting to note that until about 1960 the proportions of women who were arrested for homicide and aggravated assault were similar to those arrested for larceny, but in 1972 the percentage in the larceny category had almost doubled the 1960 percentages; whereas from 1960 on, the proportions have remained roughly the same for the homicide and aggravated assault offenses.

An analysis of trends in the proportion of women arrested for selected offenses in the type II category[9] reveals that in 1972 approximately 1 in 4 persons arrested for forgery was a woman and 1 in 3.5 arrests for embezzlement and fraud involved a woman. If present trends in these crimes persist, approximately equal numbers of men and women will be arrested for fraud and embezzlement by the 1990s, and for forgery and counterfeiting the proportions should be equal by the 2010s. The prediction made for embezzlement and fraud can be extended to larceny as well. On the other hand, if trends from 1958 to 1972 continue, fewer women will be arrested for criminal homicide and aggravated assault.

In summary the data on arrests indicate the following about women's participation in crime: (1) The proportion of women arrested in 1972 was greater than the proportion arrested one, two, or three decades earlier. (2) The increase was greater for serious offenses than it was for all type I and type II offenses combined. (3) The increase in female arrest rates among the arrest rates for the serious offenses was caused almost entirely by women's greater participation in property offenses, especially in larceny.

The data show that contrary to impressions that might have been gleaned from the mass media, the proportion of females arrested for violent crimes has changed hardly at all over the past three decades. Female arrest rates for homicide, for example, have been the most stable of all violent offenses. Further probing of female arrest rates in the type II offenses revealed that the offenses that showed the greatest increases were embezzlement and fraud and forgery and counterfeiting. The increases were especially marked for the period from 1967 to 1972. None of the other offenses included in either type I or type II, save larceny, showed as big a shift as did these two white-collar offenses. Should the average rate of change that occurred between 1967 and 1972 continue, female arrest rates for larceny/theft, embezzlement, and fraud will be commensurate to women's representation in the society, or, in other words, roughly equal to male arrest rates. There are no other offenses among those contained in the uniform crime reports, save prostitution, in which females are so highly represented.

Two final observations: (1) it is plausible to assume that the police are becoming less "chivalrous" to women suspects and that the police are beginning to treat women more like equals; (2) police behavior alone cannot account for both the large increases in larceny, fraud, embezzlement, and forgery arrests over the past six years and for the lack of increase in arrests for homicide, aggravated assault, and other violent crimes.

The more parsimonious explanation is that as women increase their participation in the labor force their opportunity to commit certain types of crime also increases. As women feel more liberated physically, emotionally, and legally, and less subject to male power, their frustrations and anger decrease. This explanation assumes that women have no greater store of morality or decency than do men. Their propensities to commit crimes do not differ, but, in the past, their opportunities have been much more limited. As women's opportunities increase, so will the likelihood that they will commit crimes. But women will be most likely to commit property, economic, and financial types of offenses. Their greater freedom and independence will result in a decline in their desire to kill the usual objects of their anger or frustration: their husbands, lovers, and other men upon whom they are dependent, but insecure about.

CROSS-NATIONAL ARREST STATISTICS

A brief comparison of female arrest statistics in the United States with those collected by the International Criminal Police Organization for 25 countries all over the world in 1963, 1968, and 1970 shows that the United States moved from eighth place in 1963 to fourth place in 1968 to third place in 1970.

But the heterogeneity of the countries that rank directly above and directly below the United States makes it difficult to draw any conclusions about the types of societies that are conducive to high female arrest rates. Among those countries closest to the United States, there is, on the one hand, the West Indies, Thailand, and Burma; and, on the other hand Portugal, West Germany, Luxembourg, France, Austria, and Great Britain.

Perhaps more sense can be made of the rankings when they are broken by types of offenses. The offense categories that are included in the International Criminal Statistics and their definitions are listed in note 10. Table 3 compares the United States' female arrest statistics with other countries' for offense categories I, III (A and B), IV and VI.[10]

For property and financial crimes—such as larceny, as defined by the FBI statistics, and fraud—the United States ranks second and first, respectively. Countries that rank directly above and below are those of Western Europe such as West Germany, Austria, and the Netherlands. For crimes of violence and drugs, American women rank sixth and seventh and are surrounded by a heterogeneous collection of countries that include the West Indies, New Zealand, West Germany, Scotland, and Canada. The positions of the United States and the countries of Western Europe in the larceny and fraud rankings are consistent with the hypothesis that, in those societies in which women are more likely to be employed in commercial and white-collar positions and to enjoy legal and social rights, they are also more likely to engage in property and economic types of crimes.

CONVICTIONS AND SENTENCES

Examination of convictions and sentencing patterns between men and women over time is difficult because of the absence of judicial statistics at the level of state courts. The federal statistics that are available from 1963 to 1971 are consistent with the arrest data in that they show that over the eight-year time span, the highest proportion of women have been convicted for fraud, embezzlement, and forgery. These same offenses also show the greatest increase in the proportion of females who have been convicted between 1963 and 1971.

California statistics from 1960 through 1972 do not show that the increase in convictions has followed the increase in arrests for the same types of offenses.[11] Although there has been an increase of 31 percent in the proportion of women convicted for all types of crimes from 1962 to 1972, that increase has been due solely to the higher conviction rates for violent offenses.

New York State statistics on the proportion of female commitments

Table 3
Ranking of Countries by Percentage of Women Arrested for Various Crimes: 1963, 1968, 1970

Country	All Crimes		Murder		Major Larceny		Minor Larceny		Fraud		Drugs	
	Rank	Percent	Rank	Percent	Rank	Percent	Rank	Percent	Rank	Percent	Rank	Percent
West Indies	1	28.9	11	13.3	13	3.4	11	16.3	5.5	15.4	—	—
New Zealand	2	25.3	4	16.9	8	4.2	6	19.6	5.5	15.4	5	14.2
Thailand	3	17.3	19	4.2	15	3.0	14	14.4	13	10.1	11	4.6
West Germany	4	16.4	8	15.0	10	3.8	1	25.5	2	21.8	3	14.6
Luxembourg	5	16.2	—	—	2.5	8.7	13	15.4	14	9.5	—	—
United States	6	15.2	6.5	15.4	7	5.3	2	24.8	1	23.5	7	11.1
Austria	7.5	13.8	3	22.0	2.5	8.7	4	22.6	3	20.8	4	14.3
France	7.5	13.8	12	12.8	1	8.8	8.5	16.6	4	18.7	—	—
England and Wales	9	13.5	6.5	15.4	16	2.6	7	18.5	8	14.4	—	—
Tunisia	10	12.8	1	27.0	4	8.5	18	7.3	20	4.6	12	3.5
Israel	11	12.1	22	2.8	17	2.5	19	6.8	17	6.6	8	7.7
Korea	12	11.5	2	22.4	9	4.0	16	10.0	15	8.2	2	23.1
Scotland	13	10.9	10	13.4	11	3.7	8.5	16.6	7	14.5	—	—
Netherlands	14	10.4	15	8.1	13	3.4	3	23.5	9	13.1	—	—
Ireland	15	10.1	13	12.5	5	6.5	10	16.5	11	10.6	—	—
Monaco	16	7.5	—	—	—	—	—	—	—	—	—	—
Tanzania	17	6.9	9	14.1	19	2.2	21	4.2	21	2.1	—	—
Cyprus	18	6.7	17	6.5	18	2.4	17	7.7	19	4.7	9	6.8
Finland	19	6.6	16	6.9	13	3.4	12	15.9	12	10.3	—	—
Japan	20	4.6	5	16.5	20	1.2	5	20.5	16	7.0	1	24.1
Malawi	21	4.2	20.5	4.0	22	.9	23	2.6	22	1.7	14	1.0
Hong Kong	22	3.0	20.5	4.0	21	1.0	22	4.1	18	5.5	13	2.2
Fiji	23.5	1.9	18	4.5	23	.3	20	5.1	23	.8	—	—
Brunei	23.5	1.9	—	—	—	—	—	—	—	—	10	4.8
Canada	—	—	17	10.0	6	5.5	15	13.4	10	11.8	6	13.9

to correctional institutions by type of offenses from 1963 to 1971 reveal an overall decline and no significant changes within any of the offense categories.

The proportion of female commitments to all state penal institutions declined between 1950 and 1970 from 5.1 percent to 4.7 percent.

On the whole, using the rather meager statistics that are available, it appears that the courts have not been adapting their behavior to meet the changing roles that women, and perhaps tbe police in their interactions with women, are performing. In interviews that were conducted with about 30 criminal trial court judges in the Midwest in the winter of 1974, we found that most of the judges had not observed, and did not anticipate, any changes either in the numbers or types of women or in the types of offenses that women were likely to be charged with in the immediate future. Most of the respondents said that they expected to continue to be easier on women than on men, when it came to passing sentence.

WOMEN AS VICTIMS OF CRIMES

This section shifts the focus of this article and turns the issue on its head by examining the role of women as victims of criminal acts. One of the issues to which the woman's movement has directed much of its efforts has been the treatment of women who are victims of rape. The movement has been critical of the legal system and has demanded changes in the standards of proof and identification that are required. It has pointed to the police and demanded that they behave more humanely. It has insisted that medical and psychological facilities be made available and has called for changes in the manner and circumstances under which women who claimed they had been raped are examined. It has also demanded that the services of a therapist be made available to the victim as soon as possible after she reported the attack. The movement itself has been instrumental in setting up "rape hot lines" in many communities.

For all the attention that has been devoted to the female as "rape victim," it is interesting to note the proportions of men and women who have been victims of all types of criminal acts. For example, Wolfgang reported the characteristics of victims of criminal homicide from 1948 to 1952 and found that 76.4 percent were men and 23.6 percent were women. In 1972, the FBI reported that 22.2 percent of all murder victims were women.

In 1971, under the auspices of the Law Enforcement Assistance

Administration, the Bureau of the Census conducted victimization surveys in Montogomery County, Ohio (Dayton), and in Santa Clara County, California (San Jose). In Dayton, 16,000 persons over the age of 16 and in San Jose, 28,000 persons over the age of 16 were victims of assault, robbery, or personal larceny at least once during 1970. The proportion of female victims in each city is shown below:

	Dayton	San Jose
Women as a percent of		
Assault victims*	31	34
Robbery victims	36	34
victims	49	30

*Includes person who reported they were raped.

It is obvious that the percentage of women victims is less than their representation in each of the communities. Even when rape victims are included in the assault categories, the proportion of assault victims is less than the 50 percent that one might expect simply on the basis of female representation in the community.

The following statistics allow for comparison between women and other categories in the two communities by showing rates of victimization per 100 population.

	Victimization Rates	
	Dayton	San Jose
Persons victimized by		
Assault*	3.2	3.3
Robbery	0.8	0.8
Personal larceny	0.4	0.2
Women victimized by		
Assault*	1.9	2.1
Robbery	0.6	0.5
Personal larceny	0.4	0.2

*Includes persons who reported they were raped.

Young men between 16 and 24 victimized by		
Assault	11.7	9.2
Robbery	1.7	2.4
Personal larceny	0.8	1.0
Minority group members victimized by*		
Assault	3.1	3.9

Robbery	1.6	1.0
Personal larceny	0.8	0.3

* Dayton figures are for black persons; San Jose figures are for persons of Spanish origin or descent.

These figures, along with the national data on homicide, indicate that women are less likely to be victims of crimes than are men, and especially young men. Of course, one might argue that the relevant comparison is not the proportion of female victims by their representation in the society, but the proportion of female victims by the proportion of female offenders. If it is men—and especially men between the ages of 16 and 24—who commit the highest proportion of criminal acts, then perhaps one should expect persons in that category to also account for the highest proportion of victims.

In their report to the National Commission on the Causes and Prevention of Violence, Mulvhill and Tumin described the results of a survey of victim and offender patterns for four major violent crimes in 17 large American cities. The crimes were criminal homicide, aggravated assault, forcible rape, and robbery (armed and unarmed).[12] The table below describes the sex of victim for one of those types of offenses.

Sex of Victim and Offender for Aggravated Assault Arrests,
17 Cities, 1967

Sex of Offender	Sex of Victim		Total
	Male	Female	
Male	56.6	27.0	83.6(727)
Female	9.3	7.1	16.4(142)
Total	65.9(573)	34.1(296)	100.0(869)

Note: The figures represent percentages; those in parentheses are numbers of offenses.

The Mulvhill-Tumin data also show the following characteristics:

1. For all four offense categories, at least two-thirds of both the victims and the offenders are men. Armed robbery is almost exclusively a male situation: 90 percent of the victims and 95 percent of the offenders are men.

2. In the case of criminal homicide, 34 percent of the interactions are intersexual, and the roles performed by the men and women are divided almost equally—16.4 percent female offender/male victim, 17.5 percent male offender/female victim. There is a greater likelihood that the victim of a homicide perpetrated by a woman will be a family mem-

ber (most likely her spouse) than when the homicide is committed by a man. Women are also more likely to kill members of their family than are men. White and black women share that propensity almost equally.

3. In the other offense categories, when the situation is intersexual, there is a much greater likelihood that the male will be the offender and the female the victim. For aggravated assault cases, the ratio of male-female victims is 3:1, in armed robbery, 2.5:1, and in unarmed robbery, 13:1.

These 1967 data are consistent with those obtained in the 1971 victimization surveys of Dayton and San Jose in that they also portray the male as being the victim much more frequently than the female. These data serve the additional function of dramatizing the extent to which violent crime is still very largely a male enterprise (males are both the perpetrators and the victims). Only 3.8 percent of all the criminal homicides, 7.1 percent of all the aggravated assaults, and 0.9 and 2.9 percents of all the armed and unarmed robberies were acts perpetrated by females against females. Finally, the 1967 data also show that, when violent offenses are intersexual, the woman's role is much more likely to be that of the victim and the male's that of the offender. Homicide is the exception.

CONCLUDING REMARKS

In the last three or four years, all of the mass media—films, newspapers, television, magazines, and radio—have agreed upon a common theme vis-à-vis women and crime. They have claimed that more women are engaging in more acts of violence than have been engaged in by American women at any time in the past. And they have attributed much of the females' greater propensities for violence to the woman's movement. The fact that, in 1970, 4 women made the FBI list for the 10 most wanted criminals served as prima facie evidence of the accuracy of their perceptions. The Patty Hearst scenario also did much to convince the mass media that the image they were projecting about the increased propensities for violence by American women was indeed an accurate one.

But examination of national statistics over several decades reveals quite a different picture and, admittedly, one that lacks the drama of the media-created image. Women's participation in crime, especially serious crime, has increased. And the increase has been especially marked from 1967 on. But the types of serious crime that women are engaging in, in growing numbers, are crimes of property. They are economic and financial types of offenses. It is larceny, embezzlement, fraud, and forgery that are proving so attractive to women, and not homicide, assault, and armed robbery.

The increase in the first group of offenses and the decline in the second are, I believe, related in the following manner. With the woman's movement, a much greater proportion of women are working outside the home which provides more women with greater opportunities to embezzle, to commit fraud, and to steal than are available to housewives. The fact that these women are working also enhances their feelings of independence. The woman's movement supports these feelings by offering women a new image of themselves; and laws have changed so as to provide women with more legal and social independence. All of these factors, I believe, reduce the likelihood that women will attack or kill their most traditional targets: namely, their husbands or their lovers, other women with whom their men have become involved, or their unborn babies.

The factors cited above have provided women with the economic independence to take care of themselves and with a legal and social status that allows them to live without the protection of a man and to determine the fate of their own bodies. At least in the short run, then, I think we will continue to see an increase in women participating in property, fiscal, and economic offenses. Violent offenses will remain relatively stable or decline. The expectation, or the fear, that large numbers of young women will turn to radical politics and become revolutionaries has little evidence to support it. The Patty Hearsts and the Emily Harrises are probably as rare a phenomenon as was Ma Barker.

Comparison by Age: Juvenile Delinquency

2

Affluence and Adolescent Crime

JACKSON TOBY

EDITOR'S COMMENT: *The alarming relationship between affluence and adolescent crime in developed countries that Toby noted over a decade ago is still valid. Juveniles in developed countries contribute a much larger proportion of total criminality than do their counterparts in societies at less advanced stages of economic development. Moreover, the youthful contribution to total criminality in the United States and many other developed countries is rising at a much faster rate than that of the adult population.*

In 1960 a United Nations Congress on "The Prevention of Crime and the Treatment of Offenders" met in London. Delegates from countries on every continent compared notes. The verdict was pessimistic: Crime rates were increasing in nearly all countries, especially among adolescents, and rich countries were having as serious problems as poor countries.[1] In 1964 another United Nations Congress met in Stockholm and came to similar conclusions about adolescent crime. Economic growth, though it raised living standards, did not seem to reduce crime rates. Some criminological experts went further: Affluence was itself a causal factor in the worsening crime problems of contemporary society.

What did these crime problems consist of? Rape? Murder? Assault? From crime reports in the daily newspapers of the large cities of the world—New York, London, Tokyo—one might think that crimes of violence were rising rapidly and constituted a major component of "the crime problem." In some places this was happening, but it was not a consistent trend. For example, in Scotland and in England and Wales, there was a steep rise in the crime rate between 1927 and 1962, . . . but in neither country were crimes against the person an important factor. In Great Britain, crimes against the person consisted of less than 5 percent of crime in general. Furthermore, crimes against the person were not increasing faster than all crimes together; in Scotland, crimes against the person rose more slowly. Criminologists who disregarded the selective horror stories of daily newspapers and looked at crime statistics coldly have observed that the crime problem revolved mainly around theft. Insofar as crimes of violence increased they were mainly crimes like armed robbery rather than rape and murder. This thought may not console the gas station attendant shot during a holdup attempt, but it helps to explain the motivation of people who behave in ways summarized in the unrevealing category, "crime."

CRIME AND THE REVOLUTION OF RISING EXPECTATIONS

The preponderance of crimes against property sheds light on the tendency of crime rates to rise in the most affluent countries. People steal, not because they are starving, but because they are envious, and they are more likely to be envious of the possessions of others in countries with rising standards of living. Why should this be so? Because the rise in living standards is associated not only with an improvement of the style of life of elite groups, it is associated with the trickling down of television sets, refrigerators, transistor radios, and automobiles to segments of the population who had not anticipated such good fortune. Industrial societies, which produce the new luxuries, distribute them more democratically than the less affluent agrarian societies did. Paradoxically though, the trend toward increasing equality in the distribution of consumer goods generates expectations of further equality. When expectations are rising faster than the standard of living, the greater availability of consumer goods makes for greater rather than less dissatisfaction. This revolution of rising expectations is both cause and effect of the soaring ownership of automobiles, television sets, and radios not just in the United States or even in Europe but in Africa, Asia, and South America (see table 4). Traffic jams are now fully as serious in Tokyo as they have long been in New York and London; rivers of cars flow to-

Table 4
INDICES OF AFFLUENCE FOR SELECTED COUNTRIES, 1963

Country	Number of Radios per 100 Population	Rank	Number of TV's per 100 Population	Rank	Number of Cars per 100 Population	Rank
United States	97	1	33	1	36	1
Canada	48	2	25	2	25	2
Sweden	39	3	24	3	20	5
Denmark	35	4	20	5	13	11
Belgium	33	5	12	10	11	13
Luxembourg	33	6	5	21	15	7
West Germany	31	7	15	8	13	9
Finland	31	8	10	11	7	19
France	30	9	9	12	17	6
United Kingdom	29	10	24	4	14	8
Norway	29	11	8	14	10	14
Austria	29	12	6	17	9	15
Switzerland	28	13	6	18	13	10
Iceland	28	14	*	*	12	12
Netherlands	26	15	13	9	7	18
Argentina	25	16	6	20	3	22
Chile	24	17	0.4	31	1	30
New Zealand	24	18	6	19	24	3
Israel	24	19	*	*	2	25
Panama	22	20	4	22	2	26
Australia	20	21	16	7	23	4
Japan	20	22	16	6	1	29
Venezuela	20	23	7	16	4	21
Ireland	19	24	7	15	8	16
Italy	19	25	8	13	8	17
Peru	18	26	1	26	1	31
Mexico	17	27	3	24	2	28
Jamaica	13	28	1	30	3	23
Spain	13	29	3	23	2	27
Portugal	12	30	1	27	2	24
Greece	9	31	*	*	1	32
Paraguay	9	32	*	*	0.4	36
South Africa	7	33	*	*	6	20
U.A.R.	7	34	1	29	0.3	39
Ghana	7	35	*	*	0.4	37
Brazil	6	36	2	25	0.1	40
South Korea	6	37	†	34	†	—
Turkey	5	38	†	35	†	—
Philippines	4	39	0.2	32	0.3	38
Ceylon	4	40	*	*	1	33
Iraq	2	41	0.7	28	1	34
Burma	1	42	*	*	0.1	35
India	1	43	†	36	0.1	42
Nigeria	1	44	†	33	0.1	45
Pakistan	0.5	45	*	*	0.1	41

ward Tokyo every morning from as far as Mount Fuji.[2] Suburbanization is no longer an American phenomenon; the automobile has transformed the world. Table 4 reflects the level of affluence in selected countries—at least insofar as radios, television sets, and automobiles can be regarded as indices of affluence. Thus table 4 shows the United States, Canada, and Sweden to be among the countries of the world rich in durable consumer goods whereas India, Nigeria, and Pakistan are among the poor countries. But for persons interested in the effect of affluence on crime, it is not only the level of affluence that is important, but the rate at which affluence is increasing. The rate at which affluence is increasing is comparatively slow for the richest countries. Thus, the rate of increase of ownership of radios in the United States and Canada is of the order of 12 percent per year. India's annual rate of increase of radio ownership was 36 percent in the decade 1954–1964, and Nigeria's was 89 percent. True, these countries started from very low levels of ownership. Still, if we are interested in the impact of affluence on the revolution of rising expectations, the increases are dramatic. The situation with respect to automobile ownership is somewhat different. The richest countries have a comparatively slow rate of increase in automobile ownership. But it is not the poorest countries that have the fastest rate of increase but countries of the second rank: Italy, Greece, Spain. (Germany and Japan also have high rates of increase, but this can be interpreted as due to "catching up" after the Second World War.) The poorest countries have annual rates of increase only slightly higher than the richest countries, doubtless because an automobile is such a large investment in poor countries. If the increases in ownership of durable consumer goods contribute as much or more to envy as the level of ownership, this would help to explain why crime is increasing in most countries of the world. Industrialization and suburbanization may be thought of in relation to the world of adults. But the revolution of rising expectations has consequences for the young too. As car registrations grow, so do the desires of adolescents to drive (as well as to own cameras, transistor radios, and new clothes). Few adolescents can get legitimate access to a car, partly because of the age of licensing drivers, partly because of the cost of vehicles. In Japan, for example, the custom is to pay workers in accor-

---

*Statistics not available.
†Less than 0.05 per 100 population.

SOURCE: *United Nations Statistical Yearbook, 1964* (New York: Statistical Office of the United Nations, 1965), pp. 23–42, 391–98, 714–16.

dance with age as well as skill; so adolescent workers (as well as school-boys) have almost no chance to buy a car unless they come from rich families. Relative to adults, they are impoverished despite the growing affluence of Japanese society. Interestingly enough, the crime rate in Japan has risen most rapidly for the 14-to-17 age group, and has not increased at all for adults.[3] In 1941, the Japanese police apprehended 334,417 suspects of whom 7 percent were 14 to 17 years of age; in 1964, 726,910 suspects were apprehended of whom 19 percent were 14 to 17. Although table 5 shows the crime trend for the entire 14-to-17 age group, in 1954 the 14 and 15 year olds and the 16 and 17 year olds were separated in Japanese crime statistics, making it possible to study arrest data since then in greater detail.[4] For ages 20 to 24, the crime rate was 17.1 per thousand persons of those ages in 1955, and it was still 17.1 in 1964. For ages 18 and 19, the crime rate increased from 13.1 per thousand persons of those ages in 1955 to 17.8 in 1964. For ages 16 to 17, the crime rate increased from 8.8 per thousand in 1955 to 14.5 per thousand in 1964. For ages 14 and 15, the increase was the greatest of all: from 5.8 per thousand persons of those ages in 1955 to 14.1 in 1964.

Can the increase in the crime rate of Japanese 14 and 15 year olds be fully explained by a desire to share in the new affluence? Probably not. There are other factors, including the decreased authority of adults over children since the defeat of the Japanese in the Second World War. A case history of a Japanese delinquent shows some of these interrelated motivations in vivid form. The following are excerpts from three days of conversation with a 19-year-old boy interviewed recently in a training school for delinquents near Tokyo.[5]

At 15, Toshiko graduated from junior high school and enrolled in a vocational school to learn how to drive and repair cars. He stayed six months although the course was supposed to last one year. He said that his friends urged him to quit in order to "live an adult life." He wanted to smoke, to stay out late at night in the entertainment districts of Tokyo, to play *pachinko* (a popular Japanese slot machine game), and to wear fashionable clothing. Before he was imprisoned Toshiko wore bell-bottomed trousers and short jackets, the costume of a *chimpira* gang. He and his friends wished to feel superior to other Japanese and therefore wore what they thought to be American style clothing. Toshiko's mother disapproved, but his father, a hard-working clerk, did not say anything. Like his friends, Toshiko wore thin underwear instead of the

Table 5.

INCREASE IN JUVENILE CRIME IN JAPAN

Age of Suspects	Suspects Apprehended by the Japanese Police in													
	1941		1946		1951		1956		1961		1964	
	Number	Percent	Number	Percent	Number	Percent	Number	Percent	Number	Percent	Number	Percent
Over 20	281,708	84	333,694	75	452,602	73	427,192	77	422,430	66	488,080	67
18 and 19	19,780	6	51,910	11	58,030	10	48,301	9	62,758	10	55,208	8
14–17	22,731	7	47,479	11	75,626	12	52,457	9	96,126	15	135,334	18
Under 14	10,198	3	12,401	3	32,777	5	26,663	5	57,572	9	48,388	7
Total	334,417	100	445,484	100	619,035	100	554,613	100	638,886	100	726,910	100

SOURCE: "Juvenile Problems in Japan," (Tokyo: Central Council on Juvenile Problems, Prime Minister's Office, 1962) p. 38, "Summary of the White Paper on Crime, 1965," (Tokyo: Training and Research Institute of the Ministry of Justice, March 1966), pp. 17–18.

heavy underwear worn by the older generation. (There is very little central heating in Japan, and heavy underwear is protection against the cold, damp climate.)

After leaving the vocational school, Toshiko and his friends maintained their interest in cars. They broke into at least 11 cars over a period of several weeks, using a master key to get inside and shorting the ignition wires to start them. They picked up bread in the early morning from in front of grocery stores and ate it while driving around. When the gasoline was used up, they would abandon the cars—first taking care to remove the radios, which they sold for as much as 2,000 yen ($5.50) each.

Toshiko and his friends also broke into shops at night. They would select a little shop without a watchman. It would have to be located where a car, previously stolen for the purpose, could be parked nearby while the break-in was in progress. There were usually three to five in the group, one or two looking out for the police. They would either jimmy the door or apply a chemical paste to a window and set it aflame, enabling it to break easily and quietly.

Sometimes they picked a quarrel with a drunk, beat him up, and went through his pockets. Aside from drunks, however, they did not usually bother conventional people. More usually, they would extort money from members of rival chimpira groups. Toshiko would walk down the street until he saw a likely victim. Two confederates would be nearby but not visible. "Hello, fine fellow. Lend me your face." This was a challenge for the victim to go to a less busy place for a fight. Not seeing Toshiko's friends the victim would agree: he was angry. After the fight started, the confederates would join in, using wooden bats as well as fists. Soon the victim had enough and was willing to agree to give the victors what they wanted. They preferred money. But the victim might not have any. If not, they would take his fountain pen, watch, railroad ticket, and even his clothing. If he had on expensive shoes or a new suit, they might accompany him to a pawn shop where he would exchange these things for old clothes and cash, the latter for Toshiko and his friends. (They would give a small amount to the victim, 10 percent or less.)

Since Toshiko was stealing and extorting yen with his friends, he had enough money to spend long evenings in the entertainment districts of Tokyo. Subways and buses stopped running at midnight, whereas he did not usually leave his favorite bars until 2 *a.m.*, so he was forced to pay expensive night rates to taxis in order to get home. This dissatisfied him; he preferred to pay for beer and whiskey or, if he was looking for cut-rate intoxication, for sleeping pills rather than for transportation. He asked his father to buy him a car so that he might drive himself home in the small hours of the morning. His father was outraged. Toshiko did not work, he slept until noon or later every day; he spent his nights in the bars of Shibuya (an entertainment district); and he had the effrontery to ask his father, a poorly paid clerk, to buy him a car. (His father did not himself have a car.) A violent argument ensued in the course of which his father hit him; he hit his father back.

This blow must have been even more surprising to Toshiko's father than the original request for a car. While paternal authority is not now what it was once in Japan, it is still considerable. In traditional homes, the wife and children do not eat with the father, who is served literally on bended knee. That a son would dare to argue openly with his father is a sign of the increased equality between the generations in urban Japan. That he would hit his father, no matter what the provocation, is, to a Japanese, almost unbelievable.

Toshiko's father ordered him out of the house. He left home and moved in with a friend where he stayed for a week. Then he came home and apologized. His father would not forgive him. For a few weeks he stayed first with one chimpira and then with another. As soon as he found a girl who worked in a bar as a hostess and could help support him, he rented an apartment. (Such a girl is called a *dambe* in Japanese slang meaning "one who pulls money in on a string.") It was important to him that she not become pregnant because she could not continue to work, so Toshiko was careful to use contraceptives during sexual intercourse. This was not his usual practice with casual pickups.

The significance of Toshiko is not that he is Japanese or even that he is delinquent but that he represents one aspect of the revolution of rising expectations: the dissatisfaction of adolescents with their share in the new affluence. From this point of view, Toshiko is an international phenomenon that can be observed in Stockholm and Tel Aviv, as well as in Tokyo and Newark. Sweden offers an unusual opportunity to observe the effect of affluence on delinquency because circumstances that tend to raise the delinquency rates of other countries are, for the most part, absent from the richest country in Europe. Sweden was not a belligerent during the Second World War and did not suffer the disruptive effects of bombing and population loss, as did Japan. Sweden has no ethnic minorities, except for Lapp reindeer herders in the northern section, and therefore need not be concerned about prejudice and discrimination as a cause of crime. Sweden is culturally homogeneous; except for temporary workers from Latin countries, there has been no large-scale immigration for centuries. In the United States and Great Britain, on the other hand, an appreciable part of the crime problem results from the limited economic and social opportunities of colored persons. In Israel, much crime results from "melting-pot" problems. Since immigrants from the Middle East and Africa are more difficult to educate and to train for industrial occupations than those from Europe and America, young Israeli from "Oriental" backgrounds are more likely to feel materially deprived. Statistics show that Oriental youngsters become delinquent more frequently than European youngsters.[6] The following are excerpts from an interview with a 20-year-old Yemenite prisoner in an Israeli reformatory; they illustrate one by-product of the revolution of rising expectations in a culturally heterogeneous society:[7]

Happy's parents came to Israel in 1939 from a town in Yemen when they were young adults. Born in 1944, Happy does not seem to have many pleasant childhood memories. He mentioned two birthday parties when he was very young. I think he mentioned them to suggest how little his parents did for him as he grew older. He stopped going to synagogue at the age of 10. By the age of 15, he began smoking and gambling on the Sabbath. This was shocking behavior to his Orthodox parents, and they objected. "But I did not hear." Happy finished elementary school at 15 and went for a year to a vocational school.

When he was free, he lived in Tel Aviv. He would wake up about 10:30 A.M. Although his mother was in the house, he would take something to eat for himself. Then he would go to a street with trees and benches where he would meet his friends. If any of the boys had money, the would go to play snooker (a form of pool) or to a day performance in the movies, taking a girl if possible. If there were unaccompanied girls near the meeting place, who didn't work and had nothing to do, they might be picked up. If the boys had no money, they sat, talked, got bored, and annoyed people. If there was a plan to steal a car in the evening and break in, they talked about the job. If no job was planned, they talked about girls, about jobs they did pull or would pull.

Happy wanted to be considered *bomba* (tough) rather than *fryer* (a sucker). A fryer wants to be accepted by the gang, but he never succeeds. "This kind of boy hasn't had the kind of childhood we had, and he doesn't know how to take care of himself." He is permitted to associate with the *chevra* (gang) because he gets money (presumably from his parents) for gasoline, for a party, or to pay the bill in a restaurant. A bomba, on the other hand, is daring and aggressive. He steals the latest model cars, and he is successful with *fryereet* (girls who are easy to seduce). The chevra gambled three or four evenings a week for about five hours at a time, playing poker, rummy, 21, coin tossing, dice, or a game with a numbered board called "7 times 3." Happy was not usually very lucky. He lost as much as $50 in an evening. Gambling usually started on Friday evening, stopped at 2 or 3 A.M., and began again at about 10:30 A.M. on Saturday morning. The gambling stopped by Saturday evening when the chevra went to the movies or to a dance club. Sometimes a boy won too much, and the others suspected him of cheating. They might beat him up and take his money.

Happy and his friends drank liquor at every opportunity, sometimes during a card game, sometimes at a coffee shop, sometimes at a party. They drank Stock 84, for which they paid $1.20 to $1.40 for a half pint. When they had little money, they bought a big bottle of medicinal brandy for 70 cents.

Alcohol increased the probability of fights. "When you are a little drunk, sometimes you start pushing someone around." Once Happy kicked a dog when he was "high." The lady who owned the dog shouted at him; he shouted back. The owner's husband joined the argument. Soon the *doda* (literally "aunts" in Hebrew but meaning "police") were called. But fights occurred for other reasons. Happy recalled one time when he was playing cards out-of-doors on a Saturday afternoon. A member of an extremely Orthodox sect came over to the chevra and told them to stop gambling on the Sabbath. In the course of the furious argument that ensued, the Orthodox man threw a nearby bicycle in the middle of the game. They stopped the game and beat him up badly. If members of the chevra made remarks about a girl in the movies, and her boyfriend resented them, this could start a fight. Or sometimes a member of the group took a couple of friends and *laredet alay* (literally "went down on" but meaning "beat up") a boy who was saying insulting things about him or about the group.

On Happy's right hand is a tattoo consisting of a half moon and three stars, which (he said) means, "We are against the law." Although he made this tattoo in the reformatory, this could well have been the motto of his chevra in the community. Car thefts were a favorite activity. At first cars were stolen only for joyrides. The competition consisted of stealing newer model cars and large cars. "The car is always full—as many as the car will hold." Girls were sometimes reluctant to come for fear of getting involved. Once Happy left his straw hat with a feather in a car he had tried to start unsuccessfully. The gang went back to get the hat after having stolen another car. The doda gave chase; but Uri, the driver, outdistanced them. After a while, they decided to use the cars they stole to help in burglaries. For example, they broke into a super-market through air vents in the back—forcing the grill—and took ciga-rettes and cognac and chocolate away in the car. Then they went back to the room of one of the boys and had a party.

Once, when they passed a Willys station wagon filled witb appli-ances, they stole them and sold them to a client (fence) recommended by a friend. The loot consisted of clothes, irons, fans, transistor radios, and electric shavers. Four boys each got $200. Happy has his share under a tile in the courtyard of his house and continued to ask his mother for a pound or two (33 or 66 cents) for spending money. Happy spent all of his share in a month. (He kept the clothes he bought in a pal's house—so as not to arouse his mother's suspicions.) This success aroused the interest of the chevra in transistor radios, and they broke into appliance stores, preferably from the back but sometimes from the front when the street was clear. Sometimes they broke into two stores in a week, some-times none at all. They also broke into dry goods stores—but this was not profitable. From every car they stole, they took the radio. Sometimes they stripped cars without moving them.

In some ways, the crimes of Happy and his gang are not startling. They remind criminologists of the Irish, Polish, and Italian juvenile gangs in Chicago a half century ago—or of Negro gangs today in Phila-delphia, New York, or Cleveland. Gangs consisting of the sons of pov-erty-striken migrants to the city are commonplace. But the juvenile gangs of Sweden are less easy to understand because poverty, in the old sense of hunger, ragged clothes, and disease, does not exist in Sweden. As in many countries, there has been a housing shortage in Sweden, especially in the cities; this shortage dates from the postwar rise in birth rate. But existing housing is modern and pleasant. Slums cannot be the breeding place of crime in Stockholm, Malmö, or Gothenburg, the three largest cities of Sweden, because there are no slums. Neverthless, delin-quency has been a troublesome problem for the Swedes. From 1946 to 1955 the conviction rate rose 38 percent in the age group, 15 to 17; the corresponding rise for the 18-to-20 age group was 57 percent. Note that the increase in Swedish delinquency rates, unlike the increase in Japa-nese delinquency, was more pronounced among older adolescents. There may be a good explanation for this. Sweden is a radically equalitarian country, whereas Japanese tradition stresses the submission of the young to the old. Swedish youngsters, 15 to 17, are the beneficiaries of many governmental service including excellent youth clubs, and they can earn almost as much as adults if they choose to leave school and go to work. So even though they may feel deprived, they are not likely to feel as deprived as Japanese youngsters of the same age.

In spite of these favorable circumstances, Swedish adolescents commit crimes. And in addition to committing crimes they behave in ways that are, if not illegal, disturbing to adults. For example, in the 1950s gangs of *raggare* (cruisers) drove around the downtown districts of the large cities in American made cars looking for girls. At one time raggare automobiles interfered sufficiently with traffic flow in Stockholm that city officials invited leaders of the main group, the Car Angels, the Car Comets, the Teddy Boys, and the Car Devils, to City Hall to discuss the problem. On New Year's Eve in 1957, a crowd of 3,000 persons, about two-thirds of them under 21, gathered in the center of Stockholm and bombarded police with empty tin cans and other objects. They forced several cars to stop and wrenched off their doors. One car was overturned and wrecked.[8] Gate-crashing has also been a problem in Sweden, as it has in the United States.[9] As a Swedish governmental report put it, "Groups of young people force their way uninvited into a party, or break into a private home or apartment, in the absence of the owners, and proceed to break china, mutilate furniture, and deface walls."[10]

That the rise in Swedish delinquency is indirectly related to Swedish prosperity is not self-evident. But there does not seem to be any major social trend—except the increase in affluence—to blame for the delinquency problem. There are also some direct connections between delinquency and affluence. In Sweden, as in the United States, auto theft is predominantly a crime of adolescents.[11] Furthermore, while the rate of auto theft in Sweden rose from 29 per 100,000 population in 1950 to 126 per 100,000 population in 1957, the rate computed per 10,000 automobiles registered rose only from 90 per 10,000 registrations in 1950 to 116 per 10,000 registrations in 1957.[12] What does this mean? That the temptation to steal cars was proportional to the number of cars in use and the number of adolescents who felt dissatisfied with their share of them. Of course, older Swedish adolescents did not have to steal cars in order to drive them. Unlike the situation in Japan, teenage boys in Sweden who work in unskilled jobs may nevertheless earn enough to afford a secondhand car. The raggare gangs do not consist of delinquents any more than the American hotrod clubs consist of delinquents. But some raggare boys and girls are not satisfied with their share in

Sweden's high living standards. And they can be very delinquent indeed, as the following excerpts from an interview with a former member of the Road Devils show.[13]

Lappen was an unwanted child. He arrived just as the marriage of his parents was breaking up. Shortly after Lappen's birth, his father left his mother for another woman. Lappen's brother Bengt, two years older than he, was kept at home, and Lappen was temporarily sent to live with his maternal grandparents in Lapland; his mother could not take care of both children.[14] Lappen's mother earned 600 crowns a month (about $120) in a butcher shop. By Swedish standards this was a low income, and Lappen reported that he envied the clothes and spending money of some of his friends whose family earned 1,600 crowns a month (the man of the family earned a thousand and the woman 600). When Lappen was 9 or 10 years old, he and three friends from relatively poor families began stealing candy and fruit from local stores so that they could have the same things as the other boys in the neighborhood. (Stig was one year older than Lappen, Borje one year older, and Jan one year younger). The other neighborhood boys admired the courage of the thieves. "We took greater and greater chances because we had to show that we were just as good as those whose parents had a lot of money." The boys who did not need to steal stole anyway out of a sense of adventure. Lappen and his three friends became the leaders of a gang. Lappen's gang controlled 10 or 15 square blocks. Between the ages of 10 and 15 Lappen participated in many fights. As many as 200 boys were involved in some of the biggest fights. The fights were with gangs from outside the neighborhood and were usually over "honor and girls, if I may say so." Lappen differentiated between two types of boys from outside the neighborhood: boys who came from essentially the same class and boys who were *sossar* (important). Fights with boys from the same social level were relatively friendly. "We fought to show who was best. After the fight, we were all friends." In addition to fighting Lappen and his friends increased the scope of their stealing activities. They "borrowed" rowboats and bicycles. They also "borrowed" automobiles for joyrides.

When Lappen attended school he played hookey at least one day a week. He said it was because he "had it so easy. The next day I came back and knew what they had talked about." The teachers did not find out about his truancy because he would write notes to them and forge his mother's signature. His mother urged him to go to school. However, she didn't tell the teacher he played hookey when she had an interview with the teacher because "she wanted it to be good for me in school. Mother wanted me to be something, to go to the university, but I wouldn't. My interest was motors. I wouldn't sit on a book." Lappen's relationship with his mother has never been very good. "She lives her life and I live mine. I like her but I do not love her."

At the age of 15, just about the time he quit school, Lappen had his first sex experience. His gang (the South End Club) had obtained a meeting room in a local youth club. Lappen had carefully observed the caretaker's keys, and he had made a duplicate from memory. Consequently, he, Stig, and Borje had a key to the meeting room. One evening he took a girl friend into the room and locked the door. Stig and Borje were outside to see that members of the youth club did not try to come in. Other members of the gang were in the game room of the club to keep the caretaker busy enough so that he would not disturb Lappen. Since there was no bed or sofa in the room, his first experience with *knulla* (intercourse) occurred on a table. Subsequently, he engaged in knulla frequently, usually in the house of girls whose parents were working. Although he and his friends were *raggarbrud* (promiscuous), they resented it when girls were unfaithful. He told me of one member of the gang who was in love with a girl. When he discovered that he had been sharing her with numerous others, he was enraged. He told his friends. On some pretext the jealous lover and seven of his friends, including Lappen, rowed to a deserted island near Stockholm with the girl. They confronted her with her infidelity and, as punishment, forced her to remove her clothes, and then all except the injured boyfriend had sexual relations with her in turn. They rowed back to the mainland leaving her to swim back as best she could.

When he left school, Lappen got a job as a car mechanic. On and off for the next three or four years, he worked in this occupation, earning 200–250 crowns a week ($40–$50). Like many other Swedish boys of similar background, he is fascinated by cars, especially big American cars. He eventually became a member of one of the four most important raggare clubs of Stockholm, the Road Devils. Lappen and his friends drank heavily, drove recklessly, and cruised around the city of Stockholm picking up girls who were "looking for a good time." They held noisy parties and dances. Some members stole accessories for their cars. Those who did not own a car "borrowed" cars for joyrides. Lappen was probably more delinquent than most of the raggare. He rolled homosexuals and drunks. He burglarized stores with one or two confederates— usually using *schmacha* (the smash and grab technique). His last schmacha was a jewelry store window. He got enough jewelry and watches to sell to a fence for 2,000 crowns. With this money he bought his own car and gave up stealing.

As Lappen described his life as a raggare boy, it was a life of fun, of laughs. "I lived an expensive life and I done exactly what I want. If I wanted to go to Copenhagen, I gotta go to Copenhagen. When we would drive to a little town, the girls knew we came from Stockholm and looked up to us." There was dancing and singing in the streets. "When I want to dance, I dance." Every weekend there would be parties in the homes of various girls or boys that he knew. He would start out on a Saturday evening at one party and would move on to others as the inclination moved him. He would usually bring vodka or Scotch or Spanish brandy as his contribution to the merriment. Ten to 20 young people would be present at a given party at one time, but there would be constant comings and goings. For example, Lappen would usually get to three or four parties by Sunday morning. "If I didn't have fun, I'd get home by 3 or 4 A.M. If I had fun, I'd get home by 6 or 7." Sometimes however, the parties lasted all through Sunday.

In 1957 Lappen was convicted for breaking and entering and sent to Fagared, a youth prison near Gothenburg. When he was released, he did not return to Stockholm. Instead he took a room in Gothenburg and got a job as an auto mechanic. Somehow, while he was in the institution, he had fallen in love with a local girl. He distinguished his love for this 17-year-old girl from the many intimate relationships that he has had with girls in his neighborhood and in the raggare. (Girls are also members of the raggare clubs, but they rarely own cars.) "That year, 1958 I shall never forget. It was the happiest year of my life. For the first time, I had a family. I played cards with her father and listened to the radio." The girl's father, an office worker, took a liking to Lappen. He discovered that the boy was living in a lonely furnished room and offered to rent a room to him in their house. Lappen eagerly accepted. During the period when he lived in his girl friend's house, he was, according to his account, a model young man. He didn't drink; he went to bed early; he worked steadily; and he spent his spare time with his girl friend. Unfortunately she became pregnant. When they told her parents, he at first thought that they would allow him to marry her, which is what both of them wanted. But a few days later the father told him that he "was no longer welcome in the house." Without further discussion, Lappen left. The girl, being only 17, could not marry without her parent's consent. They insisted that she go to a hospital and have an abortion. Lappen returned to Stockholm. His letters to her were returned unopened. Soon he went back to his old life with the raggare. Twice he and another Road Devil broke into safes although Lappen was very nervous, and he let his partner handle the explosives.

"The boys in this place are like gamblers. If we win we get money. If we lose we get locked up. Because we are good losers, we can smile." He recognized that, when he got out of prison, he faced a choice between two very different ways of life. "I know that the right kind of life is to work and have a family, something to hope for. Maybe I had it too easy the last year now and it is difficult to get back to normal life. On the one side, I found a lot of fun and on the other side, the right side, there was only a hard life." I asked Lappen what the chances were of his not getting into trouble any more. "If I learn to trust people, I won't have any more trouble." I think what he meant was that he would not commit further crimes if he developed another relationship like the one he had with the girl from the Gothenberg and her family.

Case studies like those of Lappen, Happy and Toshiko illustrate the mechanisms whereby affluence leads to crime: through arousing feelings of material deprivation that cannot be satisfied legitimately. It is unlikely that adolescents from such different cultures would react to affluence so similarly unless there were a common causal process at work. Bear in mind though that the Lappens, Happys, and Toshikos are in the minority in their countries. Feelings of deprivation do not inevitably lead to crime. On the contrary, they are rarely acted upon. Under what conditions does the impulse to steal lead to theft? If affluence not only arouses predatory motives but gives the potential predator some prospect for "getting away with it," it greatly increases the probability that the motives will find expression in action. As the next section of this report will show, urban industrial societies do precisely that for adolescents: they loosen social controls and thus provide the opportunity for delinquency.

AFFLUENCE AND PARENTAL CONTROL OVER CHILDREN
One of the effects of affluence is to increase the life expectancy of everybody in the society, including of course, parents. This means that a child in a rich industrial society has a far better chance of having both his parents alive and well during his adolescence. Another effect of affluence is to increase the divorce and separation rate. Why? Because industrialization enables women to support themselves—and their children, if need be.[15] Hence marital unhappiness is more likely to result in divorce

or separation in rich industrial societies than in poor underdeveloped societies. But the most important effect of affluence on the family is to strip it down to jet-age size (mother, father, and their dependent children) and to isolate it physically and emotionally from other relatives. This is not true of all families even in the United States. And some industrial societies—Japan is a good example—have gone less far in deemphasizing generational ties than have Sweden, Israel, and the United States. Still, families in industrial societies are characteristically small; they move from community to community as employment opportunities arise; they lack the bulwark of kinship and communal support that poorer societies had.

These effects of affluence on the family help to explain why delinquents come from broken or inadequate families in industrial societies. Broken and inadequate families cause delinquency in rich societies because these societies assign major responsibility to parents for the control of their children. In poorer rural societies, where in addition to their biological parents, neighbors, grandparents, uncles, aunts, and other assorted relatives supervise children the death or divorce of parents does not lead to juvenile delinquency. In short, a truism of criminologists that delinquents come from less stable families than nondelinquents, is a truism only for affluent industrial societies. And even for us it is not clear why it is true. Two quite different mechanisms have been suggested by experts to explain this relationship between parental inadequacy and juvenile delinquency:

Mechanism 1. Parental rejection and neglect damage the personality of the developing child. Lack of impulse control results from pathological socialization. The psychopathic or neurotic boy reacts with violence to trivial provocations, sets fires, and steals purposelessly.

Mechanism 2. Parental inadequacy and neglect, by reducing family control, thereby orient the boy toward his age mates in the neighborhood. The family and the peer group are in a sense competing for the allegiance of boys in high-delinquency neighborhoods. If the peer group is delinquent, a boy's desire for acceptance by his peers tempts him to participate in delinquent activities.

Some evidence supports both mechanisms; research is needed to distinguish the more important one. Such clarification would be useful because if mechanism 1 predominates, juvenile delinquency will probably continue to rise in all urban industrial countries It is unlikely that most family catastrophes can be prevented. Assuming that the emotional scars resulting from death, divorce, or the mental illness of a parent cause delinquency, then delinquency may be part of the price of living in a rich society. On the other hand, if mechanism 2 predominates, more effective programs of delinquency control can be designed than are available at present. Assuming that the main problem is a breakdown of family control over the child, thereby exposing him to the corrupting influences of the street corner gang, then supportive institutions can be developed to backstop parents.[16]

Supportive institutions may be needed anyway. After all, although "problem" families have less effective control over adolescents than "normal" families in affluent societies, under contemporary conditions, all families have weak control over adolescents, especially over boys. This weakness of adult control is most obvious under pathological circumstances such as slum neighborhoods or broken homes. Its ultimate source, however, is not pathology but the increasing social fluidity resulting from the allocation of education, recreation, work, and family life to separate institutional contexts. These changes in social organization affect everyone in contemporary societies, but their impact is especially great on adolescents because adolescence is a period of transition. Youngsters must disengage themselves from the family into which they were born and raised and establish themselves in a new family unit. They must eventually withdraw from the system of formal education and assume an occupational role. While preparing to make these transitions and learning preparatory skills, many adolescents are socially adrift—except for such solidarities as they form with youngsters in the same situation as they. This is one reason for the development of "teenage culture." It is not the whole explanation. The affluence of industrial societies creates the material basis for an adolescent market. That is to say, adults in the United States, Sweden, Great Britain, the Soviet Union, Israel, and other industrial societies give adolescents substantial discretionary purchasing power, which enables adolescents to demand (and obtain) distinctive clothing, motion pictures, phonograph records, recreational facilities, and eating and drinking places.[17]

Teenage culture helps to ease the transition between the family into which the child was born and the family the young adult will create by marriage. Peers give the adolescent an emotional anchorage, but they constitute an unpredictable influence. Unless adolescents are organized under adult sponsorship, as boy's clubs, Scouts, and church youth groups are, they may mutually encourage one another to engage in a wide variety of unconventional or rebellious behavior. Delinquent gangs represent an antisocial development of adolescent autonomy; they are of course less pleasing to adults than scouting or 4-H clubs. Gang formation is possible in contemporary societies because the institutional structure, in adjusting to the requirements of urban industrial life, has (unintentionally) undermined effective adult supervision of adolescents. Of course, some families maintain better control over adolescents than others; and adolescent girls are generally better supervised than adolescent boys. The very technology of industrial societies emphasizes the independence of the adolescent from parental observation. In the age of the automobile, an adolescent's home may be the place where he sleeps and little else. The car is not the only means of avoiding adult surveillance, but the car symbolizes the looseness of the ties between adults and adolescents because it is such an effective instrument for escaping the eyes of adults.

The increased freedom of adolescents from adult control cannot be revoked. Not only technology but ideology is on the side of youthful independence. Contemporary societies are organized with the unit of participation the individual rather than the family. The child is not a representative of his family in the classroom or in the play group; as an adult he will participate in the economic and political systems as an individual also. This principle of individualism, implicitly embodied in social organization, is explicitly defined (outside the Iron Curtain countries) in the concept of "freedom." Adolescents are jealous of this prerogative. The freedom offered to adolescents is not always used wisely; the freedom to choose is the freedom to make mistakes. Delinquency is one mistake. On the other hand, many adolescents use their period of unsupervised freedom creatively: to establish commitments to educational and occupational goals, to learn how to relate to the opposite sex, and ultimately, to marry and have children. It would be throwing out the baby with the bath water to attempt to establish preindustrial control over adolescents to prevent some of them from using their freedom destructively.

AFFLUENCE AND EDUCATION COUNTERVAILING FORCES ON DELINQUENCY

The new affluence has an important impact on the material aspirations of young people: on the desire for cars, transistor radios, cameras, and clothes. But affluence has also an impact on education. Substantial proportions of adolescents in industrial countries now remain in school instead of going to work, which was the usual pattern up to a generation ago. Even for the United States, the first country to embark on mass secondary education, the change is recent.

Why does affluence have this effect on educational aspirations? One reason is the increased public support of education made possible by large national incomes. Another is the greater resources of individual families, making it possible for them to forego the financial contributions of working adolescents. Both of these factors make for an increased supply of educational opportunities. Education is a substantial investment, both for society and for the individual family; rich countries can make this investment more easily. The demand for education—as opposed to the supply—depends on the motivation of young people themselves. This has been negatively demonstrated in recent crash programs in slum schools (e.g., the Higher Horizon program in New York) where substantial new resources did not make dramatic improvements in student accomplishments. Research is needed to clarify the conditions under which students are motivated to seek as much education as they can master. It is known that parental encouragement is important. And what if parents are not encouraging? Can teachers and other school personnel make up for this deficit? To some as yet unknown extent, they can.

The potentialities of fostering education can perhaps be gauged by an unplanned experiment in the consequences of high aspirations. American children of Japanese, Chinese, and Jewish backgrounds do extraordinarily well in school and go to colleges and universities in disproportionate numbers. They also have extremely low delinquency rates.[18] What is the connection? These same ethnic groups are often considered drivingly ambitious. Do not their educational aspirations reflect this ambition? Japanese, Chinese, and Jewish parents want to insure their children a share in business and professional occupations; education is the means to this end. Being members of minority groups, they are perhaps more keenly aware of the necessity of education for socioeconomic success, but they are motivated in essentially the same way as white Anglo-Saxon Protestants. The connection between higher education and high-income employment is well understood and provides a principal motivation for college attendance.[19]

What about Negroes? Unlike the Japanese, Chinese, and Jews, American Negroes show massive educational disadvantage. But recent studies prove that Negro educational retardation does not reflect lack of interest in education. Negro school children, even though they may be performing poorly in the classroom, are as likely as white children to say that they want to go to college.[20] They are less likely to perceive education as feasible for them; hence they are less likely to plan on going and to put in the consistent studying that can make college attendance a reality. In the light of their underutilization of the educational escalator, it is not coincidence that Negro adolescents have a high delinquency rate. Whereas education is a legitimate opportunity for Japanese adolescents, delinquency constitutes for Negro adolescents a tempting alternative to poverty—what one sociologist has called an "illegitimate opportunity."[21] It would be oversimplifying to maintain (1) that all delinquents are envious and (2) that they would not be delinquent had they realized that education could get them a high standard of living. Some delinquents are not envious. Some envious adolescents are not delinquent. Some adolescents are not willing or able to wait for the economic payoff of education; they share the sentiments of a famous economist who said, "In the long run we are all dead."

Table 6.

BOYS BORN IN STOCKHOLM IN 1940 WHO, BY THE AGE OF 21,
ACQUIRED A RECORD IN THE CRIMINAL REGISTER, BY
EDUCATIONAL ATTAINMENT

Highest Educational Attainment	Boys with Criminal Records		All Boys
	Number	Percent	
Gymnasium	10	2.0	488
Realskola	34	9.9	445
Primary school	185	20.2	918
Unknown	7	14.3	49
Total	236	12.4	1900

SOURCE: Unpublished study of comparative adolescent delinquency being conducted by Jackson Toby, Carl-Gunnar Janson, and Shuichi Miyake.

Nevertheless, there is fragmentary but consistent evidence from various industrialized countries that the longer a youngster stays in school the smaller are the chances that he will commit crimes. For example, table 6 presents some Swedish data showing that the criminal conviction rate for boys in Stockholm in 1940 was 10 times as great if they completed primary school than if they completed gymnasium. The data in table 6 are unusually clear-cut; few countries have as good criminal records as Sweden where it was possible to trace 94 percent of the cohort of Stockholm boys from birth until the age of 21.

Table 6 shows clearly that educational accomplishment prevents criminality, but it does not tell why. Therefore it does not immediately suggest policy recommendations. Would raising the age for compulsory school attendance reduce adolescent delinquency? Not unless mere custody of children in school is the reason for the correlation between educational attainment and nondelinquency. This is rather unlikely to be the case. The correlation almost certainly reflects the motivations of young people themselves. That is to say, the significance of graduation from gymnasium is that graduation from gymnasium fulfills the aspirations of Swedish young people. Most of them were interested in obtaining business and professional occupations. Some may have been interested in education for its own sake. But committing crimes would be incompatible with the fulfillment of either of these goals. Arrests label a boy to himself as well as to his classmates and teachers as belonging to a different world, a world the values of which are opposed to those of the school and incompatible with it.

Table 7 is a refinement of the data of table 6 taking into account the fact that the 1,900 boys came from different socioeconomic circumstances. It is known that boys from working-class families are less likely to seek higher education than boys from business, professional, and white-collar families. It is also known that boys from working-class families are more likely to be arrested for delinquent behavior than boys from more elite occupational backgrounds. Table 7 examines the joint effect of socioeconomic background and educational attainment on criminality, thus providing an answer to the question: Which takes precedence? The answer is fairly clear. Those Stockholm boys who graduated from gymnasium had a low offense rate, and it did not make much difference whether their fathers were high status or low status. Three of the 71 working-class boys who completed gymnasium had a criminal record as compared with 2 of the 235 boys from upper-class families. At the minimal education level, on the other hand, parental status had an appreciable effect on criminality. Whereas 21 percent of the 618 working-class boys with minimal education had a criminal record, none of the 25 upper class boys with minimal education had one. What are the implications of this finding? That a youngster who commits himself to education is unlikely to become delinquent regardless of his family background.

Table 7.

THE CRIME RATES OF BOYS BORN IN STOCKHOLM IN 1940, BY EDUCATIONAL ATTAINMENT AND THE SOCIOECONOMIC STATUS OF THEIR FAMILIES

Highest Educational Attainment	Boys with Criminal Records					
	Upper Class		Middle Class		Working Class	
	Number	Percent	Number	Percent	Number	Percent
Gymnasium	4	1.7	3	1.6	3	4.2
Realskola	4	5.3	15	8.6	15	8.0
Primary school	0	–	57	20.0	128	20.7
Unknown (49 cases)	–	–	–	–	–	–
Total	8	2.4	75	11.8	146	16.6

SOURCE: Unpublished study of comparative adolescent delinquency being conducted by Jackson Toby, Carl-Gunnar Janson, and Shuichi Miyake.

But why does educational commitment have this effect? Criminologists do not know for sure. One likely possibility is that youngsters who pursue successful careers at school are consciously doing so in order to enjoy the "good life" as adults. They desire to share in the material rewards of an affluent society, just as delinquents do, but they utilize a legitimate path to socioeconomic advancement. This is probably not the whole explanation. Whatever the initial motivation for desiring success at school—to please concerned parents, to obtain a well-paying job as an adult, to learn—involvement in the school program has consequences for the student's conception of the world. A relatively uneducated delinquent does not know as much about the pleasures an affluent society can offer as a university student. The university student may obtain pleasure out of reading a book, attending a concert or ballet, visiting a museum, appreciating natural beauty, fighting for social justice— as well as out of driving a powerful car, getting "high", and wearing fashionable clothes. Delinquents in affluent societies characteristically desire material pleasures intensely—so much so that they are willing to risk freedom for them—but they are aware only of a small part of the opportunities for gratification that their societies offer. Furthermore, opportunities they are unaware of are those that are awakened or cultivated by the educational system. These considerations suggest that another reason that education prevents crime is that education broadens that range of desires of young people and stimulates some desires that bear little relation to money income. This is, of course, speculation. Research is needed to establish the precise mechanism whereby educational achievement prevents crime.

CONCLUSION

Poverty is nothing new. It is affluence that is new. But the relationship between subjective dissatisfaction and objective deprivation is more complicated than was first thought. Poverty cannot cause crime but resentment of poverty can, and curiously enough, resentment of poverty is more likely to develop among the relatively deprived of a rich society than among the objectively deprived in a poor society. This is partly because affluent industrial societies are also secular societies; the distribution of goods and services here and now is a more important preoccupation than concern with eternal salvation. It is also because the mass media to which television has been a recent important addition—stimulate the desire for a luxurious style of living among all segments of the population. These considerations explain why the sting of socioeconomic deprivation can be greater for the poor in rich societies than for the poor in poor societies. They also throw light on the high crime rates of affluent societies and on the increase of adolescent delinquency rates with the increase in general prosperity. Relative to adults, adolescents feel like a poverty-stricken and powerless minority and how they feel has consequences for how they behave. The fact that adolescents mostly go to school and adults mostly go to work helps to explain the phenomenon of "teenage culture." It is not the whole explanation. The affluence of industrial societies creates the material basis for cultural differentiation. That is to say, industrial societies allocate to adolescents substantial discretionary purchasing power, and this enables adolescents to demand (and obtain) distinctive clothing, motion pictures, phonograph records, recreational facilities, and eating and drinking establishments. From the viewpoint of understanding delinquency, however, the extension of formal education is probably more important than the development of the adolescent market. The reason for this is that mass formal education has created serious problems of life goals for adolescents with educational disabilities. For academically successful adolescents, school is a bridge between the world of childhood and the world of adulthood. For children unwilling or unable to learn, school is a place where the battle against society is likely to begin.

Orientation to consumption seems to be an increasing characteristic of industrial societies. It permeates most strata, not merely adolescents, and it contributes to other phenomena besides delinquency, e.g., ostentatious expenditures for food, clothing, travel, housing. However, the impact of commercialism is greatest on working-class adolescents because the impact on them of the educational system is less positive than for middle-class youth. If they leave school as soon as they legally may, they have less opportunity to experience art, literature, serious music, science, religion, and meaningful work than they have of being attracted to the gadgets and entertainments available in the marketplace. This isolation of school-leaving youths from what are generally conceded to be the accomplishments of industrial civilization may partially account for violent crime. As Nelson Algren put it in his paraphrase of a literary idea of Richard Wright, "when a crime is committed by a man who has been excluded from civilization, civilization is an accomplice of the crime." [22] Selective exposure to industrial society is not merely an internal problem. Anthropologists have called attention to the selective "diffusion" of culture traits to underdeveloped societies or even religion.

H. G. Wells once remarked, "Human history becomes more and more a race between education and catastrophe." Is delinquency a catastrophe? Some might argue that delinquency is a small price to pay for life in a rich society where most people, including adolescents, have the freedom to choose the direction of their destiny. It is true that delinquency is rare in subsistence economies (where there is less to envy) and in totalitarian states (where social controls coerce would-be rebels). On the other hand, crime does cost a society something, not only the losses to victims but also the wasted years of delinquent youths. Most ex-delinquents regard the years spent in raising hell on the streets as well as those in prison as irretrievable mistakes. Mass education can prevent some of this waste. The appeal of education, like adolescent delinquency itself, is stimulated by affluence. But affluence needs reinforcement if youngsters from homes where parents do not value education are to believe that education is for them too. The primary benefit of education is of course intrinsic: the greater realization of the potentialities of young people. But a secondary consequence is to deflect adolescents from the destructive possibilities open to them in a free society. If the experience of American society with its Japanese, Chinese, and Jewish minorities is any precedent, the indirect consequence of educational upgrading will be the reduction of adolescent delinquency. True, these ethnic groups possessed special cultural values favorable to education, which were transmitted to children without planning. However, it seems likely that planned programs of educational upgrading, adequately financed and enthusiastically publicized, could duplicate the Japanese, Chinese, and Jewish unintended experiments in delinquency prevention. Is it worth a try?

3

Youth Crime in Postindustrial Societies: An Integrated Perspective

PAUL C. FRIDAY and JERALD HAGE

There has been a considerable growth in youth crime since the end of the Second World War. In fact, this kind of crime appears to be one of the problems of modern postindustrial societies. It affects capitalist countries such as the United States, and socialist countries such as the U.S.S.R. as well as nations like Sweden that lie somewhere between. The following patterns appear to be clear: (1) youth crimes are most frequent in urban, industrial, affluent societies, and within these societies are concentrated primarily in urban areas; (2) the perpetrators of the majority of offenses are young males under the age of 24; (3) the offenses themselves are generally against property; and (4) the majority of these youthful offenders do not continue in crime but eventually lead relatively law-abiding lives.

Theories attempting to explain crime have focused primarily on conventional youth crime. These theories fall into three major areas of analysis. The first emphasizes wide structural and societal origins such as urbanization,[1] geographical areas,[2] and social class opportunity structures.[3] The second stresses the importance of immediate origins or of family socialization,[4] family structure,[5] gang associations,[6] or the general exposure to deviant and nondeviant patterns.[7] Finally, the third stresses conditions surrounding the act itself, such as how youth "drift" into sporadic acts,[8] the conditions affecting the development of adequate commitments to conformity.[9]

43

No one set of theories or single level of analysis is adequate in and of itself as an explanation of crime. The current trend in criminological theory has been to concentrate on either the subcultural or situational variables affecting the young urban male, rather than on the wider societal origins such as urbanization and industrialization. More important, these explanations have not addressed themselves to what might be the structural condition in postindustrial society that are affecting the other levels of analysis. One should simultaneously attempt to explain the concentration in urban areas, the young age of most offenders, the meaning of the criminal act, and the fact that the youth do not make careers of being criminals. Thus, the intent here is to develop an integrated perspective on the problem of youth crime by looking at all levels of "cause" and the way in which each etiological force affects adolescents. The objective is to indicate what factors influence youth reliance on groups supporting delinquent values by considering the patterns of role relationship of adolescents[10] and how these subsequently affect youth's integration into society.

In spelling out the patterns of role relationships that affect how well youth in general and young criminals in particular are socially integrated, it is hoped that the perspective can provide the necessary missing link between macro- and microdeviance analysis.

Patterns of role relationships become the common denominator through which wider origins affect associations, and associations help define the self-concept and the situation. Durkheim, especially in his seminal work *Suicide*, provided much of the inspiration if not many of the concrete ideas. Our approach is quite different from that of Hirschi,[11] who was also inspired by Durkheim, but put most of the emphasis on attitudes, such as attachment, rather than behavior, as represented by role relationship variables, although a role relationship perspective is implied in Hirschi's study of juvenile delinquency. There are five major patterns of role relationships which appear to play a key role in socialization and in integrating the individual into the society. These are seen to be (1) kin relationships—including the extended family, (2) community or neighbor (3) school, (4) work, and (5) peers not otherwise defined by the four others. For example, two friends may do homework together in a student-student relationship, or they may work together unloading a truck for a grocery store. These are school and work relationships, respectively, that are quite distinct and separate from the two friends bowling or going to the movies together.

The five kinds of relationships actually imply others as well. There are quite a few potential kin and work relationships, depending upon the particular situation. For the purposes at hand it is unimportant to distinguish between uncles, aunts, mothers, or fathers, but instead to be concerned with the amount of activity and time spent across all of those relationships. Indeed, it is proposed that what is vital is not how many role partners there are but rather whether there is at least one significant relationship in each which there is considerable activity. In other words, the saliency of a given set of relationships is critical and a saliency is measured by activities.

How does one measure the activity? In a pilot research study, Marwell and Hage found that a number of role relationship variables formed a factor which they called intimacy.[12] Despite its name, all of the variables are behavioral. Those with the highest loadings include few role partners or occupants; wide variety of activities and locations; relatively high frequency of interaction; considerable knowledge about the role partners; common role sets (the role partners had common third parties); and that activities in some respects dovetailed (there was some division of labor in the role set). The general hypothesis then becomes that, if youth have intimate role relationships in all five areas or kinds, they are much less likely to engage in youth crime. Or, to put this more dynamically, as the intimacy declines both within certain areas and across all of them, the youth is less integrated into society and more likely to be involved in various kinds of crime.

Thus, the key is not so much whether a youth is unemployed, in school, has divorced parents, or lives in a ghetto—although these can be important causes explaining a lack of work, school, family, or community role relationships—but whether or not he has these relationships at all and how involved he is in them. The more involved one becomes in these relationships, the less likely he is to engage in deviant acts and especially to be involved in major crimes that often lead to detection and prosecution.

What affects the probability for adolescents to have certain role relationships? One ought to look for factors that would seem to create special situations for adolescents in particular, rather than for either children or adults. As youth grow older, their capacities for role relationships increase. Thus, looking at the normal adolescent, one would expect the gradual development of such relationships in all five areas. What factors, then might retard this natural growth?

With increasing industrialization, there appear to be a steadily lengthening period of adolescence and a greater isolation of youth from

45

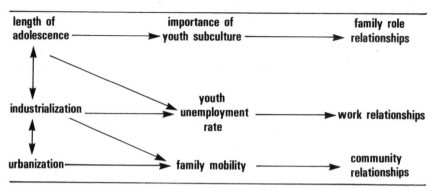

Fig. 1. The societal forces of industrialization and urbanization and their consequence for role relationships

diverse role patterns. This phenomenon appears to be a natural requirement of an affluent and urban society. Also, industrialization has created a new social category, youth unemployment, and it has done this in several ways (see figure 1). First, technological advances have been eliminating the need for unskilled labor.[13] As a consequence, individuals who drop out of high school have increasing difficulty in finding work. Even with good academic credentials, the first job usually proves the hardest to find. The more employers that are concerned about skills, the more that work experience and education become critical. This emphasis is the sine qua non of postindustrial society.

Youth unemployment, in turn, signals significant change in society, the lengthening period of time before youths can expect to have their first jobs. For those who do find jobs, their position in the labor force is more likely to be anomic, or forced, in the Durkheimian sense, subsequently reducing the probability of developing integrative relationships in the work sphere. Employment certainly is not the primary source of integration for youth, particularly the young ones. The conditions creating youth unemployment must be considered, however, since these are the structural forces which tend to isolate youth and restrict the development of integrative relationships.

As technology increases, the skills required for economic and social participation in the larger society also increase. The time between childhood and meaningful, working adult involvement becomes longer. More years of formal schooling are required before gainful employment is attained. Adolescence is becoming socially longer even as there is evidence that biologically the maturation period is becoming shorter. It is the lengthening period of an ill-defined position and status that has made delinquency such a common characteristic of contemporary society.[14]

Since the skills required for economic participation come from formal schooling, this suggests the third factor inhibiting integrative role relationships—the development of meaningful school roles that are not derived from authoritarian figures. In earlier eras, alienated youth could leave school and be absorbed into the vast unskilled and semiskilled labor force,[15] but the numbers of such jobs and the willingness to occupy them are decreasing.[16] In general, adolescents as a social category become systematically restricted in social participation: they are prohibited from integration in the adult society by virtue of age, talents, and skills.[17] Since many youth cannot work, their isolation is increased; and, as Coleman has stated, they "are cut off from the rest of society, forced inward toward their own age group, and made to carry out their whole social life with others of their own age." [18] The saliency of the peer group is increased, yet the peer group is least likely to be integrative and to develop the necessary commitments to conformity.

Adolescents create their own culture—not a counterculture, but a youth subculture with its own fashion, speech, musical taste, and the like. In part this culture is necessary, given the structural constraints against work integration in postindustrial society and the increased alienation at home and school. Postindustrial society has tended to make fewer and fewer demands on youth, creating perhaps the world's largest leisure class without the wherewithal to utilize it. As Friedenberg states, "society seemingly asks so little of him (a youth), merely that he 'grow up,' finish school, and get on the payroll." [19]

The creation of a youth subculture could be one of the barriers to family relationships. The quite strong negative correlation between family interaction and friend or peer interaction, noted in a study by Friday,[20] suggests that youth may choose not to interact with their own families as a consequence of having their own subculture. The loss of this role relationship does not matter as long as there are other relationships besides those of peers. The fewer there are, the greater the probability of some youth crime.

Finally, industrialization and urbanization have affected the development of community relationships by increasing the rate of family mobility. Mobility has eroded the sense of community, diminishing opportunity for the development of role relationships based on roots in a neighborhood. It is important to have a variety of role contacts, particularly across age groups; yet increasingly in urban areas adults interact with friends who are scattered throughout the metropolitan area and not with individuals who live in the same building or block. There is a reduction of long-term interest in youth on the part of conforming adults outside of the family. Young people are mobile, meeting friends away from home and away from the neighborhood where informal social controls are more likely to be exercised. Once a certain proportion of the population has developed this postindustrial pattern, one can no longer speak of it as a community.

Many theories which have been proposed to explain youth crime have done so by analyzing relationships of youths with societal institutions and the role and impact the latter play in the individual's adaptation to structural demands. Such theories focus on family, school, and peers in the socialization process. For example, Hirschi has emphasized attachments or attitudes toward these institutions as factors in youth crime.[21]

The role relationship model is consistent with these theories, but stresses the interrelationship and interaction across all institutions instead of focusing on only one role group. The model also underlines the frequency of interaction (behavior) and not simply attachments (attitudes). The key is how many opportunities there are to be socialized to the dominant norms of society. This is a question of how many relationships, especially in different areas, the youth is involved in and, most important, how intimate these are. Particularly crucial is the spread across family, community, work, and school because it is in this way that the individual becomes wedded to societal norms and values.

The theory of differential association, for example, suggests that the ratio of the exposure to criminal and noncriminal norms is critical in understanding youth crime.[22] The behavioral outcome is a function of the frequency, priority, duration, and intensity of the exposure to the criminal or noncriminal pattern. The role relationship model attempts to go beyond this general theory and suggests that the dominance of either conforming or criminal patterns is a function of the total role set. The role relationship perspective interprets differential associations as arguing implicitly that one has only a few relationships, primarily peer ones, and that these become critical. Insofar as one has a wide variety of intimate contacts no single one, even if it involves deviant norms, can become too important. The greater the variety of relationships, the more likely will be a counterbalancing and/or strain toward conformity to the norms of the larger society. Conversely, if only one or two role relationships exist, these become more critical. If they involve socialization to

deviant norms, then under these circumstances the differential association thesis should hold.

What evidence is there to support at least circumstantially these
ideas? In a study of Swedish adolescents, Friday found that the greater
the interaction with family, the less the frequency of serious theft, and
the greater the interaction with either a teacher or a boss outside of
school or work, the less the self-reported theft.[23] This study did not systematically measure all of the possible role sets, but it did report that
greater interaction with friends correlated with greater theft. Hindelang
reached a similar finding.[24] Social class controls did not affect the correlation.

For those theorists who have emphasized the importance of a positive self-conception,[25] a diversity of intimate role relationships appears
to correlate with a positive view of self. The loss of interaction opportunities in the family can have a considerable impact on self-image. A
low frequency of interaction between sole partners, particularly parents
and children, is a reflection of little sentiment or affection[26] and reinforces self-worth, or the lack of it. The importance of family interaction
patterns has been stressed as more significant in the etiology of delinquency than in the physical structure of the familial unit.[27]

This finding is supported by Vaz and Casparis in their comparison
of Canadian and Swiss youth.[28] They indicate that the Canadian sample
tended to be more peer oriented and also more deviant, while the Swiss
favored parents and engaged in less criminal acts. They interacted, tested
frequency of interaction, and found the Swiss boys interacted more frequently with adults than with their peers. Kobal, studying delinquency
in Yugoslavia and England concluded that there tended to be more
openness and communication between youth and adults in Slovenia
than in London.[29] Likewise, Clinard and Abbott found crime rates
higher in Africa in areas less likely to have stable family relationships.[30]
Finally, a report from the criminological institute at Ljubljana on the
living conditions of delinquency states that one of the characteristics of
families producing juvenile delinquents is a "lack of emotional ties between parents."[31]

Unfortunately, none of this research has attempted to tap the many
different variables involved in what is here called the intimacy factor.

In examining the nature of the interaction, and not simply the attachments, the variety of activities, the amount of self-discourse, and the
integration of role partners and activities are particularly critical. Data
on these variables would considerably improve the measurement and

the strength of the findings. While interaction frequency is important, other ways in which one can be integrated may be more so. Equally significant is that none of this research has attempted to "add across" role relationships or deal with the total role pattern; further, there has been an overemphasis on the family and not enough on the school and work place or the overlap between them.

The integrating function of schools is frequently taken for granted. The conclusions of an 11-year longitudinal study found the school to be the third most important factor contributing to delinquency.[32] Only the family and peer group had more pervasive effects. The most general societal function of schools is the transmission of knowledge, norms, and values. In essence, Durkheim maintained, the school functions as the primary regulator of moral education for a nation and "the school is the sole moral environment where the child can learn methodically to know and love."[33]

The role of school and its opportunities for creating role relationships have not been adequately researched. As long as a youth has significant relationships in school, whether he is doing well or not, school is likely to be an important element in a youth's life. It may be a relationship with a teacher, coach, librarian, girl friend, or another student; but if there is a role relationship, then the adolescent is likely to be motivated and to strive to stay in school. Relationships with teachers are generally impersonal[34] which may be due in part to the changing expectations in school. The society demands more skills to be taught, and teachers have become accountable economically in terms of pupil performance. Subsequently, these pressures tend to alienate the poor student, decreasing the probability of developing integrative relationships and commitments, let alone the skills required for participation in the economy.

There is an interaction between the home and school in the ability of the school to facilitate and reinforce integration. Social background and class-based socialization processes determine to a great extent children's behavioral patterns and personality structures before they enter school. Once in school, these behavioral patterns are observed and evaluated by a teacher whose expectations may reinforce the youth's identity or tend to alienate that youth from the socialization and norm transmission role of the school. The alternative for youth is to accept the social role definitions given by the dominant interactive partners in the school, or to reject those definitions thereby reducing the impact of the school relationships in fulfilling their integrative function.

If integration is facilitated ideologically by feeling and being a part of the whole society, work is one mechanism whereby such participation and feelings may or may not develop, depending upon the situation. As Durkheim suggested, "the individual becomes cognizant of his dependence upon society; from it come the forces which keep him in check and restrain him. In short since the division of labor becomes the chief source of social solidarity, it becomes at the same time the foundation of the moral order." [35] The nature of the work and the ability of the work situation to facilitate meaningful relationships are crucial. Durkheim cautions, however, that the division of labor may not produce solidarity if the work is anomic, i.e., isolated from a glimpse of the total meaning of the labor, is forced upon the individual, or if the functional activity of each worker is insufficient. [36]

Work role relationships are critical because work, having a job, and earning an income are important parts of male social identity. Being in a college preparatory class or preparing for a technical career is a structural equivalent to being employed. It is this loss of work, being defined as being unemployed or seeing no future potential for work, that probably most deeply affects the adolescent's sense of powerlessness. [37]

The impact of the work situation on delinquent behavior is illustrated by a study of the stages of industrialization in Poland. [38] Looking at four different stages of economic development, Mosciskier stressed that particular stages—such as rapid growth and mobility in the development of the work situation—temporarily facilitated delinquency, while in situations where the youth were part of the workers' councils and developed what is referred to as socialist social relations, delinquency rates did not increase.

The importance of the work situation is also seen in studies from Japan. Kiefer concluded that "responsible behavior is secured in Japan by developing the allegiance of the individual to the work group in such a way as to legitimate its disciplinary claims on him and intensify his feelings of obligation not to offend against it." [39] Since the work group seems to dominate personal life in Japan, criminality is reduced to the extent that one is integrated behaviorally into the group.

The work group is important because of its potential as an integrating force. The extent to which the work situation is anomic or forced affects its ability to function as an integrating mechanism. While work is integrative, forced work or a forced division of labor exacerbate the tension between individuals and the needs of society. This tension will result in anomie to the extent to which individuals are not morally aligned with the new collective conscience of organic solidarity.

An eight-hour-a-day job, depending upon the kind of work, may provide many opportunities to have meaningful social relationships, as well as occasions for youth to see and hear how adult males behave. Indeed, this is, in the absence of school, the main way in which males are integrated into society.

Beyond the consideration of the adolescent and his role relationship in the family, school, and work place it is necessary to explore the opportunities for neighborhood integration. Children who do not have playmates on the block and siblings in the family have lost another opportunity for social integration into meaningful relationships. In many cases, children in a neighborhood do not go to the same school, to the same voluntary groups, or more significantly, do not interact with each other's family or other neighbors. Where such interaction is common, the probabilities of delinquency are reduced.[40] Maccoby, in an analysis of two working-class neighborhoods, found a strong correlate of criminality to be the extent of integration in the ongoing interaction system of the local community.[41] Facilitators of such integration would be the church, boy scouts, YMCA, and the like. Each of these provides a wide range of relations across age groups.

Clinard discusses the importance of neighborhood or community integration. He refers to communicative integration as the extent to which contacts permeate the group. Neighborhood integration was seen to operate on both the individual and organizational levels.[42] On the individual level, integration involves the extent to which relationships are limited to the community, the commitments individuals have to others in the community, and the number of acquaintances one has in the community. These community relationships decrease as family and school relationships become more alienating or absent due to migration. Criminality was found by Rogler in Puerto Rico[43] and by Clinard and Abbott in Africa[44] to be higher in areas with little community integration.

What are the consequences of having little intimacy in family, school, work, or community role relationships? What happens when role relationships are lacking across groups? The saliency of peer group role relationships increases, and the youth spend more time in the group (see figure 2). Indeed, there is little else to do. The peer group becomes more significant to the extent that a youth is isolated from or unable to obtain sufficient reward for conformity in the family, school, or other conforming groups. Karacki and Toby found a lack of commitment to an adult way of life to be at the root of the delinquency problem.[45] Looking at youth gangs, they found that those who appeared nondelinquent tended to be boys who had changed from the youth culture to adult roles and norms and those who had successfully returned to school or work.

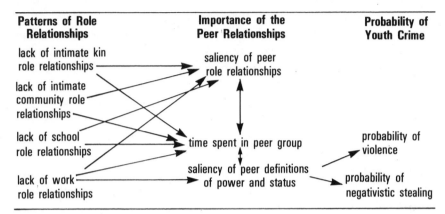

Fig. 2. Patterns of role relationships, the importance of the
peer group, and the probability of youth crime

Because of the excessive amounts of time spent in the peer group, its saliency, and the lack of a job and work relationship, both power and status as defined by that group become much more important than would otherwise be the case. Youth who are unsuccessful in meeting the performance standards of school may often compensate by achieving prestige among peers. Friday found a strong negative correlation between interaction in the family and interaction with friends (-0.81),[46] indicating that given a lack of familial relationships, there is a turning to one's peer group.

The model presented here suggests that, if an aggregate of adolescents having few role relationships with adult role models start to interact, they will develop group norms relative to powerlessness and status, exhibiting behavior that establishes their identity and success.

Given the dynamics of interaction in nonintegrated groups—that is, youth peer groups which have little contact with the rest of society—the concern about power and status becomes focal. Youths differentiate among themselves, and they appear to do so on the same criteria as adult groups—wealth and power. This, in turn, increases the probability of stealing and, one might add, it can also lead to violence, since gang wars and fights essentially flow from concerns about power and status—

in this instance, male identity rather than social prestige. Studies of gang activities in Chicago clearly indicate that the precipitating event of many deviant acts was most frequently a threat to youth power and status.[47]

While many thefts by adolescents may appear on the surface to be nonutilitarian, Friday found in Sweden that such thefts could be seen to reflect concerns about status.[48] Items most frequently stolen were gasoline, cigarettes, condoms, and sharp clothes. Each of these items in the Swedish market (with the exception of condoms) is expensive and can be directly related to status, wealth, and prestige in the youth group. Condoms possess status rewards, though not economic, in that their possession and conspicuous display imply the opportunity to use them, and in such a way define one's masculine role, particularly for the younger adolescent. Though unable to compete effectively for power and status in the adult world, adolescents still appear to employ the same general criteria of that world, but define them in their own unique fashion. These criteria are reinforced by the increased materialism and consumption required by advanced industrial societies.

One important way of testing this line of reasoning is to ask what happens when the adolescent becomes involved in meaningful role relationships. Although there is no direct test of this, the model does conform with another testing fact about youth crime and juvenile delinquency; after a peak in mid-adolescence, it declines with increasing age. Cessation of criminal activity most frequently corresponds in time with the development of the responsibilities of marriage, employment, or other relationships that foster conformity.

This perspective also explicates the peculiar need for adolescent conformity to youth norms. Durkheim talked about the problem of overcommitment to norms as a characteristic of altruistic suicide. Paradoxically this is also the pattern of youth groups or gangs as predicted in the framework in figure 2. With only one role relationship left, this becomes the most important thing in the lives of the members. The group's norms and concerns become central for the member. He must prove himself to his peers and will take great risks to do so. Thus, the strength of the peer group influences will depend to a marked degree on the intensiveness of peer group involvement as against other involvements and commitments. Hirschi suggests that if there is no commitment (attenuated attachments) to parents, school, and the like, an individual is psychologically more available to engage in sporadic acts of deviance.[49] Unlike Hirschi, who believes that attachments to peers and to parents are directly related to each other and that both are inversely related to delinquency, the role pattern perspective suggests that peer attachments are directly related to delinquent involvement. As the saliency of the peer group increases, so too does the probability of delinquency. Our argument is supported by Hindelang's attempt to validate Hirschi's model. Hindelang supported Hirschi's notion of attenuated attachments reducing criminality except for peer relationships—which he found to increase the probability of delinquency.[50]

Criminal youths, then, appear to have an isolated pattern of relationships, fostered by conditions in the society. Since the role relationships precede attachment or commitment, the limited role set increases the probability of commitment to deviance. At the same time, and this is the Durkheimian irony, by stealing—especially for joyriding—and by engaging in violence to prove their masculinity, youths reaffirm their own basic commitment to the importance of society and its values, signifying their acceptance of the system even though they are not part of it.

Taking a few well-known facts about youth crime, the attempt has been made to construct a more comprehensive theoretical framework that synthesizes the works of many who have proposed theories about delinquency or youth crime on both the wider origins level and on the immediate origins level. To do this, it has been necessary to employ Durkheim's ideas about social integration and to propose a new way of viewing the process of integration; namely, through patterns of role relationships. When adolescents have meaningful kin, educational, work, and community relationships, they are more likely to become socialized on the dominant norms of society. Integration is facilitated by interaction across all role patterns. An absence of these role relationships means a greater probability of "differential association" with youth, or in Sutherland's terms, greater priority being given to deviant patterns. In other words, the youth group becomes the only meaningful role relationship. The member becomes overcommitted to its norms, and with a pattern comparable to Durkheim's altruistic suicide. The peer group is more likely to be deviant to the extent to which individual members lack other integrating relationships, since they continue to employ the same success criteria, wealth and power, as the adult society without sufficient means to achieve it.

Structural conditions in the society hinder the development of an integrated role pattern. The paradox is that, as societies become wealthier, adolescents must spend longer and longer periods in isolation or in dependent relationships with the family, school, or "forced" employment. If youth are isolated from other relationships which could foster integration and commitment, there is greater probability of youth crime.

4

A Comparative Study of Youth Culture and Delinquency: Upper Middle-Class Canadian and Swiss Boys

EDMUND W. VAZ and JOHN CASPARIS

Whether or not the youth culture is a universal phenomenon we do not know. There is so little reported research on the subject outside of the United States that hearsay is apt to be our best source of information if we enquire about the topic elsewhere. Similarly, the comparative study of juvenile delinquency is just beginning. What we know of delinquency in non-English speaking countries is limited usually to the illegal conduct of lower-class boys.[1] The presence of a youth culture and the extent of delinquency among boys from upper socioeconomic strata remain largely a mystery.[2] Perhaps these boys are better behaved, less aggressive and hostile. Perhaps they do not as often run foul of the law. On the other hand, perhaps they have not yet been researched.

This paper is a cross-cultural step in this direction. It attempts an initial analysis of comparative data on selected dimensions of the youth culture among upper middle-class Canadian and Swiss boys. This includes their parent/peer orientation and also the frequency of their dating and other "social" activities; secondly it presents comparative material on the attitudes of these boys towards common adolescent situations and on their self-reported delinquencies. Discussion proceeds according to the comparative development of a youth culture and the social roles of these boys.

In April 1963 data on the self-reported delinquency and youth culture activities of boys were gathered from five coeducational high schools located in four Canadian communities. Anonymous question-naires were administered to 1,639 white, high school boys aged 13 to over 19 years in grades 9 through 13. Data were collected on delin-quency, peer/parent orientation, attitudes, values, and the participation of youths in legitimate peer-oriented activities. Two high schools were located in a medium-sized city of about 100,000 population, and two in suburban townships of an industrial city of over 250,000 people. The fifth high school was situated in a small town immediately outside the same city. The schools were located in mainly middle-class areas, and although the communities vary widely in size, each comes under the influence of the nearby metropolis. Vaz has reported elsewhere the spe-cific conditions under which this research was conducted.[3]

In June 1966 anonymous questionnaires were administered to 514 boys attending four schools in the Canton Graubunden, Switzerland. The schools included a *Kantonsschule*, a secondary school located in the town of Chuz, a secondary school and a private boys' *Gymnasium* situ-ated in a village nearby. The questionnaire (previously used in the Ca-nadian study) was translated into German and the items revised and made applicable to the Swiss scene.[4] Subjects ranged in age from 13 to over 20 years. Data on the small number of boys over 19 years are not included in this paper. The conditions under which this research was carried out parallel closely those of the Canadian project. The material presented in this paper stems from these two projects.

The Canton Graubunden is one of the most traditional,[5] least in-dustrialised and urbanised Cantons in Switzerland. Chur is the capital of the Canton and in 1960 had a population of 24,825. It is a rapidly growing Swiss town with a decennial growth rate of 28.1 percent, and gains by in-migration at the expense of the small rural villages in the mountains which have been steadily losing population through out-migration.

The religious composition of Graubunden is not markedly different from that of its capital or from that of Switzerland. In 1960, 55.3 per-cent of Chur was Protestant, 46.3 percent Roman Catholic. Of the boys studied, 72 percent are Protestant, 23 percent Roman Catholic.

Linguistically Graubunden is somewhat special since 26 percent of its population speak Romanisch, whereas less than 1 percent of Switzer-land speak this minority tongue; 16.1 percent speak Italian compared to 9.5 percent for all of Switzerland. German is the major language and is spoken by 56.7 percent of the Canton compared to 69.3 percent for the country. In Chur, German is spoken by 83.2 percent of the people and is

57

in daily use. Less than 11 percent speak Romanisch, and 7.5 percent speak Italian. Under 1 percent of the Canton speak French which is considerably less than for all of Switzerland. The schools where the data were collected teach in German and all our respondents understand this language.

Chur is a center of trade and transportation, an administrative capital, and serves a far-flung, sparsely settled rural region. Transportation and public utilities employ 12 percent of the working population; commerce, banking, and insurance 18 percent; and public administration employs 4.6 percent. Manufacturing employs 27.5 percent of the work force and is the single most important employing sector. However, only one-fifth of this is in heavy industrial factory-type employment.[6]

In order to establish the socioeconomic position of Swiss respondents, two major and one minor indicator were used in the following order: (1) father's occupation, (2) father's level of education, and (3) size of organisation in which father works. Using father's occupation, each questionnaire was reviewed, and eight occupational categories established. These were (1) unskilled, (2) semiskilled, (3) skilled, (4) farmers, (5) petty shopkeepers and artisans (*Gewerbe*), (6) clerical and sales (*Angestellte*), (7) middle managers, lower professions, staff, and technicians (*Hohere Beamte*), and (8) top professionals, top owners, and executives. The second indicator, father's level of education, was used to help overcome initial difficulties in the categorisation of occupations. For example, ambiguity regarding the classification of an occupational title into either "middle manager" or "clerical" was resolved in the following manner: if the father had completed "College Preparatory School" (Gymnasium, polytechnical school, etc.), the subject was labelled "middle manager." If the father had less education or if his education was not reported, the subject was classified "clerical." In order to overcome difficulties in categorising "unskilled" and "semiskilled" persons, if the father had completed secondary school he was classified "semiskilled", if not, he was categorised "unskilled."

On the basis of our occupational descriptive categories, four socioeconomic "classes" or groups were established. Unskilled and semiskilled occupations were grouped and comprise Class 4 ("lower class"); farmers form a separate unit and constitute Class 3 ("farmers"); skilled occupations, petty shopkeepers, artisans, clerical and sales workers were grouped into Class 2 ("middle class"); middle manager, lower professions, staff, and technicians were grouped with top professionals, owners, and executives and comprise Class 1 ("upper class").[7] The Swiss data presented in this paper comprise respondents categorised in Class 1.

Using identical indicators of socioeconomic position, Canadian data were classified according to the Blishen Occupational Class Scale. Four socioeconomic groups were established. The present analysis consists of data from the two highest socioeconomic strata which includes occupations on the Blishen Scale extending from judges (90.0) to transportation managers (60.1).[8] Although some of our respondents are categorised Class 1, it is unlikely that these Canadian public schools attract boys from the highest reaches of the socioeconomic ladder. It seems more likely that our respondents come from upper middle socioeconomic strata.

YOUTH CULTURE

It is unlikely that a youth culture is endemic to any society, but will emerge only under special conditions. Recent social and economic change in Canada has made possible a culture of leisure and an affluent and highly industrialised society. An unexpected consequence has been the emergence of a prestigious youth culture and the highly glamorised, socially celebrated role of teenager. Never before has so much organised publicity been focused on this age group. Especially conspicuous has been the vast transformation in family structure; family size has decreased;[9] no longer is there kinship support for raising children and there has occurred a redistribution of power within the family. The growing insecurity of adults in their parental roles[10] has made possible the opinions and views of adolescents to be heard and oftentimes felt. This has given increased individuality and independence to family members, made young people easily available to one another, and thereby fostered the proliferation of peer groups and cultures.[11]

Education has also felt the impact of affluence and change. More young people spend longer time in school, and enter the work world later than ever before. Academic standards have been "broadened," high schools have grown larger and have become increasingly "permissive." In part this has allowed children to remain in school longer and has provided an institutional setting for collective norms, interests, and behaviour patterns to develop. Having taken over many of the functions previously performed by the family, both the school and school teacher have become increasingly important agencies in the socialisation of young people. This has increased the demands made of the teacher and modified his occupational role. Anxious for an improved social status, the teaching occupation has been forced to assume the semiprofessional trappings of a multiplicity of roles. Half trained in most, fully trained in none, the school teacher is seldom expected to be a model of intellect to his pupils, and his scholarship has sometimes suffered most. Instead he is expected to be teacher, counsellor, judge of "problem" children, athletic coach, and "good guy." Understandably, he is jack of some roles perhaps master of none.

Big business has been quick to appreciate and influence the purchasing power of young people. Through the mass media it has promoted the "needs" of younger age groups, publicised the adolescent market and colorfully highlighted, as a moral imperative, active participation in teenage events. At the same time the increase in discretionary purchasing power of adolescents and the material wealth of an affluent society have contributed to the distinctive features of the youth culture.

As a system of interdependent cliques and groups the youth culture is a prominent going concern. It is the overlap of peer-oriented, joint participation in everyday activities, hardened by an inlay of extensively felt norm, sentiment, and common interest that encourages us to refer to a youth culture. But this is not to suggest the wholesale insulation of the youth culture from the larger society. Indeed, the overlapping culture of middle and upper middle-class youths mirrors the influence of that sector of larger adult society of which they are structurally members. Moreover, the multifarious adult associations and institutions that service its daily "needs" betray their approval thereby, and contribute to the material and psychological comfort of its members.

By their vacillation, adults have given tacit approval to the group-dominated, fun-ridden content of the teenage culture. It is not that parents have been rendered helpless, the "social group" (albeit stressful) orientation of parents is well known, also their prescriptions to children for peer-group commitment for status and recognition.[12] But in the absence of clear-cut standards and moral tenets their deeds lack confidence, their dictates want conviction. As role models they lack fibre and they are often of two minds about their roles as parents.

For teenagers, participation in relatively unserious, socially oriented activities symbolises group membership, fosters collective norms, and is especially instrumental for status gain.[13] The ratification of norms lends stability to the system, encourages the flow of predictable behaviour, and generates confidence among young people. Although the youth culture is anchored to the larger social structure, and Bernard suggests that it may soon include an even younger age group, its content is characteristically in flux.[14] Continuous effort at novelty and behavioural differentiation mirrors the significance of conspicuous consumption and the competitive quest for approval among teenagers, while its flourishing kaleidoscopic quality makes the teenage culture especially fascinating.

In Switzerland, conditions are different. Although Switzerland is one of the affluent countries of the world, it ranks objectively lower than either Canada or the United States.[15] Moreover, the Canton Graubunden is generally less affluent than the more urbanised and industrialised belt of the country. Much of the manufacturing that typifies the area is that of craftsmen and artisans employed in small shops. This hints that the area has experienced relatively slow social and economic transformation.[16] Again, Switzerland has always been a country with strongly traditional religious values, and this influence continues to prevail in the Graubunden area.[17] Here the family unit is apt to be relatively stable,[18] authority still vested firmly with the parents, and the rights and obligations governing parent-child relationships clearly defined and respected. It suggests too that the aims and methods of socialisation have remained intact, clear-cut goals are set for children, and that adults are still comparatively secure in the parental roles. Relationships between parents and children are perhaps a trace more formal than those in most Canadian families, and the inculcation of morals and the molding of character are both valued and taught with a conviction less evident perhaps among many Canadian families.[19]

While there has been an increase in the number of children who attend school in Switzerland, the percentage of youth between 15 and 19 years enrolled in Swiss schools is lower than in Canada and the United States.[20] Compared with Canadian schools Swiss institutions have undergone less change and are hardly "permissive" by our standards. A heavy emphasis is placed on scholarship, and discipline is widely institutionalised. It is not expected in Swiss schools that the sexes in the fifth and sixth grades will be overtly interested in each other. The school teacher continues to hold high status, and student-teacher contacts are conducted according to well-established role obligations. Since social distance prevails, a comparatively formal etiquette governs these contacts, and unlike the Canadian high school where teachers perform a variety of roles, the role of "good guy" is not yet available to the Swiss teacher. Swiss schools are concerned mainly with impersonal matters and relatively little organised opportunity exists for extracurricular activities. Unlike Canadian boys who can, and often do, enjoy the best of both worlds—the high school and the drive-in—and usually graduate "successfully" from both, Swiss boys, with their heavy academic load, must often forego many leisure activities and experiences in order to achieve future goals. Swiss boys who do find plenty of time for extra-curricular activities are often those who have left school early and become apprenticed to a trade.[21]

Family, school, and church function as mutually reinforcing institutions of adult authority and as carriers of traditional moral values. Parents ally themselves with teachers, not with their children, in authority and disciplinary disputes. Religion is taught in all grades in school and the responsibility and authority of the school over its students usually extends beyond the classroom and the school grounds. Teachers, parents, landladies, and the police are all expected to help enforce community regulations and curfew hours for young people. Faced with such a united moral front, it is more difficult for youth to play off one adult authority against another.[22]

Structural conditions continue to slow the growth of a youth culture among Swiss adolescents. This is not to suggest that social change has not occurred nor that the Swiss family has remained static. Toby suggests that orientation to consumption is apt to be characteristic of all industrial countries,[23] and we suspect too that Swiss youth are becoming more and more independent. Like their Canadian counterparts, they are oriented increasingly to an affluent style of life. But if a teenage culture is a culture of leisure, then the Swiss youth that we studied cannot enjoy very much of it because there is, relative to Canadian youth, not yet much to enjoy. The institutionalisation of a "social ethic" continues to battle an ascetic Protestantism and a traditional Catholic morality; school work is not yet defined as "fun" nor are the schools oriented to extracurricular activity; the Swiss family has only begun to shift values and the "submission to the group" is not a moral imperative; early heterosexual relationships among young people are discouraged and parental dictates respected. Since peers are not as readily accessible as they are among Canadian youth, they do not likely exercise as strong a scrutinising and evaluating role in their diurnal experiences and decisions. A culture of invidious distinctions, norms, and standards is less evident and the tyranny of group demands is likely less coercive. The comparative dearth of differentially prestigious social affairs suggests that social success is less important for popularity and is not apt to be defined as the seemingly unequivocal good it often appears to be among Canadian youth. Active participation in collective teenage events is not urgent.

More formal rules of etiquette guide heterosexual relationships among older Swiss youth and privacy seems more respected. This is possible since a ubiquitous jury of peers is not present. Briefly, the youth culture among Swiss adolescents is not widely institutionalised; lacking a moral mandate, it is not yet a conspicuously approved segment of the community.

PEER ORIENTATION

The conception of a youth culture implies at least the reciprocal orientation towards common values, shared interests and perspectives of a plurality of adolescents. Admittedly the youth culture is implicit in the larger common culture, but this does not deny its particular distinctiveness which, at the same time, is always a matter of degree.

The considerable fragmentation in institutional controls and the mutual accessibility of Canadian adolescents have facilitated the gradual swing away from parents towards peers. But this growing independence is not uniform for all ages. Younger lads, still under parental supervision, are permitted fewer prerogatives, more of their time is spent indoors pursuing their own interest and games. We should expect, too, that they are less peer oriented than are older boys.

Vaz has demonstrated the peer orientation of Canadian,[24] and Coleman of American, middle-class boys.[25] Less is known of boys from the upper socioeconomic strata. Two items were used to measure the degree to which Canadian and Swiss boys were oriented to parents and peers. The first item was as follows: "Let us say that you had always wanted to belong to a special club in town and then finally you were asked to join. But you discovered that your parents did not approve of the club. And since your best friend was not asked to join, you would have to break up with your best friend. Which of these things would be hardest for you to take?"[26]

The data in table 8 tend to substantiate our expectations. In both age groups Swiss boys prefer parents, Canadian boys favour peers. Where ages are combined the results are significant and in the expected direction.

As a second item the respondents were asked the following question: "A situation like this might face anyone sooner or later. Suppose your parents planned a trip for two or three days to celebrate their wedding anniversary and they plan to take the whole family. But then it happens that this year the town football team is playing in an important tournament the very weekend that your family is going away, and your group of friends is going to the tournament. Your parents cannot change their plans and leave it up to you: to go with them or to go to the tournament. Which do you think you would do?"

The answers to this item reveal that both younger and older Swiss boys are more strongly oriented to parents than are Canadian boys. The consistent parent orientation of Swiss boys (see table 8) undermines the probability of a structurally stable culture of Swiss youth. On the other hand 66 percent of younger Canadian boys are parent oriented whereas the majority (58 percent) of older Canadian boys continue to favour peers. The consistency in peer orientation of older Canadian boys is what we would expect. Role expectations of the older adolescent usually require fuller participation in the youth culture; involvement in social events is less incumbent upon youngsters.

Table 8.

THE ORIENTATION OF CANADIAN AND SWISS UPPER MIDDLE-
CLASS BOYS TO PARENTS AND PEERS BY AGE*

| Response Category | Percentage in Age Categories | | | | | |
| | 13–14 years | | 15–19 years | | All Ages | |
	Can.	Swiss	Can.	Swiss	Can.	Swiss
Parents' disapproval	36.0	59.2	38.5	55.7	37.9	57.1
Breaking with your best friend	64.0	39.5	60.8	42.6	61.5	41.3
	$X^2 = 9.45$		$X^2 = 9.98$		$X^2 = 19.44$	
	1df, p < .01		1df, p < .01		1df, p < .001	
N =	89	76	288	108	377	184

* Owing to a small number of rejected items columns total less than 100 percent.

On the basis of these two items, it appears that Swiss boys are oriented primarily to parents. Older Canadian boys are oriented to peers while youngsters are torn between parents and peers; their orientation varies with the item, and likely depends on the differential appeal of peer-oriented activities.

YOUTH CULTURE ACTIVITIES

The things that boys do, their interests and time-consuming activities are seemingly infinite in variety. But active membership in a youth culture means that teenage conduct must ultimately pass muster before a jury of peers. And peer-group affiliation tends to corral a boy's activities, temper his behaviour, and influence his taste in emotions. Most boys engage in some activities, few are likely to participate in them all. In spite of, or perhaps as result of, the time they spend in school, nonacademic interests loom large in the lives of Canadian boys. Among others Vaz has shown that girls, sports, "having fun," "socials," parties, and cars stand out among their concerns while scholarly interests rate low.[27]

Seeley et al. have noted that in and out of the home Canadian boys are tutored early for later adolescent roles;[28] they soon become peer oriented and eagerly look forward to active involvement in teenage events. Recurrent experience in this common round of adolescent affairs helps breed normative consensus, and strengthens peer orientations. But Swiss boys are quite strongly tied to parents, and youngsters are seldom encouraged in heterosexual relationships. Experiences of this kind will occur later and differ in kind and frequency. Since the Swiss high school is seldom the institutional catalyst for teenage events that is the Canadian school, these conditions will tend to discourage extensive and vigorous teenage social activity.

Two items were used to explore the extent to which Canadian and Swiss boys engage in selected adolescent activities. The first item enquired, "How often during the week do you take out a girl or go with your friends to a dance (e.g., Saturday night dance, bar-dance, etc.)?"[29]

It appears that dating is not a major preoccupation among youngsters of either nationality. However, older boys are most interested in girls and date more often, and the results fit our expectations. Thirty-two percent of Canadian boys compared with 24 percent of Swiss boys date about once a week. Among boys who date more often, 20 percent are Canadian, 9 percent Swiss. Although Swiss boys are interested in girls, the data suggest that they are slower than Canadian boys to include girls in their regular leisure activities.

A second item was asked of our respondents: "How often do you spend some time with your friends at a local cafe or club throughout the whole week?" It is important to note that the original version of this item enquired of Canadian boys about the frequency of this behaviour occurring during the "evening throughout the whole week." In revising the questionnaire we were advised that this item was inapplicable to the Graubunden area since the early curfew for younger boys discourages their staying out late at night when school is in session. Customarily students congregate socially in public places and street corners after school and again briefly after supper. Because of the curfew, getting together in the evenings is usually restricted to older boys. Responses to this item by Canadian boys reflect the frequency of their evening activity; the Swiss responses reflect their behaviour during the day and evening.

As expected, the data disclose that Canadian youngsters spend considerably more time with their friends outside the home than do Swiss boys. However, there is no significant difference in the responses of older Canadian and Swiss boys. What this suggests is that Canadian boys spend as much time in the evenings as do Swiss boys in the afternoons and evenings. Since we know that Canadian boys also congregate socially with their friends after classes (since academic requirements are seldom sufficient to deter them), these data help underline our hypothesis.

ATTITUDES

The vigorously competitive and social quality of the Canadian youth culture influences the roles that develop and affects the kinds of persons that adolescents want to be. The "swinger," "the boy with a style," "the terrific personality," and "the sharp dresser" are informal yet popular roles among Canadian boys, and role claimants are often required to be relatively expert with the opposite sex. It is partly through conformity to role obligations and joint involvement in the teenage crowd that boys acquire common attitudes and sentiments. Perhaps differential engagement in the youth culture is correlated with the differential classification of persons and definitions of situation in ways appropriate to the sentiments and norms of the youth culture. This implies that the attitudes of younger boys towards common youth culture events will be less favourable than those of their older counterparts. We can expect also that the attitudes of Canadian adolescents will parallel "permissive" youth culture values, but differ markedly from those of Swiss boys.

The following data gathered from a set of items are suggestive of future lines of research. Each item is designed as a "life situation" more or less appropriate to the youth culture. Each situation attempts to elicit attitudes that are apt to be strongly influenced through participation in typical, heterosexual peer-oriented activities. Although the items are relatively complex, they are perhaps sufficiently common to allow the respondent to respond to each item as a "whole."

Most Canadian public schools are coeducational and many of the relationships and experiences of older Canadian boys are heterosexual in nature. The norms governing these situations, and the male-role obligations in these heterosexual relationships will accord with the presence of girls. It is likely that coeducational schools and the heterosexual content of the youth culture temper the masculine conduct and sex-role identification of Canadian boys.

Although most Swiss schools are coeducational, boys engage less in heterosexual relationships. Single-sex experiences predominate. The typical roles and behavioral styles common to such single-sex situations will differ widely from those in milieux where girls participate. Single-sex experiences will reinforce sex-role identification, require sex-typed activities, and the display of more masculine conduct. Swiss boys may thus prefer the less "sophisticated" ceremonial approaches to fighting.

Table 9

ATTITUDES OF CANADIAN AND SWISS UPPER MIDDLE-CLASS BOYS
TOWARDS FIST FIGHTING BY AGE

Two high school boys are engaged in a fist fight. Both boys are angry and determined to win, and no holds are barred in the fight. Do you think they should fight the way they wish, no holds barred? Or should they go to the gym, put on the gloves, and have another boy act as referee?

| | Percentage in Age Categories | | | | | |
| | 13–14 years | | 15–19 years | | All ages | |
Response Category	Can.	Swiss	Can.	Swiss	Can.	Swiss
They should go to the gym and fight it out	75.3	26.3	59.0	35.2	62.9	31.5
It is all right, I guess, to fight no holds barred	14.6	56.6	13.5	35.2	13.8	44.0
It is o.k. to fight no holds barred	10.1	13.2	26.7	27.8	22.8	21.7
	$X^2 = 40.31$		$X^2 = 27.38$		$X^2 = 70.59$	
	2df, p < .001		2df, p < .001		2df, p < .001	
N =	89	76	288	108	377	184

Sharp differences in response between Swiss and Canadian boys are evident in Table 9. Seventy-five percent of younger Canadian boys prefer fighting under more formal, controlled conditions; only 26 percent of Swiss youngsters favour this. The majority (59 percent) of older Canadian boys favour this compared with 35 percent of Swiss boys. Perhaps in a youth culture where conspicuous consumption and the presentation of self are vital means for social status, opportunities for "ceremonial play," e.g. fighting "like a professional boxer" in the gym with a referee, are readily perceived as a means for status gain. Furthermore, in a newly developing youth culture perhaps Swiss boys are not strongly motivated to decide for others how they ought to fight, and thus they give their conditional approval; it is noteworthy that no more Swiss than Canadian boys unconditionally approve of fighting with no holds barred.

Shared experiences among young people foster the convergence of ideas and sentiments and help develop common attitudes among them. Any curb on this commonality of experience will tend to stunt consensus and undermine the structural stability of the youth culture. An important criterion of status among Canadian teenagers is active participation in peer-group affairs and middle and upper middle-class boys are soon pressed (by both parents and peers) into heterosexual associations. The cost of nonconformity to prevailing norms is often social isolation.

Both the formal and informal organisations of life of older Swiss boys restrict these kinds of experience to an extent less common among Canadian youth, and peer-group controls are less evident over adolescent conduct. The respective attitudes of Swiss and Canadian boys are perhaps best explained by the differential impact of the quality and frequency of their peer-group experiences.

Table 10, which presents the attitudes of Canadian and Swiss boys towards dating behaviour, reveals no significant differences in response between younger age groups. But increased involvement in the youth culture will influence the attitudes of older Canadian boys, and behavioural conformity will be less an individual matter. They will be both predisposed (through early tutelage), and socially pressed to conform to existing patterns. We find that 64 percent of older Canadian boys more or less approve of this conduct on a first date.

But the influence of parents and their service as role models will likely remain strong even among older Swiss boys who increase their heterosexual relationships. Since peer-group ties are relatively weak, norms prescribing particular types of heterosexual association and varying degrees of intimacy at each stage of the relationship are likely less coercive. Table 10 shows that 44 percent of these boys approve more or less of this behaviour on a first date.

Drinking among Swiss adolescents is neither a crime nor socially unacceptable. It is customary to see older Swiss boys drinking socially. In Canada, to serve liquor to a minor in a public place is a crime, and drinking among teenagers in the home (except on "special occasions") is usually deplored. It seems likely that cultural definitions of drinking will vary widely between Canadian and Swiss boys, and that drinking will serve different functions for them. Moreover, their social roles will differentially influence their drinking patterns.

Table 10.

ATTITUDES OF CANADIAN AND SWISS UPPER MIDDLE-CLASS BOYS
TOWARDS INTIMACY ON A FIRST DATE BY AGE

Trudy and George are 16-year-old students. They are in the same class in school. Saturday night will be their first date together. After the dance on the way home George kisses Trudy. Soon he kisses her again and they begin to neck and pet. How do you feel about this?

	Percentage in Age Categories					
	13–14 years		15–19 years		All Ages	
Response Category	Can.	Swiss	Can.	Swiss	Can.	Swiss
I do not approve of their actions	43.8	48.7	35.7	56.1	37.6	53.3
It is all right, I guess, how they wish to act	41.6	29.0	40.6	28.0	40.8	28.6
It is o.k. to neck and pet on the first date	14.6	21.1	23.8	15.9	21.6	18.1
	$X^2 = 3.02$		$X^2 = 12.58$		$X^2 = 12.63$	
	2df, p < .05		2df, p < .01		2df, p < .01	
N =	89	76	288	108	377	184

With the gradual legitimation of the Canadian youth culture, drinking among boys has very likely increased and is likely a relatively institutionalised practice among older Canadian boys. Is it possible to be an active participant for very long in typical youth culture events without taking a drink? Are there not informal games (with their own rules, roles, and special rewards) which test an older boy's capacity for liquor? Does not role expertise here confer status within some groups? The orientation to "getting high" and the practice of "having a few beers" preparatory to the "big date" are often customary among these boys.[30] The following situation item includes social drinking and initial forms of physical contact among adolescents: "Max, Susy, Hans, and Bertha are 17-year-old students. Saturday evening they go to the movies. Afterwards they return to Max's house for a few beers, and listen to some music, and dance. Then they begin necking. How do you feel about spending an evening like this?"

Although the responses are consistently in the expected direction, differences between Canadian and Swiss boys are significant only when ages are combined. That proportionately more older than younger Canadian boys approve of this behaviour likely reflects the extent to which a forbidden practice (drinking among teenagers) becomes increasingly institutionalised through active participation in adolescent events, and thereby suggests the pervasive and relatively coercive influence of the youth culture. Indeed, the values of the youth culture and its many adult-organised activities help foster conducive structures for drinking among youth.[31]

We have not suggested that Swiss youth do not engage in varying degrees of physical intimacy in their heterosexual relationships. Rather, unlike Canadian boys, older Swiss youth begin their active participation in heterosexual affairs later and proceed more slowly. Ultimately some degree of physical contact becomes acceptable.[32]

Canadian parents make their disapproval of drinking among youngsters known early. The data show that 69 percent of younger Canadian boys disapprove of mild intoxication; less than 50 percent do so among Swiss lads. Peer-group influence and youth culture participation of older Canadian boys help account for the sharp increase in their favourable attitudes. More than 53 percent more or less approve of this behaviour; of these 34 percent approve unconditionally. Certainly drunkenness is not a prerequisite to social approval among these boys; however, inebriation may be less condemned since their conduct can be defined as the unsuccessful effort to conform to game rules. Where there exists a custom of social drinking among adolescents (as among Swiss boys), claims to status through drinking are less likely successful. The results show that 63 percent of older Swiss boys disapprove of the situation described, and only 9 percent approve unconditionally.

These data suggest that drinking behaviour in the described contexts is more widely acceptable to Canadian than to Swiss boys. Perhaps parties, dances, and other social activities are considered a special class of events with their own sets of norms and customs operating; however, these events are congruent with other typical teenage affairs and constitute an integral part of the Canadian youth culture.

Not withstanding the vast influence of a relatively permissive teenage culture, Canadian adolescents are not morally freewheeling. It is true that structural change has taken place, but remnants of the Protestant Ethic remain influential. Consider only the proscriptions against self-indulgence, and the prescriptions to lead the wholesome life and subordinate immediate satisfactions in the interests of long-term goals. The idea that sexual congress out of wedlock is sinful dies hard. Certainly the adult society condemns sexual conduct among teenagers although it is clear that condemnation is less serviceable in the interests of social control than adaptation to the rapidly changing situation. Nevertheless, the attitudes of adolescents towards sexual experience, rooted in deeply instilled values, are perhaps more resistant to change than are their other sentiments. This is especially true of younger boys who are less involved in the youth culture, less amenable to peer-group influence, and whose customary roles seldom require sexual knowledge or experience of them.

From the data already presented we can expect the attitudes of Swiss boys towards sexual experience will be less favourable than those of Canadian youth.

Table 11 shows that differences in response between Canadian and Swiss youngsters are not significant. The majority of both older groups

Table 11.

ATTITUDES OF CANADIAN AND SWISS UPPER MIDDLE-CLASS BOYS
TOWARDS SEX BY AGE

Vreni is a pretty 17-year-old student. But she has a bad reputation throughout the school. She is known to be free and easy. Her classmate Robert takes her to the movies Saturday night. Before returning home Robert tries to get intimate (go the limit) with her, and she does not object. How do you feel about Robert's actions?

	Percentage in Age Categories					
	13–14 years*		15–19 years		All Ages	
Response Category	Can.	Swiss	Can.	Swiss	Can.	Swiss
I do not approve of Robert's actions	64.0	72.0	50.4	53.7	53.6	60.9
Robert's actions are all right, I guess, since Vreni did not object	28.1	25.0	38.2	42.6	35.8	35.3
Robert's actions are o.k.	7.9	2.6	11.5	1.9	10.6	2.2
	$X^2 = 1.14$		$X^2 = 8.75$		$X^2 = 12.40$	
	2df, p < .10		2df, p < .01		2df, p < .001	
N =	89	76	288	108	377	184

*The last two response categories are combined for chi-square calculation.

disapprove of the situation described. The principal difference is between boys who unconditionally approve of sexual experience under these conditions. Since it is perhaps difficult for older Canadian boys to escape the unbiquitous impact of the youth culture, it is not surprising that proportionately more Canadian than Swiss approve of this activity. Twelve percent of Canadian boys favour this compared with 2 percent of Swiss boys.

DELINQUENCY

It was possible to use only 14 delinquency items as measures for comparison.[33] The items relate to behaviour that is commonly considered in law as delinquent or criminal conduct and are framed in descriptive rather than legalistic terms. Given the socioeconomic position of our respondents and our knowledge of the areas investigated, none of the items are of a violent victimising nature. Behaviour such as gang fights, theft with assault, and the taking of drugs is omitted.

Of the six significant differences among the younger age group, four items (fist fighting, serious theft, and vandalism—typically "masculine", usually destructive acts—and truancy) were committed by a proportionately higher percentage of Swiss lads. A disproportionately high percentage of Canadian boys report theft of money and remaining out all night without parents' permission. Seven significant differences are evident among the older boys; of these, fist fighting, vandalism, serious theft, being placed on school probation, and car theft are proportionately more often admitted by Swiss boys. Gambling and theft of money are committed by a proportionately higher percentage of Canadian boys.

According to our data, the "existence" of a well-established Swiss youth culture is not clearly substantiated. Family and school controls over Swiss boys remain strong, and commitment to a "social ethic" does not appear widely celebrated. The increasingly institutionalised discretion given Canadian youth in conducting their daily affairs, is not yet available among Swiss boys. But this does not deny them occasion for delinquency. Social roles contain the opportunity for both legal and illegal behaviour, and the conditions in which they spawn and flourish often structure the nature and frequency of the delinquency that emerges. Might not the differences in the social organisation and roles of Swiss and Canadian boys influence the quality and quantity of their delinquency? Might we not help account in these terms for the dispro-

portionately high incidence of relatively aggressive, masculine-type behaviour among Swiss boys?

Boys from different social classes are differentially socialised, and
the method and content of this training is recognised to be functionally
oriented to later adolescent and adult roles. Predominant among the
roles of younger boys is their age-sex role, and the performance of masculine behaviour (perhaps irrespective of social class) is a cardinal obligation. We have suggested that Swiss youngsters are given a relatively
firm moral upbringing characterised by a sober, self-disciplined orientation towards life, and the belief that work and constructive activities are
important means for the realisation of long deferred goals. Our data
suggest too that widespread social activities and heterosexual relationships are not likely encouraged. Under these conditions the sex role distinction will be highlighted. In preparation for later roles boys will be
expected to internalise (and conform to) values such as sobriety and self-
discipline, character development, masculinity, and independence. At the
same time parental rules for children are apt to be general prescriptions
of behaviour, but within the family setting these dictates will be increasingly specific and tend to "fit" the contingencies and experiences endemic to family life. Conformity here is facilitated often through the
controlling presence of parents. But the generality of parental prescriptions for behaviour often precludes their application to the daily non-
family experiences of boys. Similarly, although the family and school
very likely share similar values and agree on the role expectations of
children, specific prescriptions for behaviour usually remain implicit.
However widely endorsed values continue to prevail and strongly influence the norms, games, and practices that emerge which allow boys a
considerable choice of alternative roles.

Especially conducive to learning and performing the more masculine, aggressive forms of behaviour among these boys are those institutional single-sex settings and daily events in which only boys customarily participate e.g., male relationships, sports events, and neighbourhood
groups—situations more typical of Swiss than Canadian boys. The
emergent roles and games are fully expressive of the masculinity and
independence of boys, and the behaviour tends also to mirror claims to
the selves that these boys wish to portray, i.e., the kinds of boys they
want to be. In tune with overall values these roles support the sex role
distinction without the controlling yoke of disciplined family prescriptions.

Here the conduct of boys is considerably less restrained, and behaviour designed to claim "sophisticated" role means less since there are apt to be few complementary role takers. What then is more expressive of being a "real boy" (and thereby ensuring the approval of others) than to skip school, fist fight, destroy property, and engage occasionally in theft? Is this not the type of behaviour that reveals a boy's courage, spotlights his masculinity, and helps confirm his self-identity? Does this behaviour not mirror the manliness to which these boys aspire? In any case, the learning and preparation for this behaviour are minimal, and whatever else such conduct might reveal it will seldom jeopardise the sex role status of boys.

In general Canadian boys of the middle and upper middle classes are introduced early to the social world of heterosexual relationships with the result that in order to maintain their popularity in the youth culture they must work hard at it. They must be socially active, develop their personalities, and become refined in the subtleties of heterosexual congress—behaviour which is largely congruent with parentally endorsed values and sentiments. One study has suggested that as older middle-class boys assume more "sophisticated" roles they tend also to practise a more "sophisticated brand of delinquency"—paradoxically, a type of delinquency that springs from conformity to legitimate role expectations.[34] Conversely, conformity to "sophisticated" roles discourages destructive, aggressive kinds of behaviour. We have already noted that comparatively less fist fighting and vandalism occur among Canadian boys. Moreover, the limited data presented in table 12 show that gambling (36 percent) and taking a drink (34 percent)—both noticeably nonaggressive activities—are offenses most often admitted more than once or twice by Canadian boys. Again, sexual intimacy with a girl, and feeling "high" from liquor are more often admitted more than once or twice by Canadian than Swiss boys. These differences, although not statistically significant, are in the anticipated direction.

But heterosexual relationships and an active social life are not endemic to the predominantly masculine world of older Swiss boys, and social obligations are encountered at a later age. Although these boys increase the scope and domain of their activities, the transition to newer adolescent roles is less urgent. For older Swiss boys there appears to be a marked continuity (from earlier roles) in role expectations. The relatively less developed youth culture and the formal institutional controls over Swiss youths perhaps limit the diversity of roles available to them. The more popular roles and their typical behaviour are largely condi-

Table 12.

SELF-REPORTED DELINQUENCY AMONG CANADIAN AND SWISS BOYS

	13–14 years		15–19 years		15–19 years	
	Percent Admitting Offense		Present Admitting Offense		Percent Admitting Offense More Than Once or Twice	
	Can.	Swiss	Can.	Swiss	Can.	Swiss
Taken little things	56.2	68.4	70.5	78.7	17.0	38.0 S
Skipped school	7.9	19.7 S	40.6	51.9	12.1	17.6
Fist fight	39.3	96.1 S	52.8	92.6 S	8.0	67.6 S
Gambling	42.7	34.2	68.8	48.2 S	35.6	33.3
Remained out all night without parents' permission	14.6	4.0 S	26.4	30.6	10.7	11.1
School probation	0.0	22.4 Inval.	7.3	18.5 S	1.0	1.9
Taken things $2–$50	12.4	26.3 S	15.6	28.7 S	4.8	8.3
Tried to be intimate with a girl	18.0	13.2	39.2	30.6	18.3	15.7
Taken money	30.3	17.1 S	36.8	15.7 S	10.4	4.6
Breaking and entering	5.6	5.3 Inval.	9.0	4.6	0.69	0.93 Inval.
Taken car for ride without owner's permission	4.5	7.9 Inval.	13.9	23.2 S	3.1	10.2 S
Destroyed property	43.8	93.4 S	52.1	79.6 S	14.5	47.2 S
Feeling "high" from liquor	7.9	5.3	38.9	36.1	17.7	15.7
Taken a drink	23.6	29.0	64.6	64.8	34.3	51.9 S
N =	89	76	288	108	288.0	108.0

* S = Significant at .05 level.

tioned by the prevailing system of values, and the groups of which they are a member. The "swinger," the boy with a "terrific line," and the "big wheel"—roles intimately associated with a heterosexual-oriented youth culture are not yet widely accessible to older Swiss boys. In any case, one cannot possess a "terrific line" for long without the opportunity to practise one's skills, nor can one usually "make out" with the opposite sex unless dyadic-type dating practices are undertaken. We know that such opportunities are relatively limited to these boys. Roles demanding the subtler social skills are assumed more gradually by Swiss adolescents. Tutelage is seldom undertaken in the early teens as is common among Canadian boys.

Older Swiss boys continue in roles that tolerate the more masculine, aggressive types of behaviour, and many of their daily experiences and situations in which they engage likely foster this behaviour. We can reasonably anticipate that these boys will engage in similarly aggressive, destructive types of delinquency. The results show that among older Swiss boys admitting an offense, 93 percent report fist fighting, 80 percent admit vandalism, and although the frequency is much smaller, for serious theft the difference in responses is significant between Canadian and Swiss boys. Of the five significant differences among older boys admitting offenses more than once or twice, fist fighting (68 percent), vandalism (47 percent), and petty theft (38 percent) are reported by Swiss boys. Car theft and taking a drink are also disproportionately admitted by these boys.

CONCLUSION

There has been growing concern over the youth culture and its impact on the behaviour of young people. Although its influence in the lives of upper-class youth has hardly been studied and its relationships to the alleged increase in middle-class delinquency remains relatively unexplored, the values, attitudes, and styles of behaviour of the youth culture are so pervasive that it is soon to incorporate an even younger age group and thereby grow increasingly important.

In a previous paper it was suggested that a middle-class culture among Canadian youth gave rise to certain kinds of "sociable" delinquency and that such behaviour emerged from active participation in routine legitimate teenage affairs. Among other things where the social organisation of family life diverted youth from extensive peer-group affiliation and where, as a consequence, there was less evidence of a teenage culture there was less apt to be evidence of "sociable" delinquency.

As a first effort we compared firsthand, albeit limited, self-reported data gathered from Canadian and Swiss high school boys. Admittedly, social variables are often difficult to equate precisely when conducting cross-cultural research; furthermore, we must often make do with whatever groups of respondents we can get. Our Swiss youths come from a more "traditional" type Canton while the Canadian boys are largely suburban residents from different sized urban and semiurban communities. Because the middle-class youth culture is likely more strongly entrenched in urban than in rural areas, this might help account for some difference in Canadian and Swiss responses. In any case, our material suggests that Swiss boys are considerably less peer oriented than are

Canadian youth, and they engage less in leisure-oriented activities—behaviour which minimally requires relaxed parental controls. In keeping with the slower institutional change taking place in the Graubunden area, these findings argue against the presence of a widespread, firmly structured youth culture. The attitudes of these boys towards selected situation-type items reveal marked differences, Swiss boys being markedly less "permissive" towards heterosexual, fun-oriented activities.

The findings on self-reported delinquent acts are also in the expected direction. "Sociable" delinquencies are more typical of Canadian than Swiss boys and become their typical roles in the teenage culture. Although petty theft is prevalent in both groups, the more masculine, perhaps aggressive, acts such as fist fighting and destroying property loom large among older Swiss boys. Serious theft and being placed on school probation are also more common among Swiss than Canadian boys, although for the latter offense the difference is almost negligible among boys reporting the act repeatedly.

5

Homicide in 110 Nations: The Development of the Comparative Crime Data File

DANE ARCHER and ROSEMARY GARTNER

This project and the development of the 110-Nation Comparative Crime Data File were supported by National Institute of Mental Health Grant Number MH 27427 from the Center for Studies of Crime and Delinquency, and by a Guggenheim Fellowship to the first author. Responsibility for the findings and interpretations in this paper belongs, of course, to the authors alone.

For a number of historical reasons research on the causes of crime has tended to be unfortunately insular and even ethnocentric. For example, almost all systematic research on the social, economic, and cultural origins of homicide has been done with respect to the experiences of single societies.[1] While these investigations of an individual society are of great descriptive value, they do not by themselves result in general explanations and theories. In addition researchers interested in homicide rates have lavished repeated attention on the data of a handful of nations—e.g., the U.S. and Great Britain—and neglected the inspection of a heterogeneous range of societies.

The reason for this narrow and culturally based approach has not been lack of interest. The need for a truly comparative approach to crime has long been acknowledged,[2] and even researchers working with the data of single nations have underlined the importance of cross-cultural investigations. Although cross-national comparisons are always fraught with a number of methodological problems, the primary obstacle to such comparative research has been a dearth of information. In the past, the social sciences have not had available adequate historical (or "time series") data on rates of homicide in a large number of societies.

Without such a cross-national data base, rigorous comparative research has not been possible on a large scale. As a result, our understanding of the causes of homicide and other offenses remains, at best, provincial and primitive and, at worst, simply wrong. Illustrations of this problem are not hard to find.

For example, sociologists have for a long time suspected that wars might somehow produce a postwar increase in homicide rates.[3] However, in the absence of historical cross-national data on homicide rates, efforts to research this question have been limited to isolated case studies as the case of a single nation after a single war.[4] For example, the eminent criminologist Herman Mannheim published an entire book on this question.[5] The book was based on the only crime data readily available to Mannheim—rates for England. On the strength of the English experience after World War I, Mannheim concluded that wars do not produce postwar "waves" of homicide. Recent comparative research, however, indicates that Mannheim was almost certainly wrong, i.e., he was misled by studying a single nation's experience which turned out to be idiosyncratic.[6]

A second example concerns an apparent paradox of current interest to many sociologists. Using cross-sectional comparisons of the homicide rates of large and small U.S. cities, sociologists have repeatedly demonstrated that larger cities have dramatically higher homicide rates than smaller cities.[7] However, there is almost no longitudinal or historical research on whether a given city's homicide rate grows as its population increases.[8] Without such evidence, of course, it is difficult to explain or understand the relatively higher homicide rates observed in large cities. The reason for our continued ignorance on this question is, again, the unavailability of historical data on homicide. What one would like to have to answer this question is a cross-national file of historical homicide data for large cities in several societies.

A third example can be drawn from the area of social policy. Many legislative issues in the justice area involve an assumption that proposed changes in law are likely to affect homicides rates—e.g., gun control laws, temporary periods of "amnesty" for the surrender of illegal or unregistered weapons, and death penalty legislation. Here again, however, the poverty of available cross-national data has made comprehensive research impossible. There has been essentially no systematic research on how changes in gun ownership in other societies have affected their homicide rates, and also little recent research on how changes in death penalty legislation have affected homicide rates in other societies. This near absence of rigorous comparative research on the effect of death penalty legislation is particularly conspicuous since a great deal of deterrence research has been done using American offense rates.[9]

These three examples are, unfortunately, only a few of the important questions which remain unresearched and unanswered because the necessary time series data on homicide rates have not been available for a large sample of nations and cities. There are many other areas where the empirical foundations of existing theory about homicide are embarrassingly provincial. For example, little is known about how fluctuations in unemployment or other economic indicators affect homicide rates. There have been a small number of American studies—including the classic study by Henry and Short[10]— but virtually no attempts to explore this question using the evidence of other societies.[11] This omission in the literature is particularly unfortunate since there are recent indications that fluctuations in unemployment and other economic variables have important societal consequences in terms of individual behavior.[12]

In all these areas, our knowledge of the social origins of homicide is lamentably culture-bound. Without historical homicide data from a large number of societies, there have been no opportunities to explore the causes of this violent offense in a range of cultures, or even to attempt more modest replications of findings based primarily or exclusively on American data.

These constraints on empirical research have had predictable consequences for social theories about the origins of crime. The poverty of existing resources for comparative homicide research has created a climate in which nation-bound and ungeneralizable theory has flourished. A casual reading of many texts on crime or the sociology of violence reveals several propositions about homicide which appear to be readily disconfirmable by the experience of other societies Perhaps even worse, it is easy for a reader of these texts to form an impression that homicide and other offenses do not exist outside the United States—since so many conclusions appear to rest rather precariously on American data alone. In summary, the absence of readily examinable homicide data for large numbers of societies has retarded the development of general theories about the social origins of homicide.

The major obstacle to generalizable research on the social origins of homicide has been the absence of a dependent variable. For this reason, beginning in 1972, we undertook the creation of an archive of crime rate data which had both comparative breadth and historical depth. After several years of intensive data collection, we have assembled a 110-nation Comparative Crime Data File (CCDF) with time series rates of five offenses for the period 1900–1970. These five offenses are homicide, assault, robbery, theft, and rape. In addition to the data series for 110 nations, the CCDF also includes series for 44 major international cities as well.

The principal sources for the creation of this massive comparative file have been (1) correspondence with national and metropolitan governmental sources in essentially all societies in the world; (2) examination of documents and annual reports of those nations which have published data on their annual incidence of various offenses; and (3) correspondence with other record-keeping agencies.

The time series in the CCDF begin in the year 1900, although many of the nations in the file did not begin maintaining crime data until much later. For example, the so-called "developing" nations generally have data in the CCDF only for relatively recent periods. In addition, the records for some nations contain interruptions due to national emergencies and bureaucratic lapses. These factors mean that for any given year or period, the CCDF has effective data for fewer than 110 nations and fewer than 44 cities.

As part of the collection of the 110-national CCDF, we have reviewed the available literature on possible sources of unreliability. and invalidity in official crime data. The implications of these concerns for comparative research with the CCDF have been discussed elsewhere and efforts have been made to identify research designs which minimize these problems.[13] For example, the most conservative design using the CCDF is one which (1) examines homicide rather than other offenses; (2) examines only longitudinal trends within each of several societies and eschews cross-sectional comparisons of absolute offense rate levels across several societies, and (3) uses some kind of data quality control procedure to take into account the variable validity of the different offense indicators (e.g., offenses known versus arrests) which are present for various nations in the CCDF.

With these methodological precautions, the CCDF makes it possible to investigate the effects upon offense rates of a great number of possible antecedent variables. In addition, the CCDF can maximize the comparative rigor of homicide research by maximizing a researcher's chances of identifying both internationally general relationships and also relationships which hold only for certain types of societies.

The long-term goal of the CCDF project is to make possible a comprehensive assessment of whether, and to what degree, trends in homicide rates follow lawful and explicable patterns. Faced with a nearly infinite list of potential antecedent variables, we have chosen to treat in greatest detail the following four classes of potential social origins of homicides: (1) short-term societal events (e.g., recessions, wars, etc.); (2) long-term social changes (e.g., urbanization, unemployment rate fluctuations, etc.); (3) relatively durable aspects of social structure (e.g., resource concentration or distribution, type of national economic organization, etc.); and (4) discrete changes in policy and law (e.g., gun control legislation, changes in courtroom evidentiary procedures, death penalty abolition or restoration, etc.).[14] A study on the effects of one of these antecedents, wars, has already been published.[15]

The 110-nation CCDF makes possible for the first time a genuinely international approach to the study of homicide, and work toward this demanding objective has just begun. It is our hope that empirical research drawing upon the CCDF will provide the historical and comparative basis for truly general theories about the social origins of homicide. The rest of this paper, made possible by this massive new data archive, concerns a substantive question of both classic and current concern to sociologists.

CITY SIZE, CITY GROWTH, AND HOMICIDE RATES
Although urban crime has been a central concern of several social sciences for a long time, it remains poorly understood. Despite several generations of urban theory and descriptive research, explanations of urban crime are still beclouded by controversy and apparently contradictory research findings.[16]

Cities have long been regarded as centers of crime and violence. This unfavorable reputation is at least as old as the Bible. For example, in Ezekiel (7:23), one of the explanations God is said to have given for his wrath is that "the land is full of bloody crimes and the city is full of violence." Over succeeding centuries, many writer have contrasted the immorality of cities with the innocence and purity of rural life. In some of these accounts, the city is described as seducing its new arrivals into a life of crime. For example, Adam Smith wrote that a man of "low moral character" could be constrained to behave properly in a village environment "but as soon as he comes into a great city he is sunk in obscurity and darkness, and he is very likely to . . . abandon himself to every sort of low profligacy and vice." [17]

This image of the city has been extremely influential in the history of sociology and, with some refinement, constitutes today the dominant theory about crime in cities. In sociology, this perspective is particularly identified with Durkheim and Wirth. In *The Division of Labor in Society*, Durkheim suggested that the "common conscience" is diluted as a city grows in size: "local opinion weighs less heavily upon each of us, and as the general opinion of society cannot replace its predecessor, not being able to watch closely the conduct of its citizens, the collective surveillance is irretrievably loosened, the common conscience loses its authority and individual variability grows." [18]

Wirth accepted this view of cities and discussed the mechanisms by which cities dissolve traditional forms of social control. [19] According to Wirth, the effects of cities included an increase in residential mobility, isolation, and anonymity as well as a breakdown of kinship ties and other informal sources of social control.

In addition to this Durkheim-Wirth view of the city as a place where traditional social controls are minimized and anonymity is maximized, no fewer than six additional theoretical explanations have appeared in the literature on urban crime. These six hypotheses can be stated in abbreviated form as follows: (1) cities foster the development of criminal subcultures; (2) cities produce class, cultural, and racial conflict as a function of greater population heterogeneity; (3) cities increase criminal opportunities because of population size and the large numbers of commercial establishments; (4) cities have relatively impersonal police-civilian relations which lead to rigid law enforcement practices and therefore arrest rates which are inflated compared to those of nonurban areas; (5) the age and sex compositions of cities have been altered by the arrival of immigrants (from rural areas, other nations, etc.) who are predominantly young males; and even (6) the possibility that the population density of cities might by itself increase the likelihood of pathological behavior.

Unfortunately, empirical evidence has not matched the richness and variety of this theoretical banquet. Despite the existence of at least seven quite plausible theoretical explanations, the available evidence on urban homicide rates and their social origins is both parochial and paradoxical.

Much of the empirical confusion concerning urban homicide derives from a collision between cross-sectional and longitudinal approaches to this area. The two approaches imply questions which are radically different. The cross-sectional approach asks whether there are homicide rate implications of city size at any one moment in time; the longitudinal approach asks whether there are any implications of city growth over time.

At least until recently, the cross-sectional approach dominated research on urban homicide. This research has been based primarily on American data, and has produced results which are as consistent as they are striking.[20] For example, Wolfgang and Clinard analyzed offense rates for American cities of various sizes and found impressively higher homicide rates in large cities than in small cities.[21]

The vividness of this cross-sectional finding with American data must be seen to be appreciated. We have replicated this well-known finding, using the most recent data available and also smoothing over five years to reduce the effects of short-term idiosyncracies. Using the FBI's Uniform Crime Reports, we aggregated the mean rates of murder and nonnegligent manslaughter for cities of various size categories over the period 1971–1975. The results of this analysis produce a cross-sectional picture of the homicide rates in American cities of various sizes and this relationship is graphed using a semilog scale in figure 3.

The strength of the relationship in figure 3 indicates why this finding is one of the most widely accepted tenets of urban sociology. For cities alone, (i.e., excluding rural and suburban areas), the relationship between city size and homicide rates is monotonic and approximately logarithmic. The relationship is monotonic in that each city size category has a homicide rate higher than all smaller size categories and lower than all larger size categories. The relationship is logarithmic in that the most dramatic differences in homicide rates occur among the smaller city size categories—for more populous cities, it takes much larger city size differences to produce comparable differences in urban homicide rates.

In an earlier publication, we have called the cross sectional result a "logarithmic J-curve" because of the shape of the graph in figure 3.[22]

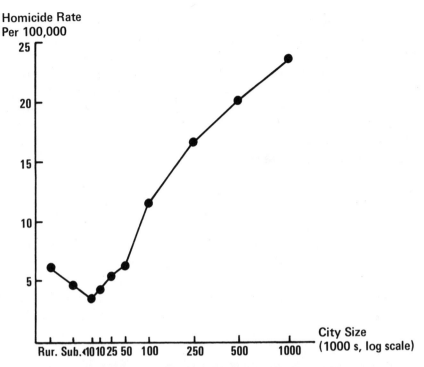

Fig. 3. City size and homicide rates in the United States,
1971–1975

SOURCE: The 110-nation Comparative Crime Data File. The cities in this trend
line are Amsterdam, Belfast, Colombo city, Dublin, Glasgow, Helsinki, and Tokyo. These seven cities have essentially uninterrupted homicide data for the entire period.

The graph is J-curve rather than linear because rural areas have homicide rates which are actually higher than the rates for smaller cities.

This finding is quite provocative, since it seems intuitively more
plausible to expect rural homicide rates to be lower than all urban rates.
In fact, none of the seven theoretical models summarized earlier can
explain the finding that rural homicide rates exceed the rates of small
cities and are as high, in fact, as the rates of cities with populations
between 50,000 and 100,000. The ecology of homicide is clearly multi-
variate in nature, and rural homicides cannot be understood without the
introduction of other theoretical variables which are, at present, uniden-
tified.

By itself, the cross-sectional approach represented in figure 3 seems
straightforward and—except for the unexpectedly high homicide rates

in rural areas—quite compatible with any of the seven theoretical explanations listed earlier. All seven theoretical models predict greater homicide rates in large cities although for different reasons, and the cross-sectional evidence appears to support this prediction. This finding only becomes a paradox when longitudinal evidence is examined.

The relationship shown in figure 3 has led many researchers to the quite reasonable expectation that this effect of city size might have implications for city growth as well. If it is true that the homicide rates of large cities exceed those of small cities, it seems reasonable to expect the homicide rates of a city to soar as the city grows from small to large. A few longitudinal studies of this question have been made, however, and the results of these inquiries constitute the other half of the paradox of cities and homicide. These few longitudinal studies are paradoxical precisely because they have not found the reasonable and the expected— i.e., they have not found that individual cities experience homicide rate increases as they grow in population size.

Three of these longitudinal studies have examined cities over a period of roughly one century. For example, Powell studied Buffalo between 1854 and 1956; Ferdinand studied Boston from 1849 to 1951; and Lane studied both Boston and Massachusetts generally from the mid-nineteenth to the mid-twentieth century.[23] These three studies of American city growth found a consistent decline in murder and other serious crime rates, despite the population gains of these cities during the century studied.[24]

There have also been some historical studies of entire societies. Although studies at this level of aggregation bear only imperfectly upon our question, they appear to support analysis done at the city level. For example, Lodhi and Tilly studied records of crimes against the person in nineteenth-century France and found that the rate of these offenses fluctuated mildly over time but had no discernible trend.[25]

This, then, is the paradox of cities and homicide rates: why do large cities currently have higher homicide rates than small cities, if there is no evidence of increasing homicide rates as a city grows? The cross-sectional evidence on city size and homicide seems at first to suggest that cities must grow to some absolute size (e.g., 100,000 persons) before having a high homicide rate. But this apparently reasonable proposition is contradicted by the longitudinal evidence which shows that cities do not in fact show homicide rate increases as they grow. In short, if larger cities currently have higher homicide rates than small cities, how did they get these high rates—if not by growing in population size?

Using the wealth of twentieth-century data series in the 110-nation CCDF, we have attempted a new interpretation of this apparently paradoxical relationship between cities and homicide rates. Our approach has been to try to provide answers to three conceptually separable questions which, we believe, provide the key in this paradox.

The first two of these questions address the cross-national generalizability of the two sides of the paradox as we have described them and the third attempts a synthesis of these findings. The three questions are (1) since much of the cross-sectional evidence has depended on American data, is it generally true—in a comparative or cross-nation sense—that big cities have high homicide rates? (2) Does comparative longitudinal evidence support the tentative indications that urban homicide rates do not necessarily increase as a city grows in population size over time? And (3) can these two designs be combined in some way to provide a historical picture of the dynamic relationship between the homicide rates of large, growing cities and those of nonurban areas over time?

City Rates and Other Rates (A Cross-Sectional Question)
As shown by the logarithmic J-curve in figure 3, there is no question that large U.S. cities have atypically high homicide rates. But in a heterogeneous society like the U.S. this finding could well be due to factors other than the size of cities per se—e.g., the homicide rate differences could easily be due to the social and economic differences between rural and large urban areas, etc. For this reason, a comparative researcher might well ask if the finding in figure 3 can be replicated cross-nationally.

The CCDF provides an opportunity to assess the replicability of this finding, although the test is somewhat indirect. In addition to aggregate data for entire nations, the CCDF includes offense data for 44 major international cities—cities which are either the largest city or one of the largest cities in their societies. This feature of the CCDF data archive makes it possible to compare homicide rates in each of these major cities with the national homicide rate of the corresponding society.

If these two rates differ, it will be a conservative test of the relationship between city size and homicide rates for two reasons: (1) the national homicide rate obviously includes the rate of the city and this artifact will diminish the observed difference between the two rates, and (2) the national homicide rate reflects both rural areas and other urban areas, in addition to the major international city itself. The effect of these two artifacts is conservative. Differences will only be observed if the

Table 13.

PRIMATE CITY HOMICIDE RATES AND NATIONAL RATES: A CROSS-SECTIONAL COMPARISON*

City Homicide Rate Lower than National Rate (n = 6)		City Homicide Rate Higher than National Rate (n = 18)	
City	Homicide rate	City	Homicide Rate
1. Guyana (1966–70)	6.18	1. Australia (1966–70)	1.28
Georgetown	5.21	Sydney	1.57
2. Japan (1966–70)	2.23	2. Austria (1966–70)	0.73
Tokyo	1.78	Vienna	0.89
3. Kenya (1964–68)	5.67	3. Belgium (1965–69)	0.29
Nairobi	5.27	Brussels	0.45
4. Panama (1966–70)	11.07	4. Finland (1966–70)	0.35
Panama City	4.96	Helsinki	0.65
5. Sri Lanka (1966–70)	6.09	5. France (1966–70)	0.45
Colombo City	5.59	Paris	0.61
6. Turkey (1966–70)	9.65	6. India (1966–70)	2.72
Istanbul	4.84	Bombay	2.85
		7. Ireland (1966–70)	0.34
		Dublin	0.35
		8. Mexico (1962, 66, 67, 72)	13.24
		Mexico City	13.34
		9. Netherlands (1966–70)	0.50
		Amsterdam	1.23
		10. New Zealand (1966–70)	0.16
		Wellington	2.32
		11. Northern Ireland (1964–68)†	0.20
		Belfast	0.35
		12. Philippines (1966–70)	7.98
		Manila	23.86
		13. Rhodesia (1966–70)	5.33
		Salisbury	7.20

* Because of national idiosyncrasies in definition and reporting, the reader is cautioned against making direct cross-national comparisons of homicide rate levels. As explained in the text, this is not a problem for urban-national comparisons within the same society.

† The period 1966–70 also shows Belfast as having a higher homicide rate. This period was not used in this analysis, however, because Northern Ireland's most recent political violence began in 1969.

SOURCE: Source for all data is the 110-nation Comparative Crime Data File. Homicide rates are given in offenses per 100,000 population. In order to smooth the effect of annual fluctuations, the rates are the means of the years shown. The difference in rates between nations and cities is conservative for two reasons: (1) the national rate includes the urban rate, and (2) the national rate also includes other urban areas (i.e., the national rates aggregate both urban and rural areas).

		14. Scotland (1966–70)	0.78
		Glasgow	1.56
		15. Spain (1964–68)	0.49
		Madrid	0.56
		16. Sudan (1961–64,68)	5.67
		Khartoum	30.25
		17. Trinidad & Tobago (66–70)	14.00
		Port-of-Spain	15.31
		18. United States (1966–70)	6.62
		New York City	11.54
Median Country Rate:	6.14	Median Country Rate:	0.76
Median City Rate:	5.09	Median City Rate:	1.57

homicide rate of the major city differs from the aggregate homicide rate for all national sectors combined—rural areas, small cities, other large cities, and the major international city itself.

Since the CCDF generally contains data for only a single major city in a given country, however, it is not at present possible to test for the fine gradations of city size categories shown in figure 3. The test will only contrast the homicide rates of very large cities and the aggregate rates of the corresponding nations.

This comparative, cross-sectional test is shown in table 13.[26] In order to smooth the effects of erratic annual fluctuations, the rates shown in table 13 are in general the averages of the most recent five-year period in the CCDF: 1966–1970.

Even though the CCDF contains crime data for 44 international cities, several of these cities could not be included in table 13 for one of two reasons: (1) one (or both) of the city and nation time series was not available in the CCDF for the period 1966–1970; or (2) even if both series were available for this period, the city reported a different homicide indicator than was available for the entire nation. However, appropriate city-nation comparisons could be made for 24 cases.

In general, the cross-sectional analysis in table 13 indicates that the homicide rates of primate cities exceed the rates of nations as a whole. This was true for 75 percent (18 out of 24) of the pairs of cities and nations. As discussed earlier, it should be noted that the differences in table 13 understate the actual differences between large city rates and nonurban rates because the national rate actually includes the major city rate and the rates of other cities as well as the rates of nonurban areas.

The exceptional cases are often provocative in comparative research and it is interesting to speculate about the six exceptional cases in table 13. Are these six cases qualitatively similar, and are they in some way unlike the societies which constitute the majority pattern in table 13. Although post hoc interpretations require more art than system, it does seem that the two types of outcomes in table 13 might be related to national levels of "development," industrialization, etc. Five of the six exceptional cases are "preindustrial" societies. Perhaps homicide rates in these societies are in some way qualitatively unique—e.g., kinship feuds, revenge killings, etc., which might characterize rural areas more than the less traditional urban areas in these nations.[27]

However, even this explanation for the exceptional cases has an exception. Japan is the only heavily industrial nation in which the large city, Tokyo, has a lower homicide rate than the national average. Despite the presence of a clear majority pattern in table 13, and also a not outrageous explanation for the exceptional cases, Japan stands out as an anomaly. Why is Tokyo, alone of the major cities in heavily industrial nations, characterized by a homicide rate below the national average? Comparative research is both a search for cross-national generalizations and also a quest for unique cases, of course, and we intend to discuss this and other unusual cases in a later publication.

With these exceptions, then, the comparative evidence in table 13 is in rough agreement with cross-sectional evidence for the U.S.—in both cases, large cities have homicide rates higher than their national averages. It is also interesting that, although all the cities in table 13 are large cities, there is obviously great variation among the homicide rates of these cities—just as there is great variation among the rates of the nations themselves. This variance indicates that absolute city size does not correspond in any direct way to the absolute magnitude of a city's homicide rate—i.e., cities of 500,000 people do not necessarily have a homicide rate of, say, 17 per 100,000 people.

This suggests the intriguing possibility that large cities have homicide rates which are unusually high only in terms of the overall homicides rates of their societies. An international city therefore can have a homicide rate which is remarkably low (when compared to other large cities worldwide) but which is still a high rate for this specific society. This pattern can be illustrated using two of the cases in table 13. Both Paris and New York City had over 7,000,000 inhabitants for the period 1966–1970. But as table 13 indicates, these two cities have dramatically different homicide rates. In both cases, however, the homicide rate of the city is higher than the rate of the entire society.

If this observation is well founded, the relationship between city size and homicide rates is relative rather than absolute—i.e. there is no formula relating specific homicide rates to specific city sizes. Sociologists are unlikely, therefore, to identify a theoretical model which can predict an international city's homicide rate purely from its population. On the basis of the evidence in table 13, it seems much more promising to pursue theories which try to explain why the homicide rates of large cities appear to be anchored to—and yet higher than—the corresponding national rates. Other evidence for this "nation-anchored" hypothesis of urban homicide rates will be discussed below.

Homicide Rates in Growing Cities (A Longitudinal Question)
As discussed above, the historical half of the paradox has been the observation that a few specific cities—chiefly Buffalo and Boston—have not experienced homicide rate increases as they have grown in size. Since the experience of a handful of cities could easily be idiosyncratic, it seems important to test the cross-national generalizability of this observation as well.

In order to provide a rough test of this longitudinal question for the international cities in the CCDF, a simple zero-order correlation was calculated between (1) the city's population, and (2) the city's homicide rate. Since almost all the cities increased continuously in population during this period,[28] this correlation provides a crude index of the homicide trend during this period. A positive correlation indicates homicide rate increases during this period; a zero correlation indicates homicide rate decreases.

Some of the 44 international cities in the CCDF have data points which are too few in number or too scattered to permit calculation of this trend. However, it is possible to produce 34 correlations, each one roughly analogous to the single-city studies of Buffalo and Boston discussed earlier. Since fewer than 100 years were available for these 34 cities, however, our analysis is not as deep as these previous case studies. This analysis is much broader, however, in that it examines 34 cities in 28 countries. The results of this analysis are shown in table 14.

As table 14 clearly indicates, there is no universal or general relationship between city growth and changes in absolute homicide rates. The correlation range from a low of -0.66 (for Bombay) to a high of 0.98 (for New York City), and the 34 cases are evenly divided into 17 positive r's and 17 negative r's. This broad scatter is responsible for the fact that the median correlation in table 14 is essentially zero (-0.01).

The inconsistency of these 34 longitudinal analyses suggests that there is no invariant tendency for the homicide rates of large cities to increase as these cities grow in size. Table 14 shows that homicide rates are just as likely to decrease with city growth as they are to increase.

Even though the time periods reflected in table 14 are shorter than the century-long studies of individual American cities cited earlier, several cities in table 14 have data for more than 50 years. This variance in time periods can be used for a kind of data quality control procedure. If one limits the comparison to the four cities with 50 or more years of data, for example, the median correlation is still only -0.46. Even for cities with a half-century or more of data, therefore, there is still no strong evidence that homicide rates increase with city growth.

It is possible, of course, that the near-zero median in table 14 conceals some lawful differences among different types of societies. There might be two different outcomes of population growth. Thirteen of the 34 correlations in table 14 are, in fact, significant at the 0.05 level, and this considerably exceeds the 1.7 cities (5 percent of 34) one would expect to reach significance by chance alone. This does support the idea that table 14 might reflect two radically different outcome patterns.

Although the fit is not perfect, there does seem to be some typological order to the scatter of table 14. Cities in "developing" nations seem to be over-represented among the positive correlations,—i.e., major cities in developing nations may be more likely than other cities to experience increasing homicide rates as they grow. This purely speculative typology does not, of course, alter the general lack of a consistent pattern in table 14.

In passing, it is also interesting to speculate about the different conclusions which would have resulted from independent studies of single cities—i.e., without benefit of the CCDF. For example, a researcher examining twentieth-century data for Tokyo would have concluded that homicide rates declined with city growth; a different researcher studying data for Amsterdam would have found no relationship between the variables of population growth and homicide rates; but a third researcher doing a case study of Manila would have found homicide rate increases with city growth and would have concluded that previous researchers were wrong. The unique strength of the CCDF for sociological research on homicide rates is that it can maximize a researcher's view of the range of possible outcomes across several societies and also indicate whether any general pattern occurs. In this case, the CCDF data in table 14 demonstrate that city growth can have an extremely wide range of implica-

Table 14.

HOMICIDE RATES AND POPULATION SIZE FOR PRIMATE CITIES: A LONGITUDINAL ANALYSIS

City	Correlation Between City Population and City Homicide Rate *	Number of Years in the Analysis	Significance
New York†	.98	8	.001
Istanbul	.88	19	.001
Manila	.79	23	.001
Quezon City‡	.64	8	.090
Calcutta	.51	16	.044
New York†	.47	12	.121
Panama City	.45	11	.167
Salisbury‡	.41	22	.058
Port-of-Spain	.38	25	.061
Johannesburg	.33	10	.360
Georgetown	.27	18	.273
Sydney	.27	40	.090
Quezon City	.26	11	.437
Wellington	.16	17	.542
Colombo	.15	74	.198
Khartoum	.13	13	.683
Amsterdam	.02	43	.911
Port-of-Spain‡	−.04	25	.851
Mexico City	−.13	12	.697
Dublin	−.15	47	.315
Brussels	−.17	27	.409
Oslo	−.18	14	.541
Salisbury	−.21	22	.361
Munich	−.26	28	.181
Vienna	−.32	21	.155
Montevideo	−.36	31	.045
Glasgow	−.38	72	.001
Paris	−.45	39	.004
Nairobi	−.50	21	.022
Belfast	−.54	52	.001
Madrid	−.57	16	.021
Tokyo	−.57	73	.001
Helsinki	−.58	43	.001
Bombay	−.66	16	.005
Median r	−.01		

* Since most of these cities have grown consistently over time, the correlations are easily interpreted. A postive correlation means that the city's homicide rate has increased over time; a zero r indicates no consistent change in homicide rate; and a negative r means that the city's homicide rate has decreased over time.

† New York City appears twice because a change in recording procedures created two series: one before 1966 and one after.

‡ Indicates that a rate for «murder» was used for this city other rates are homicide rates

SOURCE: The 110-nation Comparative Crime Data File. This analysis tests for the presence of any linear relationship between changes in population size and changes in homicide rates for these primate cities.

tions for homicide rates and that, in general, there is no evidence that cities and homicide rates grow together.

Seven of the international cities in table 14 have essentially uninterrupted homicide data for the entire period 1926–1970. These seven cities are Amsterdam, Belfast, Colombo City, Dublin, Glasgow, Helsinki, and Tokyo. The homicide rates of these seven cities can be represented, therefore, by a median rate for each year. This median rate reflects the same seven cities for each year in this period and the graph of this median rate over time therefore has an interpretable slope. The median rate for these seven cities between 1926 and 1970 is shown in figure 4.

Just as table 14 provided evidence that urban homicide rates do not in general increase with city growth, figure 4 indicates that these seven international cities do not show any consistent increase in homicide rates over time. The slope of the graph in figure 4 is essentially zero (0.006)—i.e., there is no evidence of progressively higher homicide rates

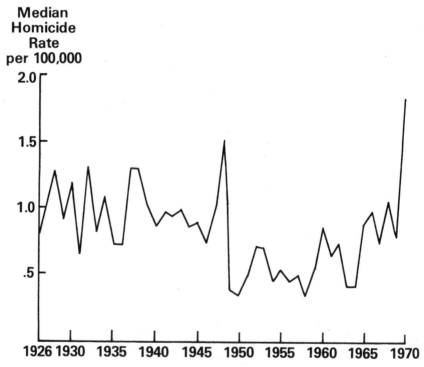

Fig. 4. Trends in primate city homicide rates, 1926–1970

SOURCE: Adapted from the FBI's *Uniform Crime Reports,* 1971–1975. Rates shown are the means of the five-year period 1971–1975.

over time. A city's population growth, therefore, does not appear to have any consistent implications for the city's homicide rate.

This completes the generalizability test of the second half of the paradox. Based on an examination of the CCDF, it does seem to be generally true that both (1) cross-sectionally, large cities appear to have homicide rates which are atypically high for their respective societies; and also (2) longitudinally, there is no consistent tendency toward elevated homicide rates as a city grows in size. The third phase of our analysis attempts a modest resolution of this apparent paradox.

Urban and Nonurban Rates over Time

The cross-sectional evidence in table 13 shows that, at a given moment in time, the homicide rates of large international cities generally exceed their national averages. Table 14 and figure 4, on the other hand, both show that there is no general tendency for urban homicide rates to increase as cities grow. The paradoxical question remains, therefore, how did large cities acquire high homicide rates if not by growing to a certain population size?

We propose to answer this question by extending the time "window" in table 13 backwards in time. Specifically, we propose to use the historical depth of the CCDF to ask whether major international cities have always had homicide rates which are high relative to their societal averages. If urban homicide rates have always exceeded national rates—despite the tremendous changes in urban size over time—then the atypically high homicide rates must be attributed to certain urban characteristics rather than others.

We have used the method of controlled comparison to provide this test of the historical relationship between urban and national rates. Because of missing data or incomparable indicators, only the period 1926–1970 could be included. For each of these years, the median homicide rate of the international cities can be compared to the median rate of the corresponding societies. This is a controlled comparison strategy since each national rate acts as a paired "control" for each urban rate—i.e., a city is only included in the median for a given year if its corresponding national rate is also available for that year. This controlled comparison prevents any bias due to the partial entry (e.g., only for the median urban rate) of homicide data from a society with unusually high or low homicide rates.

The historical relationship between the homicide rates of international cities and the rates of entire nations is shown in figure 5. The number of pairs (each pair consists of one city and one nation) in the analysis is indicated at five-year intervals.

The most striking pattern in figure 5 is that international cities have consistently had homicide rates higher than their national averages. The gap between the solid and broken lines in figure 5 is a conservative index of urban-national differences. It is conservative, again, because the dotted line actually includes the rate of the solid line, and it also includes the rates of other large and small cities as well. The difference between the two lines in figure 5 is perhaps particularly impressive because these

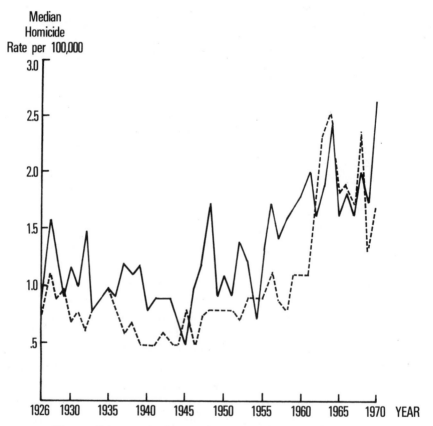

Fig. 5. Primate city homicide rates and national rates: a longitudinal comparison

SOURCE: The 110-nation Comparative Crime Data File. The solid line shows the median homicide rate of primate cities for each year; the broken line shows the median rate of the corresponding nations. The number of pairs (each pair is one city and one nation) in the analysis is indicated at five-year intervals.

international cities were much smaller—in terms of absolute population—at the beginning of this period than they are now.

The median homicide rates in figure 5 show that the main finding of table 13 (that primate cities have homicide rates anchored to, but higher than, their national averages for 1966–1970) could be "replicated" for any period between 1926 and 1970. If anything, figure 5 shows that the effect of city size was even more pronounced earlier in this century than during the period (1966–1970).[29]

The consistent differences reflected in figure 5 are our most important longitudinal findings. Although we do not have homicide data reaching back into the eighteenth and nineteenth centuries, the consistently higher rates of the cities in figure 5 encourage us to make the following extrapolation: In general, large cities have always had homicide rates higher than their national averages, and this was true even when these cities were much smaller than they are today. Even in 1926, the first year in figure 5, these international cities were still more "urban" than their societies as a whole. We are suggesting, therefore, that it is the relative size of "large" cities at any moment in time—rather than their absolute population in thousands—which is responsible for their consistently higher homicide rates.

The high rates of urban areas, therefore, must be attributed to variables other than their absolute population size. There are, of course, many other urban characteristics which could elevate urban homicide rates. Even when these international cities were much smaller in absolute terms, for example, they were still characterized by many urban characteristics: in-migration from rural areas, housing on a basis other than kinship, heterogeneity of population, stratification into rich and poor areas, etc. It is to these and other urban variables—variables which are not linked firmly to any specific city size—that we must look for an explanation of high urban homicide rates. Some combination of these urban characteristics apparently acts to inflate or exaggerate the general level of homicide in a society. Although urban rates are "anchored" near their national rates, they have consistently exceeded them—at least for the time period we have been able to examine.

A final caveat should be mentioned concerning figure 5. Because different data points in figure 5 reflect a different combination of cases—depending on the availability of city and nation data in any given year—the slope of the lines is not meaningful. Since different cities and nations are included in different periods of the table, the lines cannot provide an indication of trends for either cities or nations over time.

Our investigation of the paradoxical relationship between cities and homicide rates can be summarized as follows: (1) homicide rates and city size are strongly and monotonically related, for U.S. cities, by a "logarithmic J-curve"—with the interesting exception that rural homicide rates exceed the rates of small cities; (2) this cross-sectional result is also true cross-nationally—the homicide rates of large cities exceed their national homicide rates between 1966 and 1970; (3) however, longitudinal analysis shows that the homicide rates of international cities generally have not increased as these cities have grown in population over time; and (4) the explanation for this apparent paradox is that homicide rates of international cities have consistently exceeded national homicide rates—even when these cities were much smaller in absolute size than they are now.

The key to interpreting the paradox of urban homicide rates, we believe, is the observation that the rates of major internation cities have consistently exceeded their national rates. The determinant of a city's homicide rate, therefore, is not the absolute size of the city, but its size relative to its contemporary society. Even small cities can have relatively high homicide rates, if at any moment in history they are "urban" by local national standards. With some exceptions, any city more urban than its national environment is likely to have a homicide rate which exceeds its national average. The relative nature of this relationship, we believe, is the answer to the paradoxical question of why large cities have high homicide rates which do not grow higher as the cities grow larger.

The substantive study attempts to resolve the apparent paradox of urban homicide rates. Cross-national urban data from the CCDF show that large cities do have atypically high homicide rates, but also that there is no evidence that homicide rates increase as these cities grow in population over time. The explanation of this apparent contradiction between cross-sectional and longitudinal findings appears to be the relative population size, rather than the absolute size, of cities. Our analysis shows that cities have consistently had atypically high homicide rates, even when these cities were only a fraction of their current size. While it is true that cities have high homicide rates, therefore, these rates can only be attributed to urban characteristics other than population size.

It is our long-term hope that the CCDF will contribute to the empirical foundations of a genuinely international understanding of homicide. We believe this massive data resource can assist realization of this goal in two ways. This archive can help researchers to discover those patterns which generalize across boundaries of nation states and time periods, and also to identify exceptional cases where specific national and urban characteristics outweigh or even reverse these general patterns. An extensive program of this kind of cross-national empirical research is clearly indispensable if we are ever to see a truly general theory of the social origins of homicide.

PART TWO

SOCIAL FORCES, CRIME, AND CRIMINAL JUSTICE

6

Contemporary Crime in Historical Perspective: A Comparative Study of London, Stockholm, and Sydney

TED ROBERT GURR

Almost all authorities concerned with criminal justice and ordinary citizens in Western societies believe that common crimes against persons and property are, and have been, increasing for some years. Crime statistics by and large support this perception of rising disorder. In most countries of Western Europe, in North America, and in Australia and New Zealand, the official data document a decade or more of accelerating increase in rates of most kinds of offenses known to police, arrests for them, and criminal proceedings taken.

A common view among sociologists concerned with crime is that the data on which such judgments are based are grossly unreliable. They are a function, it is argued, of the way in which crime is defined, policed, and recorded. On this view, the perception and fear of rising crime can be dismissed as a social myth. Scholarly attention is directed away from the study of threatening behavior per se to the analysis of the interests and activities of officials who "create" crime by selective labelling and policing, and to the study of the circumstances which induce in people an exaggerated fear of crime. A corollary of this approach is that it enables the analyst to invert the structure of social responsibility. Whereas officials and private citizens blame criminals, who are mainly young and poor, for deviant acts, the critical sociologist places the onus on the authorities and citizens whose interests motivate them to "cry thief" when threatened from below.[1]

The purpose of this essay is to bring some historical perspectives to bear on the issue of public order as it is reflected, or distorted, in official data. The empirical grist for this analysis is provided by data on crime for three Western cities from the 1820s to the 1970s.

In the larger study from which this paper is derived, "disorder" means the socially threatening acts commonly called crime and civil strife. This paper deals only with crime, defined in its formal legal sense, as those individual acts which are legally proscribed and sanctioned by public authority.[2]

The beginning point for this analysis is to identify the trends and patterns in official data on crime in London, Stockholm, and Sydney, weighted for population.[3] One fundamental difficulty with such indicators is the inherent inaccuracy of official data on offenses and offenders. Crime, as legally defined, usually is covert behavior, which means that ordinary crimes against persons and property come to official attention by the reports of those victims who choose to report them, while so-called victimless crimes ordinarily are detected only through active police work, which is notoriously variable in scope and quality. Add to this the inconsistent recording practices of the police and statistical bureaus, and one has ample grounds for the kind of judgment passed by Daniel Bell, that criminal statistics in the United States are about as reliable "as a woman giving her 'correct' age." There is comparable skepticism about official crime data in other Western societies.[4]

Much of the debate over the accuracy of crime statistics results from attempts to assess the true extent of criminal behavior. Perhaps that is the wrong question to ask. In this study we are concerned with two other problems, which are equally important, and more readily answered with such data as are available. The first is how much popular and official concern there is about crime, and how much public effort is directed at it. These are precisely the kinds of conditions that are most directly reflected in official crime data. Readily available indicators and their prima facie significance include:

Indicator	Prima Facie Significance	Validity of Information
Crimes known to police per 1,000 population	Extent of citizen and police concern with crime	For crimes with victims, markedly influenced by citizen trust in police. For crimes without victims, a function of police surveillance. For both, a function of recording systems
Arrests per 1,000	Extent of police action against suspected offenders	Generally good but affected by recording and reporting practices
Committals to trial per 1,000	Extent of official concern with crime	Good, except where cases are shifted among jurisdictions or between higher and lower courts
Convictions per 1,000	Extent of official sanctions against offenders	Good

The second problem deals with how public order changes over time. On the above argument, statistics on crime and arrests in most contemporary societies are, in effect, the reports of the social and political system to itself about the seriousness of its self-defined problems of public order. As public concern mounts, more crimes are likely to be reported; as police concern rises, so will patrolling and arrests. Similarly, changes in the extent of official insecurity will likely show up in changing rates of committals for trial, convictions, and—depending on the time and place—the severity of sentences. Evidently there is a circular process in which increasing public concern is likely to generate higher rates of reported crime.

It is reasonable to assume that there is an approximate relation between changes in objective criminal behavior and changing public concern. If illegal behavior of particularly threatening kinds increases in frequency and visibility, concern and official reaction are likely to increase too, perhaps more rapidly than the behavior itself. Therefore the trends in crime indicators are revealing about the changing volume of disorderly behavior in ways that statistics, for one point in time, cannot be. The one major qualification is that changes in the law, police procedures, and court disposition of cases sometimes occur independently of the degree of concern about crime, and alter indicators as a consequence. So the practical task, when interpreting data on crime trends, is to disentangle the social reality of behavioral change from the political and administrative reality of change in the institutions which respond to and record behavioral change.

In brief, official data on crime, weighted by population, are prima facie indicators of levels of public disorder, defined as the extent of public concern about crime (indexed by indicators of crime known to police) and the extent of official efforts at crime control (indexed by data on arrests and convictions). Given enough contextual information, one may also be able to infer the relative importance of behavioral and institutional factors in causing changes in indicators of public disorder. In the aggregate, we can think of crime data as the product of two different conditions. One is behavioral: the volume of criminal acts. The other is institutional: the activities of the agencies which define and maintain public order. Both change over time, but changes in official activities are more readily observable than changes in social behavior. Given an observed set of short- and long-term trends in indicators of disorder, institutional factors are examined first to see to what extent they can account for the trends. By a process of elimination, the residual changes, if any, can with some confidence be attributed to changes in social behavior.

Optimistic celebration of the improvements in urban life was a common theme of observers of most Western cities during the second half of the nineteenth century. Improved public order was one of the celebrated accomplishments. Not only were streets increasingly likely to be paved and lighted, they were safer to travel by day and night. Not only were productivity and personal wealth increasing, property was more secure from the depredations of thieves than ever before. One can be skeptical about whether the voiceless underclasses had such a rosy perception of city life. The fact remains that the official records of crime and punishment for three cities that we have studied in depth document a sustained improvement in public order that began in the second quarter of the century and continued to 1900. In proportion to the rapidly growing populations of London, Stockholm, and Sydney, the numbers of murders, assaults, and thefts of almost all kinds which came to police attention declined irregularly, but consistently, for half a century or more. So did the numbers of persons arrested and convicted for such offenses. As public order improved, so did the quality of justice. The courts, though harsh and biased against defendants by contemporary standards, were distinctly more lenient and solicitous of defendants' rights than they had been before 1850.[5]

Public order, as reflected in the official data, continued to improve in London until the 1920s, and in Stockholm and Sydney, through the 1930s. No clear trends were evident during the 1940s, but in the 1950s a pronounced increase began in almost all indicators of crimes against persons and property, one that has continued upward to the present at an accelerating rate in all three cities. We have noted the skepticism of many sociologists about the significance of the reported recent increases in disorder; they have voiced no such doubts about the declines of the nineteenth century, indeed they seem unaware of them. The historians, for their part, generally accept the social reality of improving public order in the nineteenth century, but have not been disposed to evaluate recent developments. Our analysis summarily examines selected indicators of crime across a century and a half, with special attention to the changing institutions which generated them, as a means of assessing the validity of the historical versus sociological interpretations.

The first consistent data on criminal offenses in the three cities appeared early in the nineteenth century. By 1880 they reached, and in some cases surpassed, in detail and precision the data currently available. A deceptively difficult problem in this kind of study is matching crime to population data for the purpose of constructing indicators. Our data for London before 1869 refer to the County of Middlesex alone and to the Metropolitan Police District (MPD) thereafter. The data on Stockholm refer to the administrative city, whose boundaries have ever lagged behind suburban sprawl; in 1968, for example, administrative Stockholm included only 59 percent of the population of Greater Stockholm. Data on crime in the City of Sydney proved so scanty that we employ data on crime and population for New South Wales in its entirety; Sydney, itself, has comprised as little as 25 percent of its population (in the 1850s) and as much as 60 percent (in 1970).

This analysis is limited to "common crimes" against persons and property, because these are the offenses that typically arouse the most widespread and vocal public concern. Since people of all classes fear and excoriate offenses like murder, assault, robbery, and burglary, they can be expected to be more often reported to the authorities and more consistently policed than moral offenses or political crimes.

To simplify comparison, we use summary indicators of crimes of aggression and crimes of acquisition. These are constructed by aggregating more detailed categories of offense. For London, for example, the summary indicator for crimes of aggression includes murder, manslaughter, attempted murder, wounding, and assault (but not rape or armed robbery). The summary indicator of crimes of acquisition includes burglary, robbery, larceny, receiving stolen goods, fraud, embezzlement, forgery, and similar offenses.[6] For London and Sydney (New South Wales) the analysis is restricted to more serious (indictable) offenses of these two kinds, because data for lesser offenses are not available for the entire period of interest. Only for Stockholm are data on petty as well as serious offenses available for the entire period—more precisely, from 1830 onwards.

The criminal justice system has been likened to a funnel in which the police record many more offenses than they clear by arrest, and many more people are arrested than are charged, tried, and convicted. For each city and general category of offense, we sought indicators representing what was happening at two distant points in the funnel: crimes known to police and convictions. For New South Wales, statistics on crimes known are too sparse, so arrest data are used instead. The two kinds of indicators are not uniformly available for the full century and a half. With some exceptions, only convictions data were reported during much of the nineteenth century and only offenses known for the most recent period. Moreover, the two indicators usually differ markedly in magnitude, crimes known being invariably more numerous than convictions. Nonetheless, for periods when both were reported, they prove to be closely correlated; that is, they have similar peaks, valleys, and trends.[7] This simplifies the task of studying long-term trends because it shows that known offenses and convictions can be used cautiously, as interchangeable indicators of trends in disorder.

London. Historians of crime and public order in England have pointed to the Victorian era as one in which civil order greatly improved. Trends in indicators of court convictions for serious crimes of acquisition and aggression are entirely in accord with the historical judgment and, we might add, with the opinions of contemporary Londoners who committed their views to paper. The 1830s and 1840s were disorderly times, matched by strenuous efforts at official control, including the founding of the Metropolitan Police in 1829 and the high conviction rates reflected in our data. By the 1850s, however, conviction rates declined markedly and continued to do so, though more gradually, throughout the Victorian and Edwardian eras. By the first decade of the twentieth century, the conviction rates for both categories of serious crime were approximately one-quarter of what they had been in the 1830s and 1840s.

Most data series for the MPD were interrupted by the Great Depression, but there is evidence of a substantial increase in known crimes of both types beginning in the late 1920s. Data after the Second World War are for known offenses only, not convictions; nonetheless, indicators of all categories of known crimes show marked increases. (So do measures of total convictions, not shown here.) As of 1930 known crimes of aggression were about 7 per 100,000 population, compared to about 12 per 100,000 in the early 1950s. The most dramatic changes in all the London data are the increases in offenses known after 1955. Between that year and the early 1970s the indicator of crimes of acquisition increases by a factor of four; assaults and similar crimes by a factor of seven; and the murder rate more than doubles. Official data through 1975, not graphed here, show no levelling off of the upward trend.[8]

Stockholm. The crime data for Stockholm are somewhat different from those of London, but trace a similar pattern. Convictions for assault and breach of the peace, though quite variable in the nineteenth century, were higher than in the first half of the twentieth century by a ratio of about 4 to 1. Statistics on convictions were not reported after 1947, but the overlapping indicator of assaults known to the police shows a fourfold upturn after 1950. Murder and manslaughter are, and have been, relatively rare crimes in Stockholm, but convictions and reports for them (not shown here) showed a similar decline from the mid-nineteenth to the early twentieth century, and a marked increase from 1950 to 1965.

Indicators for theft in Stockholm include both serious and petty offenses, but not the white-collar crimes, like fraud, that are included in the indicators of crimes of acquisition for the other cities. The convictions data show that, as in London, the 1830s and 1840s were times of unprecedented civil action against offenders. The long-term trend thereafter was one of decline, interrupted by marked, but short-term, increases about 1870 and 1918. In the 1920s and 1930s the conviction rates were half what they had been between 1890 and 1915, and one-fifth their levels a century before. Statistics on known offenses were reported only after 1865, but generally show the same gradual decline—and sharp, short-term increases—as the data on convictions. Beginning in the 1940s, concern about property crimes seems to have increased as drastically as it did in London, judging by the indicator of offenses known. They more than double during the 1940s, decline briefly, and then double and redouble in the next 20 years. The convictions data are available only through 1964, but trace the same variations: by 1964 the conviction rate was four times what it was in the late 1930s. The sheer scale of the contemporary problem is suggested by the fact that one serious (indictable) theft was reported for every 20 Londoners in 1974, and one theft for every 11 inhabitants of Stockholm in 1971.[9]

Sydney. Sydney was founded as a penal colony in 1788. Until the end of transportation of convicts from England in 1840, a sizeable proportion of its inhabitants were convicts or ex-convicts, who were unquestioningly assumed to have criminal proclivities by the nonconvict population and whose behavior was subject to careful policing and harsh sanctions. One consequence was the very high—absolute and relative—level of convictions for serious crimes in early nineteenth-century New South Wales. Despite the distinctive composition of the population and its antipodean location, the nineteenth-century trends in New South Wales are remarkably similar to those in London and Stockholm. Conviction rates began to decline in the 1840s rather than later, but from then to the end of the century, their steady decline was marked only by slight perturbations. If 1840–41 is used as a base period and conviction rates then are compared with those 20 and 40 years later, these approximate ratios are obtained:

	1840–41	Early 1860s	1880
Serious crimes of acquisition	6	2	1
Serious crimes of aggression	10	2	1

The twentieth century data show that the trend continued through the 1930s. Underneath the marked year-to-year fluctuations, it is apparent that by the early 1930s the conviction rates for those two categories of offenses had declined by nearly half from their levels in the 1880s.

In the 1940s, in what is by now a familiar pattern, the conviction rates for serious acquisitive crimes began to increase substantially; they tripled by 1970 and showed no signs of levelling off. Convictions for serious aggressive crimes also increased but not so sharply: their average in the 1950s and 1960s was about double the rates of 1935–40, and they do not increase significantly after the early 1950s. The arrest rate for such crimes (not shown), however, increased much more sharply and continuously throughout the 1950s and 1960s, and in the latter decade was 600 percent of the arrest rates in the 1930s. The apparent discrepancy is readily explained: one of the institutional responses to rising arrest rates in New South Wales, as in England, has been to shift less serious cases from the higher courts to magistrates' courts, which can dispose of them in less costly and more efficient fashion.[10]

All three of the cities share the Western cultural tradition, and two of them—London and Sydney—have institutions of public order rooted in the English common law tradition. In other respects, though, the cities are dissimilar: they vary in ecological setting, size, political history, economic activities, class composition and stratification, social policy, and services. It is all the more singular, therefore, that the trends in their indicators of crime over a century and a half can be summarized, without serious distortion, in figures 6 and 7. The first figure represents the changing incidence of convictions for crimes of acquisition and violence against the person from the 1830s through the mid-1960s. Figure 7 shows the trends in crimes known during the 60 years for which such data are regularly available.[11]

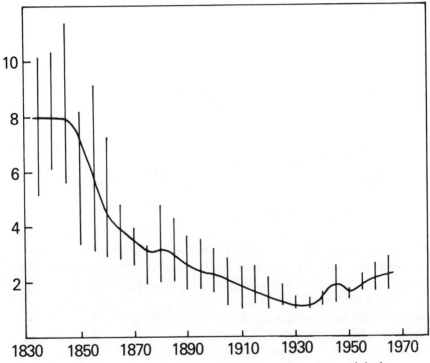

Fig. 6. The common trend in convictions for crimes of theft
and violence in Western societies, 1835–1965

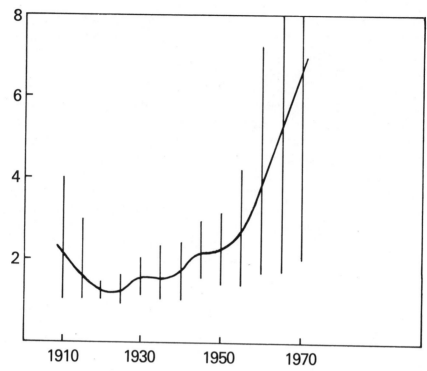

Fig. 7. The common trend in known crimes of theft and
violence in Western societies, 1910–1970

The fateful question is, What do these trends in public disorder
signify? Since official data on public disorder present at best a diffracted
image of criminal behavior, one must ask whether the trends can be
attributed to changes in the institutions of public order. Such institutional effects must be discounted before one can attribute the trends—if
any remain—to a changing social reality.

The first question is whether there have been substantial redefini-
tions of criminal behavior in any of the Western societies during the past
150 years that might account for declining crime indicators in the nineteenth century or their increase in the last several decades. Much nineteenth-century legislation aimed at controlling economic and political
dissent by the working class, but most of it has long since been repealed.
There also has been great variation in social and legal definitions of deviant and immoral conduct. The list of social behaviors that have been
the subject of recurrent attempts at regulation is similar in all three societies and includes—among others—vagrancy, lack of regular employ-

ment, infidelity, homosexuality, abortion, prostitution, public urination and profanity, insulting behavior, gambling, alcohol consumption, and the use of drugs other than alcohol. Vagrancy and similar conditions are now rarely a criminal offense, and most sexual acts between consenting adults have been decriminalized—formally in England and Sweden, by de facto nonenforcement in New South Wales. Most of the other offenses listed remain on the books.[12]

The changing scope of criminal laws governing collective behavior and social conduct is evident in the spasmodic rise and decline of conviction rates for those offenses. When we turn to crimes of violence and theft, the picture is different. Many revisions have been made in the laws relating to these offenses in all three societies. In England the principal changes occurred in the 1820s and 1830s. In Sweden there were wholesale recodifications in 1865 and 1965. In New South Wales the criminal law has grown by accretion, with fairly substantial revisions in 1883 and 1900. But none of these legal changes, nor any others, have in any substantial way broadened or narrowed the prevailing definitions of what constitutes murder, assault, theft, or fraud. Most people in these three societies, dominant groups and ordinary citizens alike, enter the last quarter of the twentieth century with much the same distaste for these kinds of behavior as was found in the nineteenth century.[13]

Measures of crimes known to the police depend on public trust in the police and police efficiency. By the same token, arrests, and hence conviction rates, tend to vary with police manpower and efficiency. Therefore we must ask whether changes in the scope, efficiency, or activities of police systems might account for crime trends.

The long-term decline in the crime indicators in the nineteenth and early twentieth centuries cannot by any stretch of the imagination be attributed to declining police efficiency. The greatest declines in the crime indicators, in fact, followed or coincided with the establishment of modern, centralized police forces in all three cities. In London the Metropolitan Police was established in 1829, replacing a patchwork of uncoordinated and mostly unprofessional police and watch services. From then onward they employed increasingly well-trained officers and new methods of detention, winning the grudging respect and, ultimately, the admiration of London's citizens. Increased efficiency and growing public support coincided with declining rates of committals and convictions, not increasing ones. In New South Wales there was a marked increase in the efficiency of police following the establishment of a colony-wide force in 1862, and the conviction rates increased distinctly and sharply in the next few years. But this is a relatively small fluctuation around the long-term declining trend. In Stockholm the police establishment was centrally organized and given expanded duties and resources in 1850; and the following decade was characterized by sharply declining rates of conviction for theft. Subsequent reorganizations mainly took the form of the addition of specialized departments, until 1965, when all local police forces in Sweden were placed under national control.

Since increased police efficiency contributed to, or at least coincided with, the improvement of public order in these three cities, it challenges the plausibility of the argument that police efficiency accounts for the contemporary increase in record crime. But the argument needs to be tested more directly. One way in which reformed police procedures might cause increases in crime indicators is by way of change in recording systems. Such a change occurred in London in 1931–32, when police were required to enter into the official records a host of offenses about which they earlier had taken only informal notes. This change caused a doubling in the total number of indictable crimes recorded by police. But we can identify no comparable changes between 1955 and 1972 that might account for the 400 percent increase in known thefts in London. In fact there is a countervailing tendency: there have been recurring increases in the threshold value of goods stolen, distinguishing indictable from nonindictable offenses.

Another example comes from New South Wales, where officials put an end in 1970 to keeping the "Paddy's Book," in which petty offenses were informally recorded. Thereafter, such offenses were to be included in the official totals, which means that increases in reported theft after 1970 will be inflated by comparison with pre-1970 data. But there were no recording changes which conceivably could have accounted for reported increases between 1960 and 1970: 200 percent in larceny, 300 percent in breaking and entering, 600 percent in armed robbery. One last example comes from Stockholm, where the rate of reported murders, attempts, and manslaughter (not shown here) increased by a ratio of about 1 to 5 between the early 1950s and 1967, and then, in the next four years, fell by 3 to 1. This improvement in public security reportedly was due to a change away from the practice of using the label "attempted murder" for the more serious cases of assault.

Increased police efficiency historically coincided with declining indicators of common crime in these three cities. Nonetheless, critics of modern police forces often suggest that the recent increases in known offenses, arrests, and convictions are the result of increasingly diligent police dipping into the dark figure of previously unrecorded crime. We have three kinds of evidence to bring to bear on this hypothesis. One is the evidence of police force size: if rising crime indicators follow the expansion in police manpower, then the argument gains plausibility. Elsewhere we have reported on statistical tests of this relationship. Between 1870 and 1940 there are nine instances of particularly rapid short-term expansion in the absolute and proportional size of the police forces in the three cities. During this era, periods of police expansion were followed by short-run declines averaging 3.9 percent per year in indicators of aggressive and acquisitive crime. Between 1941 and 1970, we identified five further instances of rapid police expansion. In this recent period, police expansion was followed by increases averaging 3.8 percent per year in the summary crime indicators. Analysis of the specific circumstances, however, shows that in each case, as in many earlier ones, a sustained increase in reported crime provided the incentive for police expansion. In Stockholm, for example, the ratio of police to population remained roughly constant until 1962; in the next eight years it was expanded by a third. Crime rates had been rising for a decade or more prior to police expansion. In New South Wales the police force declined in size in the 1950s and early 1960s, then underwent a modest expansion beginning about 1965. Here, as in Stockholm and London, police expansion reflected public and official concern about previous increases in recorded crime. The police and politicians in these three cities used crime data to justify increases in police resources, but it strains belief to argue that they created crime waves for the purpose. What distinguishes the contemporary experience is that increases in police manpower have not had any impact on the steadily rising rates of crime which prompted police expansion.

Two other tests of the "more thorough policing" explanation are provided by the crime data themselves. The great majority of crimes known to police are not detected through active police patrolling, but come to their attention through citizen complaints. The size and efficiency of the police play little part in this process. Where police efficiency does play a role is in apprehensions. If increased efficiency is a principal cause of rising crime rates, then arrests, and perhaps convictions, should rise as fast or faster than known crimes. The opposite proves to be the case. Postwar data from all three cities show that the known crimes have increased much more rapidly than arrests or convictions.

The third test is provided by comparing the rates of growth in more serious versus less serious offenses. In general, serious offenses are more likely to come to police attention than petty ones. If rising crime rates are the result of more thorough reporting, then the increase in offenses known should consist disproportionately of minor offenses. It is consistently the case in all three cities that reported assaults—a lesser offense—have increased somewhat more rapidly than murder and attempts. Where theft is concerned, however, the opposite is true: the serious offenses of robbery and burglary have increased far more rapidly than those for petty theft. So this evidence is ambiguous. Part of the rise in reported assaults (but not murder) may be a function of increased citizen reporting; the rise in various forms of theft cannot be so explained.[14]

We have identified several instances in which changing police operations caused distinct, abrupt changes in crime indicators. A part of the postwar increase in rates for assault could be due to better policing or better reporting. But the weight of the evidence is substantially against the "more efficient policing" explanation of rising crime rates in these three cities.

There are two ways in which changes in court procedures over time might significantly affect indicators of convictions for crime. We need to be especially concerned about these issues when assessing trends in nineteenth-century London and New South Wales, where we rely on conviction data alone. Expansion of defendants' rights before the courts may result in proportionally fewer convictions, but this probably can be dismissed as a significant factor in the nineteenth century because the most substantial expansion of rights in all three societies occurred late in the nineteenth century and early in the twentieth, after many decades of declining conviction rates. In New South Wales, for example, accused persons were not given the right to examine witnesses or testify in their own defense until 1891, nor was an appeals court established until 1912. English reforms of this sort were introduced in the same era. Free legal services were widely provided in Stockholm beginning in 1919, but not in London or New South Wales until much later. The expansion of defendants' rights may help explain why conviction rates have increased much more slowly than known offenses or arrests in the last 20 years, but it does not account for the nineteenth-century decline in conviction rates. Moreover, indicators of committals to trial, show the same declining nineteenth-century trends as convictions, which provides one additional kind of verification.

If defendants for a given kind of offense are brought before higher courts in one period, and given summary justice by magistrates' or police courts in another, the conviction rates for serious offenses obviously will be affected. Similarly, courts may be more lenient in one period than another. A variety of evidence shows that the severity of sentences declined substantially during the nineteenth century in all three societies. At the beginning of the 1880s the emphasis was on capital punishment for all major offenses—sentences which in England usually were commuted to transportation to Australia. By mid-century the emphasis had shifted to imprisonment. Later in the nineteenth century and especially in the twentieth century, a decided trend toward shorter sentences and greater reliance on fines set in. Probation and parole systems were introduced beginning around the turn of the century, as part of a growing interest in rehabilitation. More important for the purpose of interpreting nineteenth-century conviction statistics, the same liberalization of punishment was accompanied by increasing reliance on summary justice and probation. In other words, a given criminal offense in the first half of the nineteenth century was more likely to lead to a higher court conviction in both London and New South Wales than it was thereafter. In Stockholm, where we have the parallel evidence on reported offenses and the total volume of convictions, there are no grounds for doubting the magnitude of decline. But in London and, especially, New South Wales, part of the decline in conviction rates is a consequence of changing judicial practice.[15]

CONCLUSION

There are similar 150-year trends in the official data on common crimes in London, Stockholm, and New South Wales. We have examined the historical evidence on the operations of the institutions of public order, to test the possibility that the reversing trend was due largely, or in some substantial part, to changes in the criminal law, urban policing, or court disposition of cases. Some short-term fluctuations in crime rates can be accounted for in these terms. A part of the nineteenth-century decline in convictions for serious offenses in London and New South Wales probably was due to shifts in the disposition of cases from higher to lower courts. The recent increases in conviction rates probably are muted by the same factor. There is little evidence, though, that either nineteenth-century declines in crimes reported to police, or the dramatic increases since 1950, can be attributed to institutional factors. The major alternative explanation of the reversing trend is also the simplest one: that the volume of threatening social behavior did decrease consistently and dramatically in the nineteenth- and early twentieth-century experience of these three cities and then, in the aftermath of World War II, began an increase far more rapid than the earlier decline. This interpretation cannot be accepted beyond a shadow of a doubt, because so many distorting cultural and institutional factors intervene between illegal behavior and its official records. But it is improbable, to say the least, that these factors could simultaneously cause declines of four to eight magnitudes in different kinds of crime in three distant and disparate cities in the second half of the nineteenth century and equally great increases in the third quarter of this century. It is far more likely that the trends reflect, in a somewhat distorted way, real and profound changes in aggregate social behavior.

Two fundamental questions are raised by the findings of this study. One is whether they are generalizable to other Western societies. Few published studies have dealt systematically with the nineteenth-century records, but those which have come to conclusions similar to ours. The trends we observe in nineteenth-century London closely resemble those of all England and Wales.[16] In France, the rate of persons accused of property crimes declined by a ratio of 10 to 1 between 1826 and the 1930s.[17] Studies of Boston and Chicago show declines in diverse official indicators of crime during the latter part of the nineteenth century and the early part of the twentieth century.[18] Turning to the contemporary period, the rise in official indicators of crime since around 1950 in London, Stockholm, and New South Wales parallels the widely documented experience of most other Western societies. In a forthcoming study of trends in public order since 1945, for example, we survey official data on known offenses and convictions in 16 Western democracies. All of them have experienced accelerating rates of property crime in recent years, and most have had parallel increases in offenses against persons. Interestingly enough, the English-speaking and Scandinavian countries have experienced the sharpest and most consistent increases.[19]

The second question is one of causality. What mix of social, economic, demographic, political, and cultural changes is responsible for the common trends in socially threatening behavior in Western societies? Subsequent studies will deal with aspects of that question. The evidence of this essay, though, does challenge one approach to explanation: it provides little support for the contention that the recorded increase in crimes of theft and violence in Western societies during the recent past can be explained away by changes in the operations of the police and criminal justice systems. On the contrary, the internal consistency of the data and the cross-cultural parallels in trends in public order strongly imply an underlying behavioral reality: an upward surge in socially threatening behaviors that was first detectable in some societies in the 1930s, subsided briefly after World War II, and then accelerated with gathering momentum to the present.

This conclusion challenges at least one of the conventional views about how to control crime. Although the evidence supports the common belief that crime has greatly increased in most Western societies, it does not sustain the companion belief that the workings of the police, courts, or penal institutions have consistent effects on the magnitude of crime. The century-long decline in common crime that began in the 1840s in London, Stockholm, and New South Wales was accompanied by increased policing and less punitive, more rehabilitative penal treatment. Since the 1960s the same conditions are associated with sharply increasing crime. Leon Radzinowicz made the point well when he said, nearly two decades ago, "The potentiality of criminal legislation and penal system combined, for influencing the phenomenon of crime, has been greatly exaggerated in all countries."[20] In present perspective, it is evident that the policies of public order which seemed to work for nearly a century no longer have the salutary effects once attributed to them. If the reversing trend is to be explained, it must be by reference to the workings of more fundamental social forces.

One other homily on the state of social knowledge and research about common crime also follows. It is that those who dismiss rising rates of theft, assault, and murder as a social fiction which needs no remedy may be correct in some instances, but in general are just plain wrong. The problem is a very real one in most Western societies, and it weighs most heavily on less advantaged social groups. It is the poor and the near-poor who are most victimized by assault and theft in Western societies, and they are the ones who pay a disproportionate share of the costs of commercial theft, which are passed on as a kind of regressive tax to consumers. They are also the people most likely to be caught up in deviant behavior that becomes, at the hands of the authorities, first a stigma, then a bitter, antisocial life from which there is no exit. From the point of view of all these victims, the academics who dismiss or minimize the social reality of crime from their point of security and social advantage are accessories after the fact; and so are officials who deal symbolically rather than substantively with the issue.

7

The Modernization of Crime in Germany and France, 1830–1913

HOWARD ZEHR

Everyone knows that crime is more frequent today than it was in the rural milieu of our grandparents and great-grandparents. In fact, many would argue such a trend is inevitable. Modernity implies a decline in respect for conventions, a lessening of appreciation for the rights and property of others. What could be more logical than that delinquency should accompany the modernization process?

The city is usually considered a major catalyst in this development, for the association between city and disorder runs deep. Although the western world is now dominated by urban values and life-styles, modern man is still afraid of the city. Underlying this apprehension is a fear of violence and disorder. On the most basic, irrational level, the city brings forth images of faceless masses rushing to and fro, of dark streets where sinister villains lurk, of chaos and disorder which breed violence and crime. On a more reasoned level, this underlying negativism is reflected in much literature on urbanism: the city is then often said to be characterized by loosened social ties, by formal but rather ineffective social controls, by great social tensions, by irresistible temptations to do evil, by a frenzied and impersonal way of life. Such a situation is thought to encourage all sorts of delinquency: theft, muggings, rapes, and homicides as well as riots are associated with the city. Consequently, urban growth—which is an integral part of the modernization process—is assumed to result in large and persistent increases in crime. That criminal activity is more frequent in cities than in the countryside, that it has increased during the past two centuries, and that this increase can be attributed to the spread of urbanization or, more generally, to modernization are basic tenets of popular belief.

They are tenets, however, that increasingly are being called into question. Numerous objections have been raised in recent years to the general concept of the city which this view assumes. These are beyond the scope of this essay; suffice it to say here that the city—and urban growth—have been shown to be less impersonal, less disorganized, less disorienting, less novel, and less evil that most students prior to the mid-twentieth century assumed.[1] Moreover, the link between disorder and the city has had at best only tenuous empirical basis and lately some empirical evidence to the contrary has begun to surface for both collective and more individualized forms of disorder.[2] Clearly, the antiurban tenets do need to be tested.

Two problems, then, serve as the focus for the following discussion.[3] Was crime in nineteenth-century Germany and France really higher in cities than in the countryside?[4] What happened to crime in the course of the modernization process? Obviously we can only hope to scratch the surface of these problems here, but the conclusions reached, however tentative, suggest that traditional conceptions about criminal behavior need to be reexamined along with the other ideas about the nature of urban life and the modernization process. These conditions also indicate that past patterns of criminal behavior, rather than being exotic items of primarily antiquarian interest, have a wider significance than is usually assumed.[5]

Social historians have usually avoided the problem of crime due, in part, to a deep distrust of crime statistics. Such suspicion is not entirely unwarranted; indeed, anyone acquainted with the controversies generated by the FBI's soaring index of crime in America cannot help but question the validity of crime records. Deficiencies in FBI figures are only partially due to inadequacies inherent in the records themselves: crime statistics, like most statistical indices, offer innumerable possibilities for misinterpretation and misuse.[6] Nevertheless, obvious shortcomings in contemporary crime records have caused many social scientists to regard any attempt to study past crime rates as futile.

The biases and distortions in crime records must not be glossed over. However, a close study of various crime indices from both the nineteenth and twentieth centuries indicates that nineteenth-century criminal statistics are more plentiful and provide better indices of actual criminal activity than is commonly assumed. Crime indices are not random variables; records from the nineteenth century yield recurrent and comprehensible patterns of crime which cannot be attributed simply to biases in the records or to the activities of the agencies which compiled them. However, indices must be carefully selected and constructed, and a recognition of basic distortions is essential.

The basic pros and cons of historical crime records cannot be surveyed in detail here, but several guidelines for the use of crime records can be noted.[7] Modern scholars are pretty well agreed that police statistics—and especially records of crime made known to police as opposed to persons arrested—provide the best indices of delinquency because they eliminate fewer crimes (the so-called "dark figure") than any other category of record. Although it is often assumed that such statistics are lacking for the nineteenth century, a search of archival materials has turned up useable police statistics in some surprising places (e.g., city administrative reports). Nevertheless, in practice a compromise is often necessary; most European governments opted for court records during the nineteenth century, and thus a large body of well-organized and carefully collected court data is available on a national basis while police indices tend to be diverse and localized. Fortunately, comparisons of court and police data suggest that court records may not be such bad sources as might be expected, so long as certain qualifications are recognized. Most importantly, the dark figure in nineteenth-century court records was not only much larger than for police records, but also for certain property crimes such as theft it increased drastically during the course of the century due, at least in part, to the inability of law enforcement agencies to keep up with rises in population and crime levels and also, perhaps, to a decreasing emphasis upon the sanctity of private property.[8] Thus trends in theft rates based upon nineteenth-century court records are much too negative, causing increases in theft rates to be underestimated or even ignored altogether.[9]

A second caution is that actual crime categories to be examined must be selected discriminately. Many crimes by nature result in poor indices. Sex crimes (where the victim is embarrassed), very minor offenses (where the offense is too small to bother with or where the police are not effective enough to make a report worthwhile), or arson (where, in the absence of a suspect, it is difficult to determine whether a crime actually occurred) are examples of crimes for which statistics are virtually worthless. These crimes are rarely reported and even more rarely result in arrest and trial. In general, the records of crimes are considered to be better the more serious the offense and the more likely it is to involve a party other than the offender and victim. Homicides, serious cases of assault and battery or theft, and bank robbery are examples of crimes for which indices are considered relatively reliable.

Certain crimes, in other words, are almost impossible to study, at least using statistical sources. Moreover, the use of general indices of crime—such as total crimes against persons or property—is practically ruled out. General categories of crime give exceedingly misleading results because rates are then determined primarily by more numerous minor crimes for which indices are dubious. Also, they may group together crimes which in fact have little in common; the behavior of arson rates in Germany and France, for instance, was more similar to that of violent crimes than to property crimes, with which they are usually combined. Thus emphasis must be placed upon certain specific crime categories for which indices are relatively reliable.

But even the best indices retain certain built-in distortions. Several problems are particularly germane. International comparisons of crime rates, even for "good" indices such as homicide, are exceedingly hazardous due to variations in definitions of crime as well as in report, arrest, and trial policy. Comparisons between areas within a given legal system or comparisons of rates in one area through time are more reliable, but even here variations in police efficiency and policy must be noted. And this points to a second problem. For several reasons, the dark figure in nineteenth-century records appears to have contained an urban-rural differential which affected patterns of crime both longitudinally and cross-sectionally, i.e., through time and space. What is known about early nineteenth-century village life and traditions suggests that minor violence and malicious mischief may have been looked upon more lightly in the countryside than in the city; the social order is less fragile in small, stable communities; minor violence or pranks may have served as a traditional outlet for village tensions; and victim, offender, and law-enforcement official are likely to have been acquainted, causing cases to be settled informally. Crimes of violence, therefore, may have gone unrecorded more often in rural areas and in the early nineteenth century than in more modern, urban settings; rural gendarme reports in Württemberg in fact included no category of assault and battery until 1890.[10] On the contrary, however, village traditions protecting property as well as the relative infrequency of property crimes in the countryside (documented later) may have caused property crimes to be considered more serious and to receive more attention by both police and public in rural areas. Thus rural rates of property crimes appear inflated relative to urban while rates of rural violence are underestimated relative to urban. Moreover, the distortion operated through time as well; as society became increasingly urban, the visibility of property crimes seems to have decreased (which may explain the bias in court records noted earlier) while the visibility of violence increased. And it should be noted that, while this bias exists in all records, it was reinforced at each stage of the judicial process and thus is more serious in court than in police records.

The following discussion is based upon an analysis of three basic sets of data. Court records in France and Germany allow cross-sectional comparisons of crime rates in the 86 *départements* (departments) of France and the 83 *Regierungs-Bezirke* of Germany at specific points around the end of the century.[11] Court records also must be relied upon for an estimate of the behavior of national crime rates through time in Germany, but statistics of persons tried have been used in place of the more frequently cited index of convictions. These do not begin until 1882. No national index is possible for Germany prior to unification. Somewhat better national time-series indices are available for France: annual reports of the Ministry of Justice 1831–1910 include statistics on cases dropped by public prosecutors and by combining these with cases tried, an index which approximates crimes known to public prosecutors is possible.[12] Since a high percentage of crimes known to police was supposed to have reached the prosecutor's office, this index is clearly an improvement over court records. Finally, in addition to the cross-sectional and longitudinal analyses of national data, a number of areas have been selected from both Germany and France for closer examination. Due to the absence of local police statistics in France, the areas selected had to be departments and the crime indices court records (persons tried). In Germany, however, police statistics were available for a number of urban as well as rural areas. These statistics provide detailed information about the movement of crime rates through time in a variety of areas and thus allow a perspective absent from the cross-sectional analysis.

Eight French departments were selected as case studies.[13] These fall into four basic groups. Creuse, Loir-et-Cher, and the Vendée were predominantly rural, agricultural departments which did not urbanize or industrialize significantly during the century; population growth too was limited, and population actually declined during some periods. Pas-de-Calais and Nord, on the other hand, represent areas which industrialized and urbanized massively during the last half of the century. Loire represents a traditional but still growing urban-industrial center, while

Seine (Paris) and Bouches-du-Rhône (including Marseilles) were dynamic urban centers with long urban histories.

For Germany, 10 cities were selected for comparisons.[14] For each of these police-report statistics were available and, although the series differed in length, most fall roughly into the period 1880–1913. They can be divided into three categories. Urban centers which blossomed into large, dynamic industrial centers during this period include the Ruhr cities of Düsseldorf, Bochum, and Duisburg as well as the smaller city of Oberhausen. Berlin and Breslau represent large, older cities. Finally, Ohligs, Mülheim am Rhein, and Bonn were smaller and less dynamic cities in the western industrial area.

The best rural police indices for Germany during this period are gendarme reports from Württemberg between 1890 and 1913.[15] Taken as a whole, of course, Württemberg was still quite urban by French standards (50 percent of the population lived in cities in 1910) but, outside of Stuttgart, most of the urban population lived in small towns and the province included four rather diverse *Kreise*. Neckarkreis was highly urbanized (70 percent in 1910), even with Stuttgart excluded, and experienced the highest rate of population growth (although the rate was relatively low compared to that of most large cities). Schwarzwaldkreis and Donaukreis were both moderately urbanized (43 percent in 1910), though average city size was small, and both experienced moderate growth during the period. Jagstkreis was the least urbanized and most static *Kreis*: 29 percent of its population lived in towns, and population growth was only 2 percent between 1885 and 1910. These districts, though not as rural as the comparable French areas, do provide useful contrasts to the selected German cities.

Only two basic crime categories have been selected for attention here. Theft provides the best index of property crimes; indices of fraud and of embezzlement, the other frequent offenses involving the taking of private property, are too unreliable to be of much use.[16] As the prime index of violence, homicide—traditionally considered the best possible index of crime—has been passed over in favor of assault and battery. While a larger percentage of homicides come to public attention than any other violent crime, small numbers are involved in most nineteenth-century homicide indices; the total annual number of persons tried for homicide in France during the nineteenth century rarely topped 700, for example, and on a city or even a provincial level the numbers involved are miniscule indeed. Consequently, generalization is difficult and the possibility of sampling errors great. Also, the homicide category is somewhat arbitrary since whether or not a crime is classified as homicide depends solely upon whether the victim dies, which in turn depends upon factors such as the availability of lethal weapons or medical facilities. Assault and battery, although it is less reliably reported than homicide, is still often known to police and, moreover, involves rather large numbers; thus it provides a better index of violence than does homicide.

We will begin the specific analysis by posing a basically familiar question in an unconventional way. Almost everyone would agree that there is a profound difference between a crime of theft and a crime of violence. Instead of asking simply whether crime was higher in the city than in the countryside or whether it rose during the century, therefore, we will ask first of all how the "mix" or balance of crimes varied in nineteenth-century Germany and France. And the best way to do this is through the use of a simple theft-violence ratio [TVR = 100 × (Homicide + Assault) / (Homicide + Assault + Theft] which measures the balance between violent and property crimes with a single index. Homicide and assault are here totalled to provide an index of violence, and theft rates serve as an index of property crimes.[17] The ratio of these two basic categories indicates the percentage of all three categories which is represented by violence. A ratio below 50 would indicate that less than half of all crimes measured were crimes of violence. Similarly, a rising TVR indicates an increasing preference for violence relative to theft.

Such a ratio allows the balance between crimes in various areas and times to be compared using a single index. In fact, cross-sectional comparisons of theft-violence ratios can be made somewhat more confidently than can cross-sectional comparisons for the individual crime indices which make up the ratio. With the TVR, rates of violence in any given area are compared to rates of theft in the same area, and therefore distortions due to differing systems of law enforcement or varying definitions of crime are reduced. Here is a case, perhaps, of a chain which is stronger than its weakest link.

But, like all good things, the ratio is not without problems. Court records must be used in many cases but, as noted previously, theft rates were increasingly underestimated by such records during the nineteenth century. The slope of trends in a TVR based on court records, therefore, will be too positive, especially after 1870 and in urbanizing areas. Similarly, urban-rural biases in both violence and theft cause the TVR to be underestimated in rural or small-town areas as compared to urban. Nevertheless, when the biases are kept in mind, the TVR provides a useful indicator of the composition of crime. In spite of this bias which would tend to minimize urban-rural differences, connection between community size and the TVR did obtain in the nineteenth century. In both Germany and France, the TVR tended to be lower in the urban areas than in rural and, in the long run, to drop as urbanization progressed; violence, in other words, was lower relative to theft in the city than in the countryside and, on the average, lower at the end of the century than at the beginning.

In France, the correlation between the proportion of the population living in larger cities (i.e., at least 10,000 persons) and the TVR in 86 departments was r = −0.59, indicating that the TVR was negatively related to urbanism and that 35 percent of the variance in the TVR can be mathematically "explained" by this factor alone.[18] Traditional levels of theft-violence ratios do not appear to have been highly important; only 17 percent of the variance in the TVR in these departments in 1900–1902 can be explained by the TVR in 1838–1840. In France as a whole, the TVR was significantly higher at the beginning of the century (38.2 in the 1830s) than at the end (28.4 in 1900–1909), a drop which of course coincided with the spread of urbanization.[19] German statistics for urban-rural comparisons on such a global scale have serious deficiencies. Conviction statistics in *Landkreise* (rural districts) and major *Stadtkreise* (city districts) do show clear correlation between the TVR and urbanism in 1883–1887, however. Thirty-nine Regierungs-Bezirke contained large city districts during this period. Within these, the average TVR in the 55 major Stadtkreise was 28 as opposed to an average of 39 in the 39 Landkreise. And these results were not due to a skewed distribution or to differences in the administration of justice from Regierungs-Bezirk to Regierungs-Bezirk; in only one of the Regierungs-Bezirke (Reg.-Bez. Danzig) was the TVR in any Landkreis or small Stadtkreis lower than the TVR in the major Stadtkreise of the same Bezirk.[20]

The theft-violence ratio was negatively associated with urbanism both longitudinally and cross-sectionally, therefore. A closer look at ratios, however, shows that in neither time nor space was the correlation linear. Figure 8 shows average TVRs and the percentages of the populations living in large cities in 86 departments of France around the turn of the century. Two to three major groupings may be seen here. Highest theft-violence ratios were without exception found in the most rural departments, while all highly urbanized departments had extremely low TVRs. Departments with moderate levels of city populations, however, were grouped together with more rural departments toward the middle of the scale. Likewise, among the cities and regions selected as case stud-

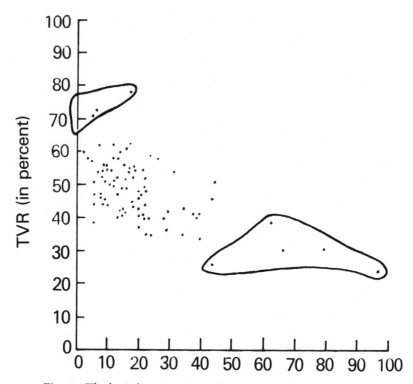

Fig. 8. Theft-violence ratios and percentages of the population living in cities in French departments, 1900–1904

ies in Germany and France, TVRs in old urban centers such as Berlin, Paris (Seine), Marseilles (Bouches-du-Rhône), and Breslau were the lowest in the groups, but middle-sized towns or urbanizing-industrializing areas had TVRs as high or higher than rural areas (tables 15 and 16). Evidently, then, it was large and/or old urban centers which, with extremely low theft-violence ratios, formed a distinctive group; while there is some evidence that the most rural areas also formed a grouping on the other end of the scale, the distinction here is less clear.

What this suggests is the existence of a modern pattern of crime, where violence is relatively low compared to property crimes, and a "premodern" pattern of high levels of violence relative to property crimes. Areas in the process of rapid change manifested patterns more similar to premodern or rural than to modern areas due either to the persistence of rural patterns of crime during the early stages of modernization or—and this is not necessarily contradictory—to high rates of violence because of the tensions of change. In urbanizing areas, there-

Table 15.

AVERAGE THEFT-VIOLENCE RATIOS IN EIGHT FRENCH
DEPARTEMENTS, 1900–1904
(BASED ON COURT RECORDS)

Departement	TVR
Old Cities	
Seine	24.4
Bouches-du-Rhône	31.5
Traditional Industrial	
Loire	39.8
New Industrial-Urban	
Pas-de-Calais	44.8
Nord	51.1
Rural	
Vendée	52.4
Creuse	67.2
Loir-et-Cher	44.9

Table 16.

AVERAGE THEFT-VIOLENCE RATIOS IN ELEVEN GERMAN
CITIES OR DISTRICTS, 1905–1909
(BASED ON POLICE RECORDS)*

City or District	TVR
Old Cities	
Berlin	15.4
Breslau	18.3
New Industrial	
Duisburg	25.2
Bochum	29.6
Small Towns	
Bonn	28.6
Mülheim am Rhein	30.8
Ohligs	47.9
Rural/Small-Town	
Donaukreis	26.3
Jagstkreis	27.1
Schwarzwaldkreis	35.3
Neckarkreis	35.4

* Data for other cities lacking for these years.

fore, the TVR would be expected to fall only after large-scale urban life
was no longer novel.

Trends in the theft-violence ratio in Germany were consistent with
this pattern. In most of the selected areas, the TVR did drop toward the

end of the century as society became more modern. Generally, however, the TVR also rose initially, reflecting the most disruptive stages of the modernization process. And in general exceptions to this pattern are consistent with the hypothesis; as would be expected, for example, the pattern was least apparent in several fairly rural districts of Württemberg and in one or two of the small towns. Only in Bochum do trends not appear to meet expectations. In Germany as a whole a similar pattern is seen (figure 9). The long-run trend between 1882 and 1912 appears to have been upward due, probably, to biases in the court records from which the national indices are calculated. As elsewhere, however, the trend was curvilinear, with an initial rise characterized by gradually falling growth rates and, finally, an actual decline in the ratio.

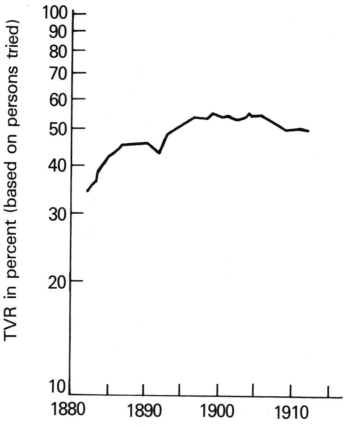

Fig. 9. Annual theft-violence ratio in the German Reich, 1882–1912

The situation is less clear in the eight French departments where dependence upon court records causes a serious distortion in trends. In the Seine, an old urban center, the TVR remained relatively steady during the century, while in Bouches-du-Rhône the TVR fell rapidly prior to 1870, then rose slightly or, if the trend is biased as expected, remained rather constant thereafter. In the Loire the pattern was similar but somewhat less pronounced. Trends in the newly industrializing departments were remarkably similar to one another but differed markedly from those in traditional urban-industrial centers. Here the ratio fell at first, rose rapidly during the early years of industrial development prior to 1870, then levelled off or possibly fell after 1870. No significant differences in timing are apparent even though large-scale industrialization did begin somewhat earlier in the Nord than in Pas-de-Calais, but otherwise patterns in these five departments held about as expected. Only in the three rural departments are movements in the TVR difficult to reconcile with the hypothesis. Overall trend patterns were shared some similarity with trends in the new industrial departments. However, the trend after 1870 was more positive in at least two of the rural departments than in the newly industrial areas indicating, perhaps, the persistence of a traditional pattern of crime, while the rise during the fifties and sixties might be explained by the population growth which occurred in these rural departments prior to 1870. Nationally, trends in the theft-violence ratio, though also ambiguous, can be reconciled with the hypothesis (figure 10). No markedly curvilinear pattern is apparent here, but industrial and urban development was much more gradual and spread out in France than in Germany, mitigating its effects upon national crime rates. Significantly, as in the departmental figures, the only period when the TVR rose markedly coincided with the industrial expansion and peak urban growth rate of the Second Empire.

But before we can make too much of this pattern, we need to know something about the behavior of the component indices which make up the theft-violence ratio. Did crime rise or fall in the long run? Were variations in the mix of crimes caused by variations in only one or in both of the component indices? The TVR alone cannot answer these questions. Thus we must also survey, though briefly, the behavior of individual theft and violence indices during the nineteenth century.

Conventional wisdom about theft is confirmed quite clearly by both German and French figures: theft rates were usually higher in cities than in the countryside, and urbanization was accompanied by relatively constant increases in theft rates. Moreover, the relationship was linear;

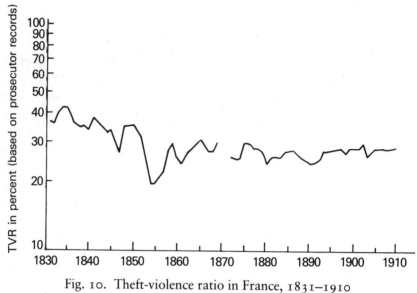

Fig. 10. Theft-violence ratio in France, 1831–1910
(1870–1871 excluded)

there is no evidence that middle-sized and/or growing cities had higher theft rates than did more mature urban centers or even necessarily that theft rates reflected the growth process rather than sheer community size.

In both Germany and France, the spread of urbanization was paralleled by an increase in theft rates. In France as a whole thefts known to public prosecutors rose 230 percent between 1831–1839 and 1900–1909. Graphs indicate that the increase was spread throughout the entire century, but the most rapid climb coincided with the period of greatest urban growth: the total urban population in France grew more rapidly in the early years than later, and the turning point in the rate for thefts also began to decline. The national index of persons tried in Germany between 1882 and 1912 does not show an increase (figure 11), but the probable downward distortions in this index have already been noted; all available local indices, including those from rural areas, for both this and the preceding period show substantial increases in theft rates. And, though it is beyond the scope of this essay to treat them in detail, trends in the areas selected as case studies in both Germany and France appear, with but few qualifications, to have directly reflected trends in urban growth.

Cross-sectional correlations confirm this pattern. Forty-four per-

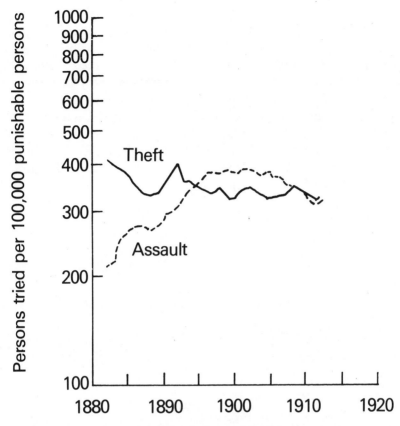

Fig. 11. Rates of theft and of assault and battery in the
German Reich, 1882–1912

cent of the variance in theft rates (r = 0.66) in the 86 French departments in 1900–1904, for instance, can be explained by the proportion
of the population living in cities, and 46 percent (r = 0.68) by the percentage of the work force engaged in industry, and this in spite of a bias
which minimizes the differences. Lowest theft rates in 1900–1904 were
experienced by Creuse, the least urbanized department in France, while
the department with highest rates, Seine-Inferieure, was among the few
which were more than 50 percent urban. Scattergraphs show the relationship to have been linear, and the relatively low correlations between
crime-prone age and sex groups and theft rates indicate that the connection cannot be explained away by the existence of larger numbers of
crime-prone groups in urban than in rural areas.[21]

Conviction statistics for Germany, grouped by Stadtkreise and Landkreise or small Stadtkreise, show a similar pattern. Theft rates in major city districts averaged 378 convictions per 100,000 punishable persons in 1883–1892, as opposed to only 273 for the remaining rural and small-town areas of Germany. Moreover, the relationship was linear; when major Stadtkreise are grouped according to size class, average theft rates increased along with community size (table 17). Most remarkably, though, these urban-rural differences were not the result of a skewed distribution since a breakdown by Regierungs-Bezirke shows that rates of convictions for theft were with but several minor exceptions higher in larger Stadtkreise than in other nearby districts.[22]

Table 17.

AVERAGE RATES OF CONVICTIONS FOR THEFT BY
CITY SIZE-CLASS IN GERMANY, 1883–1897

Community Size-Class	Average Number of Persons Convicted per 100,000 Punishable Persons
All cities with 50,000 + population	341
Cities with populations of	
50–100,000	318
100–150,000	329
150,000 +	357
All Germany	269
All but 55 largest cities	253

Even among the case-study areas which, in the case of Germany at least, are based on very diverse indices, the correlation between theft and urbanism was good. Clearly, then, urban and rural TVR patterns must be attributed, at least in part, to the behavior of theft rates but, at the same time, the curvilinear TVR pattern which was apparent through both time and space cannot.

Patterns of violence differed markedly from patterns of theft in both Germany and France. Nowhere, for instance, is there any indication of a close connection between violence and the city. Cross-sectional correlations between the proportion of the population living in cities and rates of violence around the turn of the century in French departments as well as in German Regierungs-Bezirke were insignificant; coefficients for assault and battery ranged from $r = -0.14$ for Germany to $r = 0.16$ for France, and they were quite similar for homicide. Similarly, no correlation between community size and rates of violence is apparent in the case-study areas.

More important than community size were traditions of violence. In France, where the only long-range data are available, cross-sectional correlations between rates of violence in 1900–1904, and a large number of economic and demographic variables have been checked, but the best predictor was the level of violence at the beginning of the period: 20 percent of the variance in assault rates (r = 0.45) and fully 66 percent (r = 0.81) of the variance in homicide rates in 1900–1902 can be explained by rates of the same crime in 1838–1840.

The change in the percentage of the population living in cities between 1876 and 1906 also correlated moderately with assault rates (r = 0.44), raising the possibility that, instead of being related to community size per se, rates of violence might somehow be related to the fact of social change. This possibility is best investigated longitudinally, however, and thus we must turn to time-series indices.

Overall levels of violence rose everywhere during the nineteenth century, but the increase was less than in theft. Also this trend was accompanied by a reduction in the severity of violence since, while assaults rose, homicide rates remained relatively constant or actually fell in both Germany and France.[23] More significantly, though, increases in assault were not spread equally throughout the period and there is in fact some suggestion of downward trend by the end of the century.

In general, most major upswings in violence appear to be relatable to urban-industrial growth or, more precisely, to the initial and/or most disruptive stages of the process. Rates of assault and battery rose in Germany for several decades after 1880, when the industrialization process was in full swing, then turned downward by the end of the period (Figure 11). Overall growth during the same period was lower in France (+ 21 percent using persons tried), where industrial and urban growth was much less rapid or novel than in Germany (+ 44 percent). But in France, too, trends in assault paralleled the course of modernization. Here assault rates rose throughout most of the century, but the rate of increase was considerably greater before 1870 than after, and moreover, was greater between 1855 and 1870 than before. The greatest rises in violence, then, coincided with the period when industrialization was relatively new; the large increase during the Second Empire in particular coincided with the tremendous industrial and urban expansion of this period. No tendency to decline at the end of the period is apparent in the French index, but it can be argued plausibly that the gradualness of the industrial revolution in France was responsible for this pattern in national indices.

Although evidence is mixed due, quite possibly, to the deficiencies in these indices, both cross-sectional and time-series analyses of the selected regional and city indices tend to confirm this pattern. Among the eight French departments, for example, highest assault rates were in the two newly industrializing departments and periods of most rapid increase in violence coincided with urban and industrial "take-offs." Similarly, in the German areas where long-range statistics are available, trends in assault rates were curvilinear, with increases in assault rates coinciding with periods of expansion.

Time-series analysis, in short, does suggest a connection between violence and urban growth or perhaps social change in general. But it is hard to be very precise about the relationship. Did violence increase in response to urbanization and urban growth in general or simply in response to the novelty of the change? Most evidence seems to point to periods of transition as times of unusually high rates of assault and battery, but this may depend upon the specific situation. The nature of the transition and the type of immigrant coming into the city may make a difference. How the community attempts—or fails to attempt—to deal with the transition also may affect the pattern; a tight housing situation, for example, in a rapidly growing city is certainly more conducive to violence than a situation where housing is plentiful and uncrowded. Violence rose, it can be suggested, during times of transition, then may have levelled off or fallen as adjustments were made, but the exact pattern depended upon the specific situation. At any rate, the curvilinear pattern in the theft-violence ratio, which has already been related to the modernization process, can be attributed primarily to the behavior of assault rates.

That conventional wisdom linking violence and the city is false can be said with more certainty; there is simply no evidence at all that violence was more frequent in cities than in the countryside. Many rural areas had assault rates higher than those in cities, in spite of the fact that rural rates of violence were probably underestimated by official crime records. In the long run, traditions of violence appear to have been a more important determinant of violence rates than the degree of urbanism or city size.

To summarize briefly our main empirical conclusions, crime rates in general, but especially property crime rates, rose during the nineteenth century; on the whole, crime was more frequent by 1910 than it had been in 1830. More important in the long run, however, is the declining importance of violence—and especially serious violence—relative to theft. And a transitional stage has also been observed in which violence kept up with or even outstripped rising theft rates, and this transition was associated with the modernization process.

But it should be noted that this is not the whole picture. Other alterations in the nature of criminal behavior took place during the century which must be outlined briefly. Most importantly, the response of crime to the material conditions of life changed. During the first half of the period, both property and violent crimes responded quite clearly, though in opposite directions, to fluctuations in the basic costs of subsistence. Gradually, though, this correlation loosened, although this does not mean that the connection between crime and economics disappeared; instead, there are signs that the place of basic subsistence costs was taken by more general indices of well-being, reflecting the rise in standards of living which accompanied the modernization process.

How then are these patterns, some of which run counter to common assumptions about crime, to be explained? One familiar argument clearly will not do: the idea that urbanism and urban growth breed social disorganization and anomie, which in turn breed crime, simply does not fit. The lack of a direct connection between theft rates and the urbanization process is a case in point. Most critics of the city would agree that property values were protected by the rural social order in the somewhat more idyllic age before massive industrialization. Thus it is precisely theft rates which should have been most sensitive to the social disorganization of urban growth; theft rates should have been higher in new and growing cities than in older, more stable cities and theft rates in expanding cities should have risen at first, then dropped as the conditions of urban life stabilized. No such phenomenon is apparent. And violence seems to have represented the retention, not the breakdown, of traditional values and relationships. In fact, it can also be argued that violence is actually predicated upon the presence, not the absence, of primary relationships; studies of contemporary violence, at least, indicate that most serious violence occurs between relatives and acquaintances, not complete strangers.[24] Not only does the urbanization process not necessarily result in social disorganization and anomie, therefore, but a state of disorganization would not necessarily lead to crime.

Rather than a breakdown of social order, a deterioration of social life, or a rejection of prevailing values, it can be argued that developments in criminal behavior during the nineteenth century represent the victory of the modern world, a modernization of criminal behavior. What occurred, in other words, was nothing less than the transition from premodern or preurban to modern or urban criminal patterns.

During the early part of the century, property was still protected by village tradiition and by fairly effective informal social controls. Material need may have been great, but expectations in general were low— and, as has been pointed out many times, it is expectations and desires more than objective need which determine what men will work and steal for. Thus theft rates were relatively low and fluctuations in rates closely tied to actual costs of subsistence.

The transition from a preindustrial to an urban, industrial society, though still incomplete by 1914, altered this pattern. Theft rates rose drastically not as a rejection of prevailing values, but as a result of the success of new values and new modes of social organization. Constraints are fewer in the city than in the countryside; there is more opportunity to steal in the city, less chance of being apprehended, and in general informal sanctions are replaced by less effective formal controls. Given the same tendency toward delinquent behavior, then, an urbanite may be more likely to commit such a property crime than a rural dweller. At the same time, though, an industrial society implies—and, in fact, requires—rising expectations, a desire to acquire material goods, which was not characteristic of the premodern mind. Modern industry, for example, would be unthinkable without growing markets and a work force motivated by the desire to improve itself; one of the first tasks of early industry, therefore, was to teach workers to continue working beyond what was required simply to maintain previous standards of living. And urbanization itself generates increased expectations; social classes tend to be more fluid in the city than in the countryside, contact between rich and poor is frequent, and the hope of advancement greater. Modernization as a whole, in other words, has usually implied rising expectations—expectations that society often was unable to fulfill—along with the reduction in constraints upon the individual. The motivation to steal, therefore, was greater in the city (and, as these values permeated society, elsewhere as well) because expectations were higher, and this became increasingly true as the industrialization process matured. This then is the meaning of the increase in theft rates, and it is also behind the switch in the economic correlates of crime; costs of basic staples were replaced as determinates of crime by more general indices of well-being because standards of living, and thus expectations, had increased.

In recent years the traditional idyllic picture of harmonious rural society has been seriously shaken. It is now widely recognized that social tensions are much higher in rural societies than was previously assumed. High rates of violence in rural nineteenth-century society indicate that violence (in the form of tavern brawls, family squabbles, even homicidal feuds) was a traditional outlet for frustrations, an expression of social conflict. In fact, it was often recognized as such by villagers and authorities, causing crimes of violence to be overlooked and thus omitted from records in rural areas.

While the view that urbanization brings social disorganization and therefore crime must be rejected, modernization did create social conflicts and tensions that were particularly acute during the early stages. In such a situation, violence again was a means of dealing with these tensions, especially since other avenues such as collective violence were impractical. Thus violence rose as a traditional response to new conflicts and pressures.

Modernization, it has been argued, brought in its wake an increase in expectations and, for many groups, urban life and new industrial jobs meant an actual increase in status. But many were disappointed; the conditions of urban life (e.g., housing) were demeaning and jobs were hard and often did not live up to expectations. The ownership of tangible property, considered so important in rural life, was frequently given up in the city or prior to the move. Perhaps, therefore, low-status groups felt themselves to be losing status during the early years of urban growth, leading, in turn, to high levels of frustration. As psychologists have frequently pointed out, frustration often leads to aggression— aggression which is more often directed against substitute objects such as friends or neighbors than against the actual objects of hostility.[25] Thus, rising violence, like theft, may have reflected the gap between expectations and achievement, although in different ways.

This transitional period, during which rates of crime in general soared had a potential impact well beyond its own duration. The rapid rise in crime occurred as many social groups, including the new middle class, were being exposed to city life for the first time. It could have given an empirical base to a sense that urban life was dangerous, even out of hand, and thus strengthen such important new trends as residential segregation, and ultimately suburbanization, by class. And the resultant fear of the city could outlive the actual transitional period of crime itself. It has certainly stimulated impressions of a relationship between city and crime not only in the public mind but also among many scholarly analyses of crime as well.

All available evidence points to a stabilization and quite possibly a decline in violence, particularly serious violence, after adjustments ‘to urban and industrial growth. Several explanations may be suggested. Violence is intolerable in an urban situation and thus is strongly reproved and repressed. Consequently, other methods of dealing with conflict and frustration must be worked out; these may include other forms of crime but also some other avenues such as collective action which had not been practical during the early years of city life but now became conceivable. On the other hand, however, violence may have begun to fall off because tensions and frustrations were reduced and adjustments to urbanism were made or because family and neighborhood relationships were improved due to higher standards of living. At any rate, the decline in violence reflects an acclimatization to city life, a victory for urban and social organization.

These interpretations are necessarily speculative since quantitative analysis at the national or even regional level cannot explore them with satisfactory precision. What is needed now are closer investigations of specific groups such as urban immigrants or sections of the working class, case histories of small areas such as new industrial cities, and qualitative treatments of criminal records and actual case histories. But macroanalysis does suggest that the crime phenomenon is of wider interest than has traditionally been assumed. Because crime was normally an individual act, easier to mount than organized protest it may have reflected new expectations earlier than the strikes and riots that have more commonly been the subject to historical attention. The relationship between banditry and other social unrest has been noted for groups on the verge of modernization;[26] the present study confirms this, in broad outline, for the period in which urban crime was in transition, expressing a new intensity of conflict but in rather traditional forms. We can now add the possibility that the modernization of crime, after this dramatic period, was a vital part of more adaptive social change. Judging by the larger patterns of crime, modern criminals, however much they felt out of modern society, wanted in and saw crime as a way to realize modern values.

8

Urbanization and Crime: The Soviet Case in Cross-Cultural Perspective

LOUISE I. SHELLEY

Western criminologists have traditionally observed a direct relationship between urbanization and crime both in developing and developed countries. The relationship between urbanization and crime in the Soviet Union has been given limited consideration by scholars outside of socialist countries. The Soviet Union is, however, worthy of special consideration because it demonstrates that tight social controls and centralized planning can affect the impact of urban growth on crime.

CRIMES ANALYZED

This paper discusses only nonpolitical forms of criminality. Political offenses, those that violate Articles 70 and 190 of the criminal code, account for only a small percentage of total Soviet convictions. This relatively small number of offenses about which it is difficult to obtain information could not significantly affect the general distribution of crime and the effects of urbanization discussed in this study.

No other category of crime is excluded from the discussion. Both property crimes, divided by Soviet law into crimes against personal and socialist property, and crime against the person are examined in this study. Crimes unique to socialist society, such as speculation—the purchase and resale of goods for a profit, are included in this study because the amount and distribution of these offenses are also affected by population migration and the forces of urbanization. There is no need to establish comparability between Soviet and foreign definitions of crime because the purpose of this study is to examine the impact of population movement to the cities on the full range of nonpolitical crimes in the U.S.S.R.

DATA USED

There are significant problems in analyzing the dynamics of Soviet criminality because no Soviet crime data have been published since 1928. As a result primary source material is available to only a limited number of trusted Soviet scholars who frequently compile their materials themselves at the office of the procuracy or through field surveys. The absence of comprehensive, centralized statistics is a problem not only to Western scholars of Soviet crime but to most Soviet researchers as well.[1]

Soviet criminologists are, however, provided access to the inmate population and are allowed to examine certain regional crime patterns. The data collection, over which distinguished scholars have significant control, while not providing an overall view of Soviet criminality, does permit generally accurate analyses of crime trends and the nature and composition of the criminal population.

Studies of the current state of Soviet crime and the criminal are conducted primarily by scholars affiliated with research institutes in Russia and the Baltic areas rather than with those of universities. The research institutes, affiliated with the Academy of Sciences or the police and procuracy, publish their findings in publications intended for limited circulation as well in those intended for the general reader without access to confidential materials. The conclusions in the widely circulated publications are the same as in the more classified publications but without the detail and the full substantiating materials.

The Soviet articles which provide the basis of this study are the work of scholars who have access to selective crime statistics and offender populations. These studies were published in journals available to the general public as well as in those that are intended "for internal use only" or in other words, classified. These readings have been supplemented by interviews with scholars in the Soviet Union and research reports made by Soviet scholars to the Criminal Law Department at Moscow State University.

SOVIET RESIDENCE AND MOBILITY

The extent and location of urban growth in the Soviet Union are determined by the complex population policies, passport and registration regulations that are in effect throughout the country. While the major cities in the developing countries, the United States, and Europe have experienced significant growth and population change as a result of the arrival of large numbers of migrants from rural areas, major Soviet cities, in contrast, no longer receive a large urban influx. The major cities in the Soviet Union have reached the size desired by Soviet planners, and consequently are closed to new migrants except those who marry residents or are offered work that carries with it the perquisite of residence permission. The developing cities in the remote regions of the U.S.S.R., as a result, presently receive a significant proportion of rural migrants because they readily provide these new migrants with residential permits.

The mechanism that controls the population distribution of Soviet citizens is the internal passport. While Europeans hold identity cards that are needed for travel and hotel registration in their respective countries and abroad, the internal passport of Soviet citizens governs their permanent location and ability to travel within their country. The internal passport now given to all Soviet citizens at age sixteen, records their permanent address which is the only place where the individual may reside on a permanent basis.[2] Moving between different villages, towns, and cities is difficult and consequently a Soviet citizen may spend his entire life in the place of his birth.

> The passport is issued by the local police and is updated periodically. If the holder wishes to change his place of residence permanently he must get the formal permission of the militia in his chosen area before he moves in. This is only a formality in small towns and the less desirable spots where there is little pressure on public amenities but may present a major difficulty in places like Moscow, Leningrad and the republican capitals, which have more to offer their inhabitants. It is no secret that outsiders are all but excluded from permanent residence in Moscow; for example: some people find that registration there can be procured only by bribery.[3]

Since the introduction of the passport system in 1932,[4] Soviet citizens are no longer able to choose their place of residence or to travel internally without documentation. Collective farm workers, previously barred from receiving internal passports and restricted to local travel, are presently receiving passports that provide them with internal mobility. The internal passport not only controls the individual's residence but also his travel as the internal passport is needed to purchase plane tickets and long-distance train tickets as well as to obtain a room in a hotel. Wanted criminals experience great difficulty in travelling because of the need to constantly show their passports.

As a result of the internal passport and registration system and the difficulties involved in obtaining residence permits for major cities, urban growth is presently confined almost entirely to small and medium-sized cities, frequently in geographically remote areas where the migrants can easily obtain residential permits from the police. Collective farm workers, previously deprived of internal passports and suffering from a low standard of living, were now even more eager to move than the usual town dweller. Many young males from collective farms grasped the chance to permanently settle in urban communities after their army service. In one step they gained an internal passport and joined the industrial worker class. Large numbers of these young men accepted employment at construction sites in the Far East and Far North where they are given passports and thus enabled to move to towns or medium-sized cities as places of permanent residence.

The poor living conditions on collective farms combined with the opportunity for young, unattached males to move from the farm after their military service have resulted in a large rural population, unacquainted with urban life, settling in smaller Soviet cities in less desirable locations. The influx of many youthful male migrants with little training for urban life results in severe disorientation and high rates of criminality. While this latter phenomenon is observed primarily in major urban centers throughout the world, in the Soviet Union, because of its distinct population restrictions, the negative consequences of urbanization are felt more acutely in smaller and newer cities.

Major urban centers are spared both new migrants and seasoned criminals. Since the 1920s criminals who have been incarcerated for at least five years automatically lose their right to return to their former homes in a major city, like Moscow, after their release.[5] While this rule is not ironclad, police rarely grant exemptions and sometimes refuse to register even those who have served sentences of less than five years.

The offender convicted of a major offense is severely limited in his choice of urban residence upon termination of his sentence. Individuals who are especially dangerous recidivists (convicted at least four times), individuals convicted of armed robbery, serious assaults against the person, group rape, and premeditated murder as well as many crimes against the state and economic order "are not to be granted residence permits in cities, districts and regions listed in decisions of the Soviet government until the cancellation or annulment through established procedure of their record of conviction."[6] Individuals not permitted residence in these areas can not be "employed by enterprises, institutions and organizations located in those areas."[7] Minors, serious invalids, pensioners, and women with young children are exempted from these orders. Exceptions can be made to these restrictions only with "permission of Ministries of Internal Affairs of union and autonomous republics, Board of Internal Affairs of krai and oblast Executive Committees of Soviets of Workers' Deputies."[8]

Serious offenders and recidivists are thus denied the right to return to major cities or reside in the surrounding communities. As a result, the major urban centers house few experienced criminals and cannot serve as schools for youthful offenders. Medium-sized cities, on the other hand, are recipients of a disproportionate number of first time serious offenders and recidivists.

The distinctive patterns of Soviet urbanization as a result of strict internal population controls, have resulted in crime patterns that diverge from those of other industrialized and developing countries. While the highest crime rates in the U.S.S.R. are still recorded in urban areas, major cities have comparatively low rates of criminality while smaller cities in the Baltics, Far East, and Far North have disproportionately high crime rates.

MIGRATION AND CRIME

Soviet criminologists have recently demonstrated interest in the effects of urban migration and population movement on crime. Their interest mirrors that of criminologists in other countries who have studied the consequences of the arrival of rural residents in urban areas and the migration of individuals to different countries and cultures in both developing and developed countries.

The Soviet scholarly interest in the problem of migration and crime is explained by the significant annual movement of the Soviet population. Despite the controls placed on the mobility of Soviet citizens, between 4 and 6 percent of the population, approximately eight million people, moves annually.[9] While this movement does not provide an immediate absorption problem for the region receiving these migrants, the internal migration results in a cumulative problem of significant proportions.

Soviet researchers have concluded, both in the Russian Republic (R.S.F.S.R.) and the Baltic republics, that regions with a high coefficient of migrants are areas characterized by higher coefficents of crime.[10] This is true when the migrants share the ethnic affiliation of the resident population; and the level of criminality of the migrants is even more dramatic when the migrants do not share the nationality affiliation of the resident population.

The two fundamental types of internal migration in the Soviet Union are urban migration and movement to a lightly populated area that Soviet authorities want to develop.[11] Both of these moves cause adjustment problems for the migrant and result in an increased tendency to commit acts of criminality.

Movement to a Previously Settled Area

After their arrival in Soviet cities with already established cultural and social patterns, individuals from rural areas, unacquainted with urban ways, have difficulty in locating housing and proper employment.[12] Similar problems are also found among urban migrants in developing countries of Africa and South America who, like Soviet migrants, made a rapid transition to urban communities far from their native villages. During the strenuous periods of acclimatization, Soviet immigrants encounter many difficult situations that frequently result in the commission of acts of criminality.

Migration to Lightly Inhabited Areas

Migration to previously lightly inhabited regions brings with it a different array of problems. Rural Russian migrants are frequently assigned residences in other republics or in different areas of the Russian republic with non-Slavic populations of totally different cultural, linguistic, and ethnic backgrounds.

The Russian migration to ethnically and culturally different regions is similar to that of the problem of migrant workers in Europe and Arab countries that has been examined by Ferracuti and Al-Thakeb as well as by other scholars.[13] While in Europe the migrants have a lower rate of criminality than the local residents, in Kuwait the reverse appears to be true. The patterns of Soviet migrants in culturally different areas more closely resemble those of Kuwait than of Europe. This similarity may exist because both the migrants into Kuwait and the Asian regions of the U.S.S.R. are entering homogeneous, close-knit, and traditional societies that have had low rates of criminality in the past. The new

Soviet migrant, frequently removed from his family and thrust into a region with different mores concerning social behavior and, in particular, alcohol use suffers from the culture conflict described by Thorsten Sellin.[14] While Soviet scholars maintain that these migrants increase the level of ordinary criminality among the residents, they reduce the level of "criminal vestiges of the past" (Soviet law outlaws traditional Moslem marriage and social practices) among the native population.

While Soviet criminologists have studied the effects of both forms of internal migration on Soviet criminality, their research efforts have been confined primarily to the European republics and the R.S.F.S.R. Much of the research has been done by members of the All-Union Institute for the Study of Crime and the Elaboration of Preventive Measures whose scholars are primarily Russian. It is only natural that these Russian researchers would choose to focus on the criminological problems resulting from the difficult adjustment of rural Russian residents to new settlements because their problems are more accessible to the researchers than those of non-Russian and non-European peoples.

Recent research done by Babaev, a Soviet researcher at the Institute for the Study of Crime and the Elaboration of Preventive Measures, on the residential and social conditions of migrants is reminiscent of the work done by Clinard in *Crime in Developing Countries*. Babaev used a sample of 1,000 labor camp inmates drawn from camps of different degrees of severity. Of this sample 15.3 percent were migrants—had not lived in their previous location for more than one year—and the remaining 84.7 percent were permanent residents.[15] Clinard concluded that migrants in developing countries commit an even larger proportion of the criminality than the percentage observed by Babaev in the U.S.S.R. In a study of crime in Uganda, "migrants represented 83% of a sample of 194 offenders"[16] and in other developing countries outside of Africa migrants participated in crime to a similar degree. The contribution of migrants to crime is not as significant a problem in the U.S.S.R. as in developing countries because Soviet migrants contribute 15 percent of all crime while their counterparts in Uganda and other developing countries are responsible for over 83 percent of all crimes.

The arrival of large numbers of new settlers into the urban environment is disruptive of the community's stability and frequently leads to increased rates of urban criminality. As a result, migrants in the Soviet Union and in developing countries contribute disproportionately to the crime rate in urban areas. Recently constructed regions of Soviet cities that house large numbers of workers who have recently arrived from the country often have the highest crime rates of the city. The crime rate of a whole city, rather than that of a particular region, can also be affected by the arrival of a large number of migrants. Soviet criminologists reported in 1966 that after a rapid population influx into the Novoselorskii and Birulskii regions migrants were responsible for 33 percent and 30 percent of all crimes, respectively.[17] No indication is given, however, of the proportion of newcomers to the total population.

A later study on the impact of migration on the crime rate of an urbanizing region was done in the late 1960s. The findings of these scholars corroborated those of the earlier study that demonstrated a strong correlation between the extent of population influx and the recorded level of criminality. In the 1968 study, the researchers on migration within the R.S.F.S.R. disclosed that seven of the eight oblasts and krais with the greatest number of migrants (Tiumen, Magadan, Kamchatka, Yakutsk, Tuva, Komi, Krasnoyarskii, and Primorskii) had the highest rates of criminality in the republic.[18] This relationship still holds true today because Vladivostok, the urban capital of the Primorskii krai and a port city with a highly transient population, has the highest crime rate of any city in the Soviet Union. These studies indicate that in the Soviet Union an increase in population resulting from migration into an urbanized and developing area is correlated with a concomitant increase in criminality.[19]

While migrants in the Soviet Union commit a disproportionate share of all criminality, in developing countries the contribution of migrants to the overall crime rate is even more significant. Numerous African studies conducted in Ghana, the Republic of Central Africa, Egypt, and Zambia as well as studies done in Latin America disclosed that the majority of offenses committed in cities were perpetrated by youthful migrants from the rural countryside.[20]

Crime patterns in the Baltics and some of the more remote regions of the Soviet Union resemble those of the developing countries as a result of the rapid urbanization that is presently occurring there. The impact, however, of Soviet migrants on the local crime rate is not as significant as is that of migrants in developing countries. This is true for two reasons. Firstly, the Soviet Union is not entirely a developed or developing country but shares the attributes of both kinds of societies. As a result, it can not be expected that the pattern of migration and crime observed in the Soviet Union correspond entirely to the model presented by Clinard in his *Crime in Developing Countries*. Secondly, the Soviet Union as a planned economy does not permit completely uncontrolled urban growth and, therefore, does not suffer some of the consequences experienced in developing societies that do not control their population mobility.

As a result of Soviet centralized planning, Soviet migrants differ most significantly from their counterparts in developing countries in terms of their housing conditions and educational levels. The Soviet Union, through its control over urban population size, does not have the problem of urban squatter dwellings that are the homes of many new migrants in other societies, but the Soviet migrants are not immune from the housing problems of urban migrants because they frequently reside in dormitories in close contact with other migrants and without the benefit of familial contact.[21]

The centralized educational system in the U.S.S.R. provides instructional benefits for both urban and rural residents. Whereas the migrants in many other societies leave rural areas without much education, Soviet migrants who commit crimes tend to be better educated than the urban offender who has permanently resided in the city.[22] The migrants came to the cities hoping to use the education and the technical specialties they had obtained that were not needed in their rural homes. Many of the migrants because of their specialized skills and education had much more to lose than their urban counterparts who broke the law.

It is in their association patterns and familial relations that urban migrants in the U.S.S.R. and in Asia and Africa most closely resemble each other. Babaev and Clinard found significant differences in the styles and residential patterns of offenders who were migrants and those who were long-term urban dwellers or noncriminal migrants. According to the research of both scholars, migrant offenders had less contact with their families at their new homes or their former villages than long-term urban residents or noncriminal migrants.[23] Both scholars subsequently conclude that the separation of migrants from their parents and relatives had resulted in increased rates of criminality.[24]

Association patterns of migrants in developing countries and in the Babaev study were seen as contributing to the arrest of the individual. As Clinard states, "The village migrants' lack of familiarity with urban living appears to have had a possible relation to patterns of association that ultimately ended in their arrests."[25] Babaev established this relationship between associations and patterns of criminality even more firmly. He comments that both migrants who had resided in their new community more than six months and those that had lived there less than six months were much more likely than those who resided at their present home permanently to associate regularly with individuals with prior convictions.[26] These criminal associations, like those described by Clinard, developed at the migrant's new residence.

Soviet studies on the impact of migration on crime demonstrate that there is a direct correlation between the influx of rural residents into an urban area and the recorded increase in crime. The Soviet experience with population migration and crimes lies in between that of the developing countries in Asia, Africa, and South America and that of the European countries where the process of urbanization has already stabilized.

In the developing countries, the migrants are responsible for the majority of crimes committed in urban areas whereas in Europe the foreign migrants, primarily from rural areas, have lower rates of criminality than the native population. The negative impact on Soviet crime rates of migration into urban areas more closely resembles the effects of the migration patterns in developing countries. The Soviet migrant, however, contributes a much smaller share of the crime than his counterpart in developing countries because of the internal controls and urban planning that prevent the influx of uneducated migrants into ill-prepared cities. Soviet controls over internal development help reduce but do not forestall the disproportionate contribution of migrants to the crime rate of the U.S.S.R.

URBANIZATION AND CRIME

The Soviet Union, like the United States, Europe, and developing countries, has disproportionately more crime in urban than in rural areas. In the Soviet Union, 40 percent more crime is committed in urban than in rural areas. Moreover, in the years 1963–1966, the 10 republics with the highest levels of crime are regions with the highest level of urbanization.[27] The similarities in effect of urbanization upon crime in the countries mentioned above end here. In most developed countries, the highest crime rates are found in the largest cities while in the Soviet Union the greatest crime rates are recorded in the newer medium-sized cities.

American crime statistics derived from the Uniform Crime Report of the FBI and the Law Enforcement Assistance Administration (LEAA) Victimization Survey demonstrate that the crime rate in the larger cities (population core over 50,000) is much higher than that in medium-sized cities whose population ranges up to 50,000.[28] The Soviet Union shows a contrasting pattern. Soviet criminologists have stated that crime in the largest cities of Moscow, Leningrad, and Kiev is lower than in that of the medium-sized cities of the Baltic, Siberia, and the Far East and North.[29] Soundly based estimates of the crime rate in Moscow and a smaller Baltic city, given below, demonstrate the point of Soviet criminologists.[30]

The registration system and population policies of the Soviet Union are the reasons why such a significant difference exists between the urban distribution patterns of crime in the United States and in the U.S.S.R. The limitations of movement into the large cities of the U.S.S.R. and the exile of recidivists from the major urban centers have resulted in a relatively stable, criminal-free urban population. The medium-sized cities of the Soviet Union, needing to increase their populations for reasons of economic development, cannot afford to be as selective in their populations and therefore will accept and consequently grant residential permits to many exiled recidivists and young males unaccustomed to urban life.

The population that accounts for the disproportionately higher crime rates of Soviet medium-sized cities is, however, more characteristic of the larger cities of the United States. The United States, which does not control or record settlement patterns of its residents, has the largest percentage of migrants and criminals congregating in the larger cities. Immigrants seeking the benefits of an urban environment and criminals seeking the anonymity of large cities settle in areas with inadequate housing, medical, and social services.

American crime statistics differentiate between the crime rate of the urban core and the suburban areas surrounding them. The suburbs, traditionally the privileged retreat of the middle class, have not produced many of their own criminals but instead have been victimized by the urban offenders seeking the material wealth of the suburbanites. In the Soviet Union, the relationship between the urban core and the surrounding communities is entirely different. The small towns that surround Soviet urban centers are not populated by an elite, as in the United States and Europe, but instead house those who cannot obtain police permission to reside within the city limits. Employment and educational opportunities are located within the city and, as a result, residents of the surrounding communities are forced to commute long hours to their schools or jobs.

The young males, forced to commute long distances from these outlying communities into the cities, are responsible for much of the crime committed by youthful offenders in the major cities of the U.S.S.R. A study of these commuting offenders was conducted by researchers in Leningrad in the early 1970s. They discovered that the conditions under which they commuted and the long time spent away from parental guidance were responsible for their increased criminality. While commuting, these offenders made the acquaintance of drunks, parasites, and recidivists who had significant influence over their behavior.[31] Youths spent their undirected hours of commutation drinking and gambling and the poor condition of the commuter trains made it difficult for them to fill their time more constructively.[32]

This study of the criminality of Leningrad commuters demonstrates that the crime problems associated with urbanization cannot be studied solely by examining the population residing within a city's limits. The population policies of the Soviet Union that have prevented migrants from settling in the most desirable urban areas have forced the settlement of the most crime prone age groups outside the confines of major cities or in newly developed areas that are only beginning to experience the consequences of urbanization.

CONCLUSION

The Soviet Union shares the increased crime problems experienced by other countries that are also undergoing the process of rapid urbanization. However, the U.S.S.R. has redistributed its urban crime problems away from its major cities and had avoided some of the extreme negative consequences of rural population influx into urban areas that typify the phenomenon of urbanization in developing countries. Soviet population policies, implemented through the internal passport and registration system, have shifted urban crime to the medium-sized cities of the U.S.S.R. that can not select their resident population. Soviet urban planners, while not entirely successful in averting the dislocation problem of recent migrants from rural areas, have avoided the extreme crime problems of developing countries that have permitted uncontrolled rural influx into ill-prepared cities.

The Soviet Union, while still demonstrating a strong association between the phenomenon of urbanization and crime, has shown that the provision of housing and employment to urban immigrants helps alleviate many of the worst criminological consequences of urbanization. The Soviet case strongly suggests that the affirmation of social and familial ties is necessary to achieve a reduction of criminality among rural migrants to urban areas.

9

UNITED NATIONS CRIME SURVEY (1977)

INTRODUCTION

The present report, designed to present a worldwide analysis of the problems of crime and the administration of justice, is based on the information received from the governments of the following States: Algeria, Argentina, Australia, Austria, Bahamas, Bahrain, Barbados, Belgium, Canada, Chile, Colombia, Costa Rica, Cyprus, Czechoslovakia, Denmark, Ecuador, Egypt, El Salvador, Ethiopia, Finland, France, Gabon, German Democratic Republic, Germany, Federal Republic of, Greece, Guatemala, Guyana, Iceland, Indonesia, Iran, Iraq, Ireland, Italy, Jamaica, Japan, Kuwait, Libyan Arab Jamahiriya, Luxembourg, Malaysia, Maldives, Mauritius, Morocco, Netherlands, New Zealand, Norway, Oman, Pakistan, Peru, Philippines, Poland, Qatar, Saudi Arabia, Seychelles, Singapore, Spain, Sweden, Syrian Arab Republic, Trinidad and Tobago, Turkey, United Kingdom of Great Britain and Northern Ireland, United States of America, and Yugoslavia. Information was also received from the following nonmember States: San Marino and Switzerland.

The report consists of four sections: the first section gives the background and scope; the second provides an overall view of the current crime situation and of the existing methods and means for preventing and controlling crime, including both the measures and personnel involved,[1] the third contains an analysis by region, of the world crime situation and of the measures for coping with it; and the fourth considers the policy implications and the role of the United Nations in this regard.

This report represents a pioneering effort in that it seeks to meet a long-standing need for a survey of the world crime situation (see Economic and Social Council resolutions 155 C (VII) of 13 August 1948 and 390 F (XIII) of 9 August 1951) based on detailed quantitative data and other information provided by Member States and focused particularly on special crime problems and new forms and dimensions of criminality not previously analysed from a broadly based, factually supported comparative perspective. There are, however, some intrinsic limitations which should be noted as bearing upon the completeness and accuracy of the presentation: first, many replies were not complete; secondly, the terminology used in the various replies differed either in meaning or in nuance; thirdly, gaps in the statistical data sometimes made generalization difficult. Therefore generalizations either have been avoided, when they appeared debatable, or have been carefully qualified.

Three important general conclusions emerge from the preparation of this report. First, crime is increasingly becoming a major world problem: its extent, variety, and impact, both nationally and internationally, cannot be underestimated. Secondly, in view of the seriousness of the problem and of its ramifications and repercussions which extend far beyond national frontiers, international cooperation in relation to crime must be strengthened. Lastly, the United Nations has a primary and unique role to play in this direction, not only in the sharing of common experiences and the dissemination of reliable and internationally comparable data, but also in providing advice and technical assistance services to requesting countries in the development and promotion of relevant research and in the elaboration of policy guidelines and planning strategies in specific areas of common concern.

BACKGROUND AND SCOPE

As societies change, expand, and develop, crime assumes new dimensions and new forms. Experience may vary, but in nearly every country juvenile delinquency, crime in the streets, violence, and corruption are often matters of concern and of great public awareness. Not only crime, but also measures adopted to prevent and control it have given cause for concern. Traditional methods developed over the ages to deal with crime have not only proved largely unsuccessful, but have sometimes tended to aggravate the situation. Reactions to crime may vary between rigid support for "law and order," on the one hand, and permissiveness advocated by those recommending minimal legal intervention, on the other.

The Secretary-General, on 10 July 1974, sent a note to Member States and to certain nonmember States inviting them to provide information on the situation concerning crime prevention and control and the measures being taken. The low rate of responses and their generality did not provide an adequate basis for a report. Therefore, the Secretary-

General, on 3 June 1976, reiterated his request, addressing to Member States a detailed questionnaire on which this report is based with follow-up notes sent on 8 October and 9 December 1976.

The questionnaire was so structured as to elicit information on both the dimensions and forms of criminality, as well as on the measures and means employed to cope with it. More specifically, concerning the crime situation, countries were asked to report from available statistical information the total number of offenders recorded officially, whether male or female or juvenile offenders, for the years 1970 through 1975. In addition, they were invited to report, from available sources, the total numbers of offences officially recorded; and they were provided with a number of crime categories into which to classify their data. These were intentional homicide, assault, sex crime, robbery, kidnapping, theft, fraud, drug abuse, illegal traffic in drugs, and alcohol abuse.[2] In most cases, both offender and offence statistics were provided by responding countries from police statistics for the period 1970 through 1975. National appraisals based on informed evaluations were also requested, to complement the statistical data or to supplement it for the most recent years. In addition, specific information was requested on certain new forms of criminality. Information on the measures and means employed for the prevention and control of crime was obtained by inviting countries to report on the numbers of criminal justice personnel, to comment on their adequacy in various respects, to indicate new measures and programmes for the prevention and control of crime with the aim of assessing their impact, and to describe their activities in relation to the forecasting of crime with a view to incorporating crime prevention into national planning. The answers obtained were therefore based both on available statistical data and on national appraisals and assessments. The statistical data have been processed by computer to allow for quantitative analysis, while the evaluative information has been used to integrate, clarify, and supplement the numerical data.[3]

This survey represents a decided step forward in the collection of national statistics for use at the international level. The high response rate is evidence both of an increasing willingness to cooperate internationally in the field of crime prevention control and of the existence of reliable national data bases. This applies especially to developing countries. Thus, while occasionally still suffering from a certain imprecision, the data obtained are rich enough to provide an informational basis which has not existed in the past.

To this, other observations may be added regarding the degree of reliability of crime statistics. These may be briefly summarized as follows:

1. There is a consistent number of offences that escape the knowledge of the community and of police enforcement agencies; typical of this category are crimes of corruption and various so-called victimless crimes.

2. Victims, or other persons who are aware that a crime has been committed, may fail to refer the offence to the authorities because of fear of being exposed to the reaction of the offender or of suffering from other negative consequences, or because of a lack of confidence in the overall political system and, specifically, in the criminal justice system.

3. Use of discretion or arbitrariness on the part of the law enforcement or prosecuting authorities may result in a crime not being prosecuted and/or recorded.

4. There may also be other difficulties stemming from the shortcomings of systems for collecting and recording crime data.

The numerous attempts that have been made in this field have stressed the great difficulty of achieving comparability, not only because of the differential effect of the limitations mentioned above on the statistics of different countries, but also, most crucially, because of the variety of definitions used in national laws to refer to the same type of behaviour. Although this problem applies to all crime data, it may be especially pronounced in the case of juvenile crime. For example, the age ranges covered by the term "juvenile" vary in different countries. This difference occurs at both ends of the age scale: the age at which criminal responsibility begins, and the age at which a young person is reclassified from "juvenile" to "adult." In some countries the lower age limit is 0, in others 16, with almost all ages between 5 and 16 being found more than once. The upper limit varies from 15 to 21, with 18 as the most frequent.

Another aspect in which countries vary considerably is in the degree to which young offenders are dealt with by agencies other than those of criminal justice; in that case they frequently do not appear in the criminal statistics. This factor, together with the age cutoff point variation mentioned above, can imply that the numbers for juvenile delinquents probably appear to be lower than they really are.

Because of the constraints indicated above, care has been taken not to make direct comparison between individual countries. However, because countries have provided a very extensive set of crime statistics and other valuable information, it has been possible, for the first time, to go beyond the traditional intuitive and impressionistic posture. Whatever the limitations of the collected information, such an attempt undoubtedly represents a considerable advance.

Since decreasing crime is comparatively rare today, it is interesting to know those countries that reported it. Egypt, Ireland, Maldives, and Turkey reported a decrease in intentional homicide; Chile, Ecuador, Ireland, Jamaica, Kuwait, Morocco, and Oman a decrease in assaults; and Egypt, Ireland, Kuwait, Qatar, and Singapore a decrease in robbery. Iceland, Morocco, and New Zealand reported a decrease in both theft and fraud, and Algeria and Ireland a decrease in drug-related offences and alcohol abuse.

Because of the difficulties of collecting official statistics at the national level on special and new forms of criminality, evaluations on this were solicited. The answers provided can be summarized as follows:

Organized crime seems to be primarily a problem for developed countries (48 percent), rather than for the developing countries, of which 30 percent reported it as serious. There was little indication of whether the laws to combat it were stringent enough, or rigorously enforced. There seems to be no concerted effort among any countries to combat this type of crime. The problems of definition with this type of crime have been noted before.

Crimes against the environment were reported as posing a problem primarily in the developed countries (44 percent) compared with 17 percent in the developing countries. Only very few countries reported stringent ecological laws and their rigorous enforcement.

Political crimes were regarded as a serious problem by approximately 20 percent of both developing and developed countries, and similar proportions reported that stringent laws had been introduced and were rigorously enforced. Again, definitional problems occurred in the recording and reporting of this class of crime.

Illegal possession of firearms was reported as a serious problem by 48 percent of the developed countries and 34 percent of the developing countries, with similar proportions reporting that their laws were stringent and rigorously enforced.

OVERALL VIEW OF THE PROBLEM

Crime Patterns

World Crime Situation

On the basis of the information received on crime rates measured by the number of offenders, it is possible to conclude that the overall rate for the years 1970–1975 was approximately 900 offenders per 100,000 population and that the offender rate increased steadily by approximately 2 percent annually. For the period considered, the total increase has thus been about 15 percent.

It can clearly be seen in figure 12 that the overwhelming proportion of the adult offenders were males, with a rate 10 times that for females. For juvenile offenders, the male rate was 5 times greater than that for females. Figure 12 also demonstrates that the offender rate was higher for adults than juveniles. However, it should be recognized that these rates are computed using the total population as a base, rather than specific age groups of the population.

Male   Female
Adult Offenders

Male   Female
Juvenile Offenders

Fig. 12. World rate of criminal offenders (per 100,000 population), 1970–1975

Table 18 presents the overall rates of reported offences for the years 1970–1975. It can be seen that theft accounts for by far the greatest proportion of all offences reported and that the crimes of kidnapping and intentional homicide have comparatively low rates. If the crimes are

Table 18.

WORLD RATES (PER 100,000 POPULATION) OF
REPORTED OFFENCES, 1970–1975

Intentional homicide	3.9
Assault	184.1
Sex crimes	24.2
Kidnapping	0.7
Robbery	46.1
Theft	862.4
Fraud	83.3
Illegal drug traffic	9.8
Drug abuse	28.9
Alcohol abuse	67.8
Total offence rate	1,311.2

grouped together into the three broad categories of crimes against the person, crimes against property, and crimes involving drugs, it can be seen from figure 13 that crimes against property make up by far the greatest portion of all crime.

The rates at which the various crimes have been increasing are also of considerable interest. Over the six-year period, intentional homicide has increased 20 percent, theft 46 percent, robbery 179 percent, and drug abuse 114 percent. The world increase in the robbery and drug abuse rates must be seen as very serious.

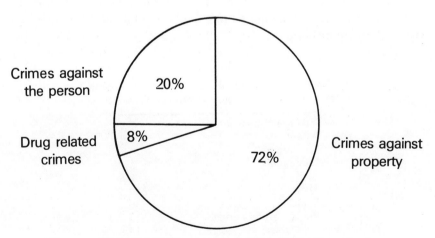

Fig. 13. The world crime picture: proportions of total crime according to broad crime categories

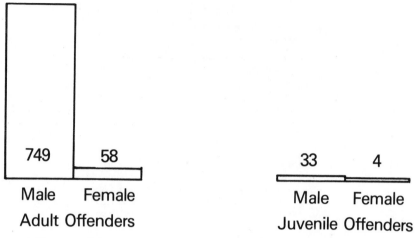

Fig. 14. Crime rates (per 100,000 population) for developing
countries by offender characteristics, 1970–1975

Crime in Developing Countries

The overall rate of criminal offenders for the period 1970–1975 was approximately 800 per 100,000 population. It can be concluded from the information provided that the number of offenders increased at an annual rate of approximately 2.5 percent. The rate of increase for females was 30 percent higher than that for males.

It can be seen from figure 14 that the overwhelming proportion of adult offenders were males, with a rate 12 times that of females. For juvenile offenders, the rate for males was 8 times greater than for females. This chart also demonstrates that the adult offender rate was higher than the juvenile rate.

Table 19.
CRIME RATES (PER 100,000 POPULATION) OF REPORTED
OFFENCES FOR DEVELOPING COUNTRIES, 1970–1975

Intentional homicide	5.1
Assault	253.1
Sex crimes	24.3
Kidnapping	1.2
Robbery	58.8
Theft	354.3
Fraud	30.1
Illegal traffic in drugs	14.9
Drug abuse	14.8
Alcohol abuse	30.4
Total offence rate	787.0

Table 19 presents the overall rate for reported offences for the years 1970–1975. Kidnapping and intentional homicide have comparatively low rates, but crimes of assault and theft are extremely high. If crimes are grouped into the broad categories of offences against property, offences against the person, and drug-related offences, from figure 15 it appears that crimes against the person and crimes against property account almost equally for a total of 90 percent of all reported crimes in developing countries.

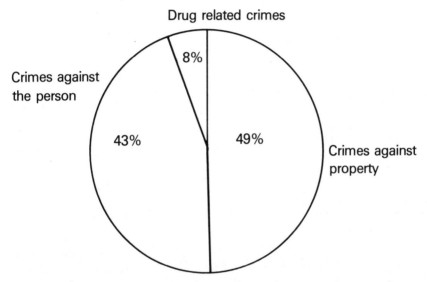

Fig. 15. Crime picture for developing countries: proportions of total crime according to broad crime categories, 1970–1975

The rates of increase in the various crimes are also of considerable interest. While the rate of increase in intentional homicide has been only 4.6 percent over the six-year period, theft and robbery have increased by 43 and 43 percent, respectively. We may conclude that these increases in theft and robbery are substantial and serious. Furthermore, drug abuse has also seriously increased at a rate of 113 percent over the six-year period.

Crime in Developed Countries

The overall rate of criminal offenders for the period 1970–1975 was approximately 1,000 per 100,000 population. The number of offenders has increased steadily at an annual rate of 1 percent. The rate of

Fig. 16. Crime rates (per 100,000 population) for developed
countries by offender characteristics, 1970–1975

female offenders has increased 50 percent more rapidly than that of the
male.

It can be seen from figure 16 that the overwhelming proportion of
adult offenders were males, with a rate eight times that for females. For
juvenile offenders, the rate for males was five times greater than for females. This chart also demonstrates that the adult offender rate was
much higher than the juvenile rate.

Table 20.

CRIME RATES (PER 100,000 POPULATION) OF REPORTED
OFFENCES FOR DEVELOPED COUNTRIES, 1970–1975

Intentional homicide	2.7
Assault	115.3
Sex crimes	24.0
Kidnapping	0.2
Robbery	33.3
Theft	1,370.5
Fraud	136.4
Illegal traffic in drugs	4.7
Drug abuse	43.1
Alcohol abuse	105.1
Total offence rate	1,835.3

Table 20 presents the overall rates for reported offences for the years 1970–1975. Crimes of intentional homcide, kidnapping, and illegal traffic in drugs have comparatively low rates, but crimes of theft, fraud, and assault are by far the predominant crimes in the developed countries.

Grouping crimes according to the broad categories of offences against the person, offences against property, and drug-related offences, offences against property accounted for an enormous 82 percent of all crime (figure 17). However, this picture should be seen against the rate of increase in some of these crimes. While intentional homicide and theft have both increased substantially—by roughly 35 percent over the six-year period—robbery has increased by 322 percent. The increase in robbery is very serious indeed, even though it accounts, comparatively, for a small portion of total reported offences. Similarly, drug abuse has increased by 138 percent over the six years, providing evidence of another seriously growing crime problem for developed countries.

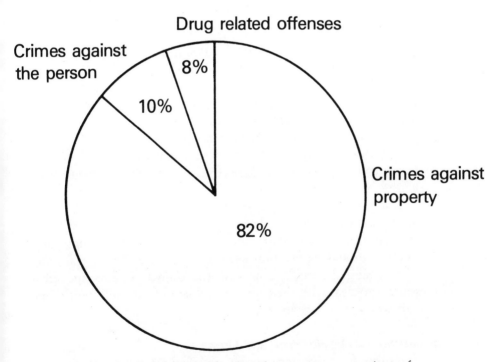

Fig. 17. Crime picture for developed countries: proportions of total crime according to broad crime categories

Country Assessments of the Crime Situation

The complementary information provided by Member States, based on national appraisals of the situation, supports the conclusion that crime increased over the 1970–1975 period by amounts ranging from slight to great. At least half of the respondents made the assessment that crime had definitively increased, while one-third considered that it had remained relatively stable. Only a few countries reported a decrease, but this varied according to crime types.

Views were also provided as to those crimes which, while not necessarily the most troublesome now, might be expected to become so in the future, especially in an international context. The three categories of crimes were singled out.

> *Criminality involving drugs.* Although drug abuse is seen primarily as an internal national problem, illegal trafficking is by its nature both international and criminogenic. Estimates of the amount of crime created as a side effect of drug trafficking vary, but countries of every region perceive it as a dangerous and, sometimes, the most dangerous threat to their economies and general social quality of life. The survey leaves no doubt that drug-related crimes, if not actual drug usage, are considered likely to be such a social threat that a major effort to coordinate and stimulate worldwide cooperation against drug trafficking should be a high priority, at least for the most affected countries.
>
> *Political crime and terrorism, including hijacking, especially but not solely, of aircraft.* Most countries are signatories to one or more of the conventions on this subject and most mentioned this problem.
>
> *Transnational crime of a fraudulent "white-collar" kind, including tax evasion, offences against consumers, and computer abuse.* In order to cope with these categories of crimes, the strengthening of international cooperation was urged. In particular, several countries requested specific help from the United Nations and other sources to deal with the pressing problem of extradition of criminals who take refuge in other countries.

Socioeconomic Development and Crime

Measures for crime prevention and control must obviously be adopted with specific reference to the factors influencing criminal phenomena. It is well known that studies and research on the aetiology of crime and delinquency have not succeeded in pinpointing unequivocal crime causes, especially as far as their generalization is concerned. Multifactorial theories support the idea that specific elements become criminogenic only when they combine with each other and when they operate in the context of given cultural and social conditions. The extreme variability in the complex interplay of aetiological factors is the real obstacle to the construction of theories of general application which can be used for the formulation of effective policies. In this regard much remains to be done by criminology and the related social sciences. For the time being, however, the more the covariations between crime trends and other types of behavioural and social phenomena are explored, the more relevant researchable areas can be identified.

In this connexion, it may be interesting to summarize the results of an analysis carried out as part of this study, correlating different crime rates with certain socioeconomic and demographic indicators.[4] The indicators used were[5]

1. The proportion of the work force in agriculture;
2. The infant mortality rate;
3. The school attendance ratio;
4. The gross domestic product per capita;
5. The proportion of the population which is illiterate;
6. The rate of population increase, because it could be that a rapid increase in population will naturally account for a higher crime rate;
7. The proportion of the population between 15 and 24 years of age (called "youthful"), as this age range is well known to be crime prone.

It must be stressed that the results are tentative and provisional and, therefore, do not allow any definitive conclusion. The patterns which seem to emerge may be summarized as follows:

1. A high rate of homicide tends to occur in countries having a low gross domestic product per capita and a high proportion of their work force in agriculture.
2. In contrast to homicide, a high rate of assault is more frequent in countries with a low proportion of their work force in agriculture. For both violent crime categories, however, the proportion of the population between 15 and 24 years of age was also an important indicator.

3. All indicators were highly related to the property crime rates so that it was difficult to isolate one of them. However, countries with a high rate of property crime often had a high gross domestic product per capita and a low proportion of the work force in agriculture.

4. Drug offences presented a similar pattern of statistical relationships as those of property crimes, although probably the most important feature was that countries with a low proportion of the work force in agriculture tended also to have low rates of drug crime.

5. It appears that some countries which have high rates of illiteracy also have low rates of juvenile crime. This finding is highly speculative, however, as the data are difficult to interpret, owing to the limitations of juvenile-offender data outlined earlier. However, the finding is supported by the observation that low juvenile-offender rates are also displayed by countries with a high proportion of the work force in agriculture.

Social and economic conditions were identified by the respondents in developing countries as the main factors related to the increases in crime. Developed countries singled out no particular elements, suggesting mostly that the causal factors were multifaceted.

The factors seen as being most related to lower crime trends were the presence of a close kinship system (30 percent of both the developing and developed countries) and the controlling effects of religion (again, the same proportions for both country groups). The developed countries saw the presence of community organizations and other local groups as having a beneficial effect upon crime prevention. People's courts, for example, in socialist countries, were seen as having a useful effect in five cases, four of these in developed countries.

REGIONAL REVIEW

Comparative Analysis

For a more detailed understanding of the world crime situation and of the means and measures needed to cope with it, a regional breakdown of the information received is presented below. The geographical distribution of those countries which did not reply made the usual United Nations regional breakdown difficult for this analysis. Therefore, the countries from which replies containing quantitative data as well as evaluative information were received have been divided into seven regions, on the basis of two concurrent criteria: geographical proximity and/or cultural similarity. The distribution adopted is the following: North Africa and the Middle East; Africa south of the Sahara; Asia; Eastern Europe; Latin America; The Caribbean; Western Europe, United States of America, Canada, Australia, and New Zealand.

The data for these regions were analysed in order to determine what significant overall differences could be observed with respect to crime rates, broken down as before by age and sex, offenders, and crime types. A similar, regional analysis was undertaken for numbers of criminal justice personnel. Once again, it should be emphasized that the rates given are for general groupings of countries and that there may be individual exceptions.

This section of the report begins with a brief comparative overall view based on data which presents the overall rates for 1970–1975. The data refers to only six regions, because the answers received from countries of Africa south of the Sahara[6] did not contain adequate statistical information.

The results can be summarized as follows:

1. *Offender rates.* It can be seen that adult-offender rates are extremely high for both Western European and other countries as well as the Caribbean region, with rates more than double those of other regions. This applies to both male and female adult offenders and to juvenile offenders.
2. *Violent crime.* Latin America displays the highest rate of intentional homicide, closely followed by the Caribbean. The Eastern European countries show a very low rate of intentional homicide. For assault, the Caribbean rate was roughly seven times higher than the rate for any other region, and for robbery, Asia, Latin America, and the Caribbean displayed equally high rates.
3. *Property crimes.* Western developed countries and the Caribbean displayed rates 10 times higher than most other regions.
4. *Drug-related crimes.* The Caribbean showed the highest rates for all drug-related crimes.

Regional Distribution

North Africa and the Middle East
Though this is a relatively homogeneous region with regard to social structure, religious traditions, and legal systems, the crime situation

varies considerably among countries. Some are experiencing no change or even a decrease in criminality (Egypt, Iraq, Qatar, Saudi Arabia, and Syrian Arab Republic); others have reported clear trends of increasing crime (Bahrain, Morocco, and Oman). One of the serious problems of the region is clandestine immigration, and related to this is that of the legal rights of immigrants.

The low rate of criminality in most countries of this region is believed to be due mainly to the combination of social stablility and economic advancement, and a social structure based on closely knit interrelationships, strongly underpinned by Islamic legislation and moral values. Family and religious institutions play a primary role in the social conduct of the members of the society and continue to form the strongest barrier against increasing criminality. Unemployment is the most frequently cited cause of crime.

Algeria is one of the very few countries reporting a decrease in female criminality and in juvenile delinquency, while some countries indicate a growing concern with regard to the latter (Bahrain, Kuwait, Morocco, and Oman). This tendency for juvenile delinquency to increase occurs sometimes even in countries having a clearly downward trend of adult criminality (Egypt, Qatar, and Syrian Arab Republic). A phenomenon almost completely unknown previously to the countries of the region is the growth of alcohol abuse (Bahrain, Kuwait, Morocco, Oman, Qatar, and Syrian Arab Republic), and this has been indicated as having a great impact on their crime picture. In some cases this has been attributed to changes in legislation and law enforcement practices.

Africa South of the Sahara

In many countries of this region, social record-keeping of a statistical nature has only recently begun to be instituted. Statistics of crime are thus not yet available for quantitative analysis. This lack of information was indicated as mainly a problem stemming from the lack of resources which are usually allotted to other priority needs.

In that connexion, certain socioeconomic factors were seen as contributing to a high crime rate. Against a general background of poverty, high rates of illiteracy and low levels of education, low standards of health, underemployment, and unemployment, the following factors were singled out: a growing proportion of the youth population in the most crime-prone age group; unemployment among the young; drift to the towns; weakening family ties and other social bonds; discrepancy between expectations raised by increased education and the lack of appropriate job opportunities; growing alcoholism rural as well as urban.

Among the new forms of criminality related to the economic situation, embezzlement, fraud, corruption, smuggling, illegal currency transactions, and transnational theft of motor vehicles were mentioned. The lack of resources, of qualified personnel, and of technical information was believed to make the fight against crime more difficult.

Asia

Some countries of this region have experienced a definite increase in most types of crime (Indonesia, Malaysia, and Pakistan) and in others the trends have either been stable or downward (Japan, Maldives, and Singapore). In Pakistan, considerable differences in the trends of crime have been noted between the different areas of the country.

The countries with upward crime trends indicated the following as the primary explanatory factors: unbalanced economic growth, maldistribution of wealth, poverty, family breakdown, migration to the cities, and growing unemployment. These factors were reported as being exacerbated by corruptive cultural influences, among which the effects of the mass media were stressed (Indonesia emphasized this particularly), and by the very great pressure put on inadequate resources by the population explosion.

Some countries, such as Japan, interpreted their relatively more favourable situation as depending on the resilience of the traditional social fabric, often because of its religious basis, which has not been disrupted by the processes of modernization and change. In Japan, wherever these stresses have been greatest (in the medium-sized industrial towns, for instance), there has been an increase in criminality, although nationally there has been an overall decrease. An interesting observation from the Japanese experience is that greater affluence affects various age groups differently. Increased wealth for adults is presumed to lead to greater stability and less criminality; for juveniles and young people it is seen as a stimulator of the principle of living for the pleasures of moment and as contributing to a lowering of social responsibility. The growth of female criminality in Japan is associated with increasing participation of women in community life, including working wives.

Singapore has found that the formal attempts to set up supportive local social organizations, combined with greater efficiency of the law enforcement agencies, has had a definite impact on the amount of crime. Most countries of this region indicate that increasing juvenile delinquency is a function of rapid social change.

Eastern Europe

This region is represented by only a few responses. It is, therefore, impossible to say to what extent the situation described in the available information represents the region. Moreover, in several of the socialist countries, changes in legislation and modifications in statistical recording techniques make quantitative analysis currently inappropriate.

The responses (some of which did not contain statistics and tended to use proportions as well as raw numbers) point to a decrease in crime, including the almost complete disappearance of professional crimes and the absence of gangster-type organized crimes. The number of crimes against the person, often stemming from the use of alcoholic beverages, is stable or declining; criminality against property gives rise to the most concern.

Among the factors which were cited as influencing increasing criminality are the migration of population, extensive industrialization, tourism, and urbanization; all these weaken existing social and moral controls of behaviour.

The prevention of crime in this region is felt to be contingent upon the solution of major social problems through the efforts of the entire community. The main emphasis has been on preventive aspects, so that, for instance, Yugoslavia reports that the police are trained in preventive as well as reactive techniques.

The raising of the general economic and material levels, including those of education, health, and social welfare, are considered the most important in steering citizens of all ages, but especially the young, away from crime. Special attention is focused on the protection of children and youth against adverse influences, with particular emphasis on the care of minors separated from their families. The reintegration into social life of young persons released from reformatories or prisons, with a view to providing adequate schooling or vocational training, is regarded as a priority. At the same time measures have been taken to create alternatives to imprisonment by expanding different forms of community treatment in which the role of volunteers is held to be very important. Thus, according to the information provided by the German Democratic Republic, only about a quarter of all criminal offenders receive sanctions involving postinstitutional treatment. In this regard, the German Democratic Republic places responsibility upon employers to take ex-convicts back into work, and special legislative prohibitions against job discrimination on the basis of a criminal record exist in countries such as Poland.

Latin America

The general crime trend of the region as a whole has been upward, although the level of statistical precision with which this has been recorded varies. To improve the data base and collection of criminal statistics, the United Nations-affiliated Latin American Institute for the Prevention of Crime and the Treatment of Offenders at San Jose, Costa Rica, has initiated a pilot project designed to promote the collection of adequate, comparable criminal statistics which could serve as a basis for policy formulation and planning.

In some countries, particularly, political violence poses a serious problem. Kidnapping has replaced hijacking as the prevailing terrorist mode of operation, despite regional instruments designed to discourage it. The tactics displayed, which involve mostly innocent victims, have caused extensive suffering and, in many cases, the loss of human life.

Economic crimes, that is, crimes which adversely affect the economic growth of countries, are thought to be increasing considerably, but since they are difficult to detect and prosecute, they often tend not to appear in the official records. The activities of transnational corporations are cited in this respect, as well as smuggling and the illegal trade of drugs and arms. The drug trade is characterized by the existence of an international, national, and local network; a large potential for corruption; the considerable mobility of offenders; the availablilty of bases at strategic points, such as airports or harbours; and the participation of foreign capital, or personnel, while the traffic in arms involves clients ranging from extremist groups to private citizens. The lack of cross-national uniformity in arms and drugs laws facilitates this trade, the consequences of which are of such gravity as to demand urgent attention.

It is the consensus of the countries of the region that further increases in crime may well be expected unless effective preventive measures are taken. The high birthrate in the region, the large proportion of youth in the population, large-scale migration to towns, the loosening of traditional controls (the family and religious groups are most often referred to), and other concomitants of rapid development, economic problems facing many countries, persisting social inequalities, the crisis of moral values in increasingly materially oriented societies moulded largely by the mass media, political instability, and social disruption— all these are elements considered conducive to the growth of crime. The need for appropriate preventive strategies has been stressed in the replies.

Caribbean

This region is made up of small countries which, for the most part, use as their statistical base crimes reported to the police. As it is well known that police statistical data provide a high figure compared with judicial or correctional data, it is possible that the apparently very high numbers in table 18 may be a function of these types of data. This is not to say, however, that the crime situation in these countries is not serious. As the countries of the region are so similar in size and social structure, it is not surprising that the impressions and views expressed in their replies are very similar to each other. Because the views expressed run parallel, the region as a whole is surveyed without reference to specific Member States.

Trafficking in drugs, illicit trade in firearms, and violence are mentioned as major problems. This is due primarily to the fact that the region lies along the main routes from South to North America. Tourism is particularly high in the region and a strong relationship between tourism and the growth of crime is emphasized: according to the views expressed, tourists foster expectations of higher living standards and provide an obvious target for theft; a high number of aliens apparently participate in criminal activities, especially in illicit trafficking and smuggling. The countries of this region, therefore, realize the problem posed by the competing objectives deriving, on one side, from the need for counteracting the negative, side effects of tourism and, on the other, from the need to stimulate it for the economic benefits which it brings to a country, particularly in generating employment in countries which, as do those in the region, cite unemployment as a major factor in crime.

The trends of adult crime have been more or less stable but are increasing for juvenile offenders. A shortage both of courts and trained personnel in all branches of criminal justice work is reported. United Nations help through the organization of meetings, training programmes, and other type of technical assistance is strongly urged to foster the development of a core of qualified personnel.

Western Europe, United States of America, Canada, Australia, and New Zealand

This group of countries has been considered collectively as a "region" also because of similarities in cultural history, economic systems, and social development. Overall, it has the largest rate of reported crime and has experienced aspects of criminality which have not appeared in other areas. Establishment of a statistical data base for the region is complicated by two factors: first, federalized States sometimes do not keep national statistical records (for example, Australia with respect to juvenile delinquency, Canada with respect to criminal justice personnel), even though the quality of statistical recording on the whole is high. Secondly, many of the countries for example, Austria report significant changes in statistical reporting methods during the period.

There have been general trends of particular significance. One is a slowing down in the rate of increase of juvenile delinquency; it is still increasing but less quickly, although this is not true for all countries. The rate of female criminality is also increasing, having started more recently than the surge of juvenile delinquency, and is showing no signs of abating. The juvenile delinquency rate is supposed to be related at least in part to the age structure of the population, with the bulge now passing through the high-risk age band (16–35).

The phenomenon of organized crime, with its persistence, organizational sophistication, and geographical spread, is a concern for many countries; in addition, there is a preoccupation with semipermanent or short-term, highly organized gangs, formed for one or a short series of specific crimes requiring great professional skill, which are becoming a widespread problem.

Many countries report a move away from the use of imprisonment, so that while the total number of individuals committed to prison is still rising, following the general increase in offender rates, the proportion of persons imprisoned in the total figure of sentenced offenders is decreasing. Different forms of this tendency are reported by Finland and the Federal Republic of Germany. Norway is considering the merits of a local civil police force as compared with a traditional centralized force. The most successful diversion programmes are thought to consist of the more extensive and imaginative use of probation and related measures. New Zealand reports success with a campaign to alert the public to its responsibilities and to the ways in which it can help. Austria is experimenting, following the lead of other nations, with day-fines (that is, the amount of the fine is calculated by reference to the income of the individual); the results are not yet measurable.

Countries in the region are beginning to try more systematic forms · of research, including forecasting and crime-cost assessments. Australia is considering specific attempts to reduce crime by influencing the erroneous conceptions of criminals and demonstrating the illusory character of what they perceive to be the economic benefits derived from criminal behaviour. The United Kingdom pointed out that this survey recognizes by implication the need for a coordinated approach towards the development of a criminal justice policy and for assessing the functioning of the components of the total system.

CONCLUSIONS

From the foregoing analysis it also emerges that a society in which deviance does not exist at all is a theoretical construct not likely to materialize—as history and present-day realities have borne out. The level of tolerance for deviant behaviour among countries varies, but few would probably opt for that degree of control which would be required for a totally "crimeless" society. It is true, on the other hand, that insufficient attention to problems of crime and failure to see its intimate relationship to broader national concerns and other aspects of social, economic, and political life can give rise to increases in crime which may seriously undermine the achievement of national goals and popular well-being.

The information received stresses the fact that the levels and forms of criminal behaviour are closely interrelated with all the other aspects of social life. Economic imbalances, both national and international, social inequalities and tensions, lack of opportunities preventing individuals or groups from egalitarian, democratic participation, uneven development, and unbalanced planning are all factors affecting the quality of human life and the spread of crime which may seriously impair it.

10

A Cross-Cultural Study of
Correlates of Crime

MARGARET K. BACON, IRVIN L. CHILD, and HERBERT BARRY III

EDITOR'S COMMENT: *The Bacon study of cross-cultural correlates of crime conducted nearly two decades ago could not now be replicated because the lives of many of the people included in the analysis have been changed by the sweeping forces of development that have irrevocably altered their life-*

style. This study is distinctive in probing the motivations of criminal behavior of many different national groups whose crime patterns could not be analyzed by the use of conventional criminal statistics. Though this study can not be corroborated on a mass scale because of societal change, the results it provides are important in establishing the causative factors associated with crime commission at a distinct period in history.

A number of researchers have analyzed the sociological and psychological background of delinquents and criminals and compared them with a noncriminal control population, in order to discover what conditions give rise to criminal behavior; for a recent review see Robison.[1] The present paper reports on variations among a sample of preliterate societies in the frequency of crime, in order to determine what other known features of these societies are associated with the occurrence of crime. The cross-cultural technique,[2] in which each society is taken as a single case, is a unique method for studying crime and has certain advantages: The index of frequency of crime in a society represents the average among its many individuals and over a span of many years, so that the measure is likely to be more stable and reliable than a measure of criminal tendency in a single individual. Some of the cultural features which may be related to crime show wider variations among societies than within a single society, permitting a more comprehensive test of their significance. Results which are consistent in a number of diverse societies may be applied to a great variety of cultural conditions instead of being limited to a single cultural setting.

If certain cultural features foster the development of criminal behavior, they should be found preponderantly in societies with a high frequency of crime; factors which inhibit crime should be found largely in societies which are low in crime. Thus the cross-cultural method may help us discover psychological and sociological variables which have a causal relationship to the development of crime; the importance of these variables may then also be tested intraculturally. On the other hand, variables identified as possible causes of crime within our society may be tested for broader significance by the cross-cultural method.

The possible causal factors which we have explored are principally concerned with child training practices, economy, and social structure. Hypotheses concerning these factors, as they have been presented by other writers or as they have occurred to us, will be described in connection with the presentation of our results.

METHOD

Sample. The sample used in this study consists of 48 societies, mostly preliterate, scattered over the world. They were taken from a larger group of 110 societies which were selected on the basis of geographical diversity and adequacy of information on aboriginal child training practices. The present sample of 48 consists of those societies whose ethnographies were searched and found to provide sufficient information to permit comparative ratings on criminal behavior by three independent research workers.[3]

Ratings. We have included two types of crime in our study: theft and personal crime. These two were chosen because they are relatively easy to identify and almost universal in occurrence. Also, they represent two quite different types of behavior. Thus we are able to clarify antecedents common to both types of crime and those characteristic of only one. Judgments were always made in relation to the norms of the culture under consideration. Theft was defined as stealing the personal property of others. Property included anything on which the society placed value, whether it was a whale's tooth or a song. Personal crime was defined by intent to injure or kill a person; assault, rape, suicide, sorcery intended to make another ill, murder, making false accusations, etc. were all included.

The method of comparative ratings was used to obtain measures of frequency. Three raters independently analyzed the ethnographic material on each society and made ratings on a seven-point scale as to the relative frequency of the type of crime under consideration. Thus a rating of 4 on theft would mean that the frequency of theft in a given society appeared to be about average for the sample of societies. Ratings of 5, 6, and 7 represented high frequencies and those of 3, 2, and 1 were low. Societies in which the behavior did not occur were rated as 0. Each rating was classified as confident or doubtful at the time that it was made. No rating was made if the analyst judged the information to be insufficient. We have included all societies on which all three analysts made a rating, whether it was confident or doubtful, and we have used the pooled ratings of all three analysts. The reliability of these pooled ratings is estimated as $+0.67$ for theft and $+0.57$ for personal crime. These estimates were obtained by averaging (using a z transformation) the separate interrater reliabilities, and entering this average into the Spearman-Brown correction formula.

Most writers in this field make a distinction between delinquency and crime, largely on the basis of the age of the offender. The nature of

Correlates of Crime

our evidence does not permit us to make such a clear distinction. Ratings were made in terms of the relative frequency of specific types of criminal behavior in the adult population. Since the age at which adulthood is considered to have begun varies from one society to another, ratings may in some cases have included individuals young enough to be considered adolescent in our society and therefore delinquent rather than criminal. The distinction does not appear to be crucial in this study.

The measures of possible causal variables consist of ratings which have been derived from several sources. Each will be described in the following section Except where noted (for certain variables in Tables 22 and 23), none of the three people who made the crime ratings participated in any of the other ratings.

HYPOTHESES, RESULTS, AND DISCUSSION

Our results will be presented under three main headings: Correlates of Crime in General, Correlates Specific to Theft, and Correlates Specific to Personal Crime. As this classification suggests, we have found it useful to consider the antecedents of crime as either general or specific, i.e., leading to a general increase in criminal behavior, or associated with only one major category of crime. A correlation of $+0.46$ was found between frequency of theft and frequency of personal crime. This indicates that the two variables show a significant degree of communality (p * .01) and also some independence.

Correlates of Crime in General

Our principal findings concerning common correlates of both theft and personal crime are relevant to a hypothesis that crime arises partly as a defense against strong feminine identification. We will begin with an account of this hypothesis.

In our society crime occurs mostly in men, and we have no reason to doubt that this sex difference characterizes most societies. Several writers have called attention to the sex role identification of males as especially pertinent to the development of delinquency in our society. It is assumed that the very young boy tends to identify with his mother rather than his father because of his almost exclusive contact with his mother. Later in his development he becomes aware of expectations that he behave in a masculine way and as a result his behavior tends to be marked by a compulsive masculinity which is really a defense against feminine identification. Parsons notes further that the mother is the principal agent of socialization as well as an object of love and identification.[4] Therefore, when the boy revolts he unconsciously identifies "goodness" with femininity and hence accepts the role of "bad boy" as a positive goal.

Miller has made a study of lower-class culture and delinquency which is also pertinent in this connection.[5] He points out that some delinquent behavior may result from an attempt to live up to attitudes and values characteristic of lower-class culture. He also notes that many lower-class males are reared in predominantly female households lacking a consistently present male with whom to identify. He feels that what he calls an almost obsessive lower-class concern with masculinity results from the feminine identification in preadolescent years.

Whiting, Kluckhohn, and Anthony, in a cross-cultural study of male initiation rites at puberty, found these rites tended to occur in societies with prolonged, exclusive mother-son sleeping arrangements.[6] Their interpretation of this relationship is that the early mother-infant sleeping arrangement produces an initial feminine identification, and later control by men leads to a secondary masculine identification. The function of the initiation ceremony is to resolve this conflict of sexual identification in favor of the masculine identification. The authors further predict that insofar as there has been an increase in juvenile delinquency in our society, "it probably has been accompanied by an increase in the exclusiveness of mother-child relationships and/or a decrease in the authority of the father."

The hypothesis that crime is in part a defense against initial feminine identification would lead to the expectation that all factors which tend to produce strong identification with the mother and failure of early identification with the father would be positively correlated with the frequency of crime in the adult population. The factor that is easiest to study is the presence of the father. It seems reasonable to suppose that successful identification with the father is dependent on his presence. Therefore, societies which differ in the degree to which the father is present during the child's first few years should differ correspondingly in the degree to which the boy typically forms a masculine identification.[7]

Whiting[8] has made use of Murdock's[9] classification of household structure and family composition to distinguish among four types of households which provide a range from maximal to minimal degree of presence of the father. They are as follows:

Monogamous Nuclear. This household is the usual one in our society. The father, mother, and children eat, sleep, and entertain under one roof. Grandparents, siblings of the parents, and other relatives live elsewhere. The effective presence of the father in the child's environment is thus at a maximum.

Monogamous Extended. Here two or more nuclear families live together under one roof. A typical extended family consists of an aged couple together with their married sons and daughters and their respective families. In such a household, the child's interaction with his father is likely to be somewhat less than in the single nuclear household.

Polygynous Polygynous. The polygynous household consists of a man living with his wives and their various children. Here the child is likely to have even less opportunity to interact with his father.

Polygynous Mother-Child. This type of household occurs in those polygynous societies where each wife has a separate establishment and lives in it with her children. In these societies the father either sleeps in a men's club, has a hut of his own, or divides his time among the houses of his various wives. The husband usually does not sleep in the house of any wife during the two to three years when she is nursing each infant. Thus the mother may become the almost exclusive object of identification for the first few years of life.

Table 21 shows the number of societies with low and high frequency of theft and personal crime within each of the four categories of household type. As the opportunity for contact with the father decreases, the frequency of both theft and personal crime increases. This result agrees with our hypothesis. If the family structure and household is treated as a four-point scale, it yields a correlation of $+0.58$ with frequency of theft and of $+0.44$ with frequency of personal crime; both correlations are statistically significant ($P < .01$). If we compare the extremes of the distribution—contrasting monogamous nuclear households (which provide the maximum opportunity for identification with the father) with polygynous mother-child households (which provide the minimum opportunity for identification with the father)—this relationship is clearly demonstrated; 18 of the 21 societies fall in the predicted quadrants for theft, and 14 out of 21 for personal crime.

Several results of empirical studies in our society appear consistent with this finding. One is the frequently reported relationship between broken homes and delinquency, since in the majority of cases broken homes are probably mother-child households. Robins and O'Neal, for example, in a follow-up study of problem children after 30 years, refer to the high incidence of fatherless families.[10] Glueck and Glueck report that 41.2 percent of their delinquent group were not living with their own fathers, as compared with 24.8 percent of a matched nondelinquent

TABLE 21.

FREQUENCY OF THEFT OR PERSONAL CRIME IN RELATION TO FAMILY
STRUCTURE AND HOUSEHOLD

FAMILY STRUCTURE AND HOUSEHOLD*	FREQUENCY OF THEFT		FREQUENCY OF PERSONAL CRIME	
	LOW	HIGH	LOW	HIGH
Monogamous nuclear	7	2	5	4
Monogamous extended	7	3	6	3
Polygynous polygynous	7	6	3	7
Polygynous mother-child	1	11	3	9

NOTE: Each entry in the table gives the number of societies in our sample which have the particular combination of characteristics indicated for that row and column.

The total number of cases in the left-hand and right-hand parts of this table and in the various divisions of succeeding tables varies because lack of information prevented rating some societies on some variables. In testing each relationship we have of course been able to use only those societies for which the relevant ratings are available. The division into "low" and "high" was made as near the median as possible.

*See Murdock (1957).

group.[11] These data suggest that a relatively high proportion of the delinquents came from what were essentially "mother-child" households.

A recent book by Rohrer and Edmonson is also relevant.[12] Their study is a follow-up after 20 years of the individuals described in *Children of Bondage* by Davis and Dollard.[13] The importance of the matriarchal household typical in a southern Negro lower-class group, and its effect on the emotional development of the young boy and his eventual attitudes as an adult are stressed throughout. The following passage summarizes, in its application to their (Rohrer and Edmonson) particular data, an interpretation consistent with those we have cited in introducing this hypothesis.

> Gang life begins early, more or less contemporaneously with the first years of schooling, and for many men lasts until death. . . . Although each gang is a somewhat distinct group, all of them appear to have a common structure expressing and reinforcing the gang ideology. Thus an organizational form that springs from the little boy's search for a masculinity he cannot find at home becomes first a protest against femininity and then an assertion of hypervirility. On the way it acquires a structuring in which the aspirations and goals of the matriarchy or the middle class are seen as soft, effeminate, and despicable. The gang ideology of masculine independence is formed from these perceptions, and the gang then sees its common enemy not as a class,

nor even perhaps as a sex, but as the "feminine principle" in society. The gang member rejects this femininity in every form, and he sees it in women and in effeminate men, in laws and morals and religion, in schools and occupational striving.[14]

Correlates of Theft

Although we shall consider correlates of theft in this section and correlates of personal crime in the next section, each table will show in parallel columns the relation of a set of variables both to theft and to personal crime. This will facilitate comparison and avoid repetition. How each of these variables was measured will be described in the section to which it is most pertinent.

The first variables to be considered are concerned with child training practices. Most of the child training variables have been developed in our research and described in an earlier paper.[15] These variables may be briefly described as follows:

Overall childhood indulgence. The period of childhood was defined roughly as covering the age period from 5 to 12 years, or to the beginning of any pubertal or prepubertal status change. In making ratings of childhood indulgence, factors relevant to indulgence in infancy— such as immediacy and degree of drive reduction, display of affection by parents, etc.—if operative at this later age, were taken into account. In addition, the raters also considered the degree of socialization expected in childhood and the severity of the methods used to obtain the expected behavior.

Anxiety associated with socialization during the same period of childhood. This was rated separately for each of five systems of behavior: responsibility or dutifulness training; nurturance training, i.e., training the child to be nurturant or helpful toward younger siblings and other dependent people; obedience training; self-reliance training; achievement training, i.e, training the child to orient his behavior toward standards of excellence in performance and to seek to achieve as excellent a performance as possible.

In rating the training in these areas, an attempt was first made to estimate the total pressure exerted by the adults in each society toward making the children behave in each of these specified ways (responsible, nurturant, obedient, self-reliant, and achieving). The socialization anxiety measures were based on an estimate of the amount of anxiety aroused in the child by failing to behave in a responsible, self-reliant, etc. way, and they reflect primarily the extent of punishment for failure to show each particular form of behavior. The measures of total pressure reflect both this and the extent of reward and encouragement.

Wherever boys and girls were rated differently on any of the above variables of socialization, we used the ratings for boys.

The relation of the crime ratings to these and other variables of child training has been analyzed. It is clear that theft is significantly related to several variables of child training.

First, theft is negatively correlated with childhood indulgence, i.e., societies with a high rating of childhood indulgence tend to have a low frequency of theft in the adult population; and, conversely, societies with a low rating of childhood indulgence show a high frequency of theft.

Frequency of theft is also positively correlated with socialization anxiety during the period of childhood with respect to the following areas of training: responsibility, self-reliance, achievement, and obedience. It should be emphasized that total pressures toward those four areas of socialization are not significantly correlated with theft. Therefore it is apparently not the area or level of socialization required which is significant, but rather the punitive and anxiety provoking methods of socialization employed.

These findings on child training in relation to theft may be summarized and interpreted by the hypothesis that theft is in part motivated by feelings of deprivation of love. Our data indicate that one source of such feelings is punitive and anxiety provoking treatment during childhood. Such treatment during infancy may tend to have a similar effect, as suggested by a correlation of -0.25 between frequency of theft and infant indulgence. This correlation falls slightly short of significance at the 5 percent level. It is of special interest that substantial correlations with socialization anxiety in childhood tended to occur in the areas of training in responsibility, achievement, and self-reliance. These all involve demands for behavior far removed from the dependent behavior of infancy and early childhood and close to the independent behavior expected of adults. If we assume that lack of adequate indulgence in childhood leads to a desire to return to earlier means of gratification and behavior symbolic of this need, then we would expect that pressures toward more adult behavior might intensify this need and the frequency of the symbolic behavior. Theft, from this point of view, would be seen as rewarded partly by its value as symbolic gratification of an infantile demand for unconditional indulgence irrespective of other people's rights or interests.

The results of the early study by Healy and Bronner seem directly pertinent to our findings and interpretation.[16] They found that a group of delinquents differed from their nondelinquent siblings primarily in their relationships with their parents; the delinquent child was much more likely to give evidence of feeling thwarted and rejected. It seems reasonable to assume that such feelings would often, though not always, indicate a real deprivation of parental love. Glueck and Glueck also found that their delinquents, compared with matched nondelinquents, had received less affection from their parents and siblings and had a greater tendency to feel that their parents were not concerned with their welfare.[17] It was also noted that fathers of the delinquents had a much greater tendency to resort to physical punishment as a means of discipline than fathers of the nondelinquents. This agrees with our observation that more punitive methods of socialization are associated with an increased frequency of theft.

Compulsive stealing (kleptomania) has been interpreted by psychoanalysts as an attempt to seize symbols of security and affection.[18] Thus this form of mental illness, in common with more rational forms of stealing, may be regarded as being motivated by feelings of deprivation of love.

Table 22 summarizes the relationship between our two measures of crime and a number of aspects of economy and social organization on which we were able to obtain ratings. Theft shows a significant relationship with only three of these measures: social stratification, level of political integration, and degree of elaboration of social control. Social stratification was treated as a five-point scale ranging from complex stratification, i.e., three or more definite social classes or castes exclusive of slaves, to egalitarian, i.e., absence of significant status differentiation other than recognition of political statuses and of individual skill, prowess, piety, etc. Level of political integration was also treated as a five-point scale ranging from complex state, e.g., confederation of tribes or conquest state with a king, differentiated officials, and a hierarchical administrative organization to no political integration, even at the community level.[19] Elaboration of social control is concerned with the degree to which a society has law making, law enforcing, and punishing agencies.

Our findings indicate that theft is positively correlated with each of these three measures. In other words, with an increased level of political integration, social stratification, and elaboration of social control there is an increase in the frequency of theft. These variables show no significant relationship with frequency of personal crime. Each of these insti-

Table 22.

SOCIOECONOMIC FACTORS ASSOCIATED WITH THEFT OR
PERSONAL CRIME

Factor	Theft		Personal Crime	
	N	r	N	r
1. Social stratification†	44	+.36†	40	+.16
2. Level of political integration†	43	+.34*	39	+.02
3. Degree of elaboration of social control‡	43	+.46**	40	+.04
4. Accumulation of food§				
5. Settlement pattern†				
6. Division of labor by sex†				
7. Rule of residence (patrilocal, matrilocal, etc.)†				
8. Extent of storing‡				
9. Irrationality of storing‡				
10. Severity of punishment for property crime‡				
11. Severity of punishment for personal crime‡				

NOTE: Ratings of factors 3, 10, and 11 were made in connection with the analysis of crime by two of the three raters (H. Maretzki and A. Rosman). Ratings of factors 8 and 9 were made by one of the raters (H. Maretzki) but in connection with an analysis of food and economy. Factors 4–11 showed no significant relationship with either theft or personal crime.
†See Murdock (1957).
‡Bacon, Child, and Barry (unpublished).
§See Barry, Child, and Bacon (1959).
*p † .05
**p † .01

tutional conditions seems capable of arousing feelings of insecurity and resentment, and hence may be similar in this respect to parental deprivation. Therefore the correlation of these institutional conditions with theft might be tentatively interpreted as consistent with our hypothesis about motivational influences on theft. It is obvious that other interpretations might be made from the same data. For example, a high frequency of crime may give rise to increased elaboration of social control.

Table 23 presents the relation of both theft and personal crime to certain adult attitudes on which we were able to obtain ratings. Frequency of theft is positively related to sense of property and negatively related to trust about property. This may indicate merely that the greater the importance of property, the greater the variety of acts which will be classified as theft, or that a high frequency of theft gives rise to an emphasis on property. But it may also mean that the greater the importance

Table 23.

ADULT ATTITUDES ASSOCIATED WITH THEFT OR PERSONAL CRIME

Attitude	Theft		Personal Crime	
	N	r	N	r
1. Sense of property	43	+.45**	40	+.25
2. Trust about property	43	−.31*	40	−.27
3. General trustfulness	42	−.28	40	−.40**
4. Environmental kindness in folk tales	23	−.47*	21	−.30
5. Environmental hostility in folk tales	23	+.36	21	+.56**
6. Communality of property				
7. Competition in the acquisition of wealth				
8. Generosity				
9. n achievement in folk tales†				

NOTE: Attitude 3 was rated by one of the three raters (A. Rosman) in connection with the analysis of crime. Attitudes 1, 2, 6, 7, and 8 were rated by another of the three raters (H. Maretzki) in connection with the analysis of food and economy.
Attitudes 6–9 showed no significant relationship with either theft or personal crime.
†See Child, Veroff, and Storm (1958).
*p † .05
**p † .01

of property, the more effectively does theft serve the personal needs to which it seems to be related.

Frequency of theft is also negatively correlated with environmental kindness in folk tales. This folk tale measure requires some explanation. It was taken from an analysis of folk tales made by one of the authors (MKB) without knowledge of the societies from which the sample of folk tales was taken. In making the analysis, each folk tale was divided into units of action or events as they related to the principal character or the character with whom the listener would be expected to identify. Each unit was then classified in one of a number of different categories including that of environmental kindness. Classification in this category means that the particular unit involved action or state of affairs definitely friendly or nurturant to the principal character. Thus our results show that societies high in frequency of theft tend to have folk tales which do not represent the environment as kind. Thinking of the environment as lacking in friendly nurturance seems entirely consistent with the relative absence of parental nurturance which we have already found to be correlated with frequency of theft.

Correlates of Personal Crime

Inspection of tables 22 and 23 reveals that the significant correlates of personal crime are different from those for theft. In no instance does a variable in these tables show a significant correlation with both theft and personal crime.

Frequency of personal crime shows a significant positive correlation with dependence socialization anxiety, a rating taken from Whiting and Child.[20] In making this rating, an estimate was made of the amount of anxiety aroused in the children of a given society by the methods of independence training typically employed. This estimate was based on the following factors: abruptness of the transition required, severity and frequency of punishment, and evidence of emotional disturbance in the child.

Ratings on mother-child sleeping are taken from Whiting et al.[21] In this study societies were placed into two categories: those in which the mother and baby shared the same bed for at least a year to the exclusion of the father, those in which the baby slept alone or with both the mother and father. According to our results there is a high positive relationship between prolonged, exclusive mother-child sleeping arrangements and frequency of personal crime.[22]

Inspection of the child training factors associated with frequency of personal crime suggests that the conditions in childhood leading to a high frequency of personal crime among adults are as follows: a mother-child household with inadequate opportunity in early life for identification with the father, mother-child sleeping arrangements which tend to foster a strong dependent relationship between the child and the mother, subsequent socialization with respect to independence training which tends to be abrupt, punitive, and productive of emotional disturbance in the child.

We would predict that this pattern of child training factors would tend to produce in the child persistent attitudes of rivalry, distrust, and hostility, which would probably continue into adult life. The results obtained with ratings of adult attitudes (Table 23) support this view. Frequency of personal crime is negatively correlated with general trustfulness. Frequency of personal crime is also positively correlated with environmental hostility in folk tales. Classification of a folk tale unit in this category means that the particular unit involved definite deception, aggression, or rejection in relation to the principal character. This variable was not highly related to that of environmental kindness, although the results obtained with the two are consistent with each other. The correlation between them was only −0.34, most folk tale units not falling in either of these categories. Our results indicate that societies which are rated as relatively high in the frequency of personal crime have folk tales with a high proportion of events representing the environment as hostile. If we may infer that the content of folk tales reflects the underlying attitudes of the people who tell them, then this finding, as well as those with our other measures of adult attitudes, supports the view that personal crime is correlated with a suspicious or distrustful attitude toward the environment.

An analysis by Whiting of the socialization factors correlated with a belief in sorcery is relevant to this aspect of our results.[23] He points out that a belief in sorcery is consistent with a paranoid attitude. According to Freudian interpretation, paranoia represents a defense against sexual anxiety. Whiting presents cross-cultural data in support of a hypothesis, based on Freud's theory of paranoia, that a belief in sorcery is related to a prolonged and intense contact with the mother in infancy followed by a severe sex socialization. The same hypothesis might be applied to frequency of personal crime, since we have evidence that personal crime is correlated with a suspicious, paranoid attitude in adult life, and sorcery is after all one form of personal crime. Our results for personal crime, in common with Whiting's for sorcery, show a correlation with mother-child household and prolonged mother-child sleeping. However, we found no significant correlation with severe sex socialization but rather with severe dependence socialization. We do not feel that these findings negate the Freudian interpretation, because dependence socialization, bearing as it does on the child's intimate relation with his mother, necessarily is concerned with the child's sexual feelings in a broad sense.

GENERAL DISCUSSION

We would like to emphasize the value of the cross-cultural method for exploring the possible determinants of crime. When each society is used as a single case, and is classified according to crime and other variables for the entire society over a period of years, the measures are likely to be reliable; comparison among societies provides great diversity in frequency of crime and in the other variables to be related with it.

The cross-cultural method may help us to identify variables with a causal relationship to crime. For example, our cross-cultural data suggest that high differentiation of status within a society is a favorable condition for a high frequency of theft, and that a high frequency of personal crime is associated with a generalized attitude of distrust. These relationships should be subjected to more systematic and intensive tests within our own society than has hitherto been done.

Variables which have been suggested, whether in empirical studies or theoretical discussions, as possible causes of crime within our society may be tested for broader significance by the cross-cultural method. It has been argued, for example, that within our society delinquent or criminal behavior is likely to develop if the boy has been raised without adequate opportunity to identify with the father. These suggestions have often been made in connection with family patterns that are said to characterize certain classes or groups within our society; the cross-cultural findings indicate that a high frequency of both theft and personal crime tends to occur in societies where the typical family for the society as a whole creates lack or limitation of opportunity for the young boy to form an identification with his father. Therefore the cross-cultural method supports the theory that lack of opportunity for the young boy to form a masculine identification is in itself an important antecedent of crime.

Another instance of such confirmation in a broader sense is the following: In our society delinquents have been reported to express feelings of alienation from their parents. It is unclear, however, whether this reflects their parents' actual treatment of them or merely their own subjectively determined perceptions. Our cross-cultural data (in common with some of the findings within our own society) indicate that a high frequency of theft is correlated with an actual low degree of indulgence during childhood.

Other theories about the antecedents of crime, when tested with the cross-cultural method, have not been confirmed in this broader framework. For example, pressures toward achievement were not significantly related to frequency of crime, although such a relationship is implied by theories of delinquency which emphasize the discrepancy between culturally induced aspirations and the possibility of achieving them. This negative result in our sample of societies does not deny the existence of such a relationship within our society, but it does indicate a limitation on its generality.

II

The Case of August Sangret
A Contribution to
Historical Criminology

WOLF MIDDENDORF

Historical criminology, a new and still underdeveloped branch of the science devoted to crime, has set itself the task of portraying a picture of criminality in earlier times. Crime is not merely an individual act; it is at the same time a mirror of the respective social conditions which change rapidly. Each crime must therefore be seen in its own time. It contributes to the picture of change in culture and civilization, in law, custom, religion, the state, and the economy.

It is one of my duties in the Max-Planck Institute in the field of historical criminology to collect and evaluate criminal cases which are of special importance and from which we can learn. Such a case is that of August Sangret.

On the morning of 7 October 1942, two men from the Royal Marine Camp on Hankley Common in southern England, in the course of their military duty in the field, discovered, protruding out of a little mound of earth, a human arm and a human leg. The following day, the police disinterred a dead body which proved to be that of an adolescent girl. Four kinds of marks of violence were found which later on, after a careful examination of the body, were described as follows: The first group of injuries were stabbing wounds directed to the top of the head on its left side. They were accompanied by wounds to the right forearm and hand, which were of a protective nature, as if the hand had been raised in defence of the head. The second group of injuries were blunt injuries to the mouth and the front of the face in keeping with either a blow in that region or a fall on to the face. The third group consisted of a single very heavy blunt injury to the brain. The fourth group of injuries, which may have occurred after the death, were those to the right foot. They would be in keeping with the body being dragged and the right foot catching in branches or stone projections. The body apparently had laid in situ for two or three days, after which it had been dragged up a small hill where it had been superficially buried. Erosion of the topsoil and the weight of a passing armoured vehicle apparently had later caused the right arm and left leg to become exposed. Police found an identity card and a national health insurance card, both made out in the name of Joan Pearl Wolfe. There also was a letter which revealed a relationship with a Canadian soldier of a nearby military camp. These documents led to the identification of the victim and her soldier boyfriend. She was a 19-year-old girl, the daughter of a widow living in Tunbridge Wells. Two and a half years ago she had left home, had drifted from one factory job to another, and lastly had been hanging around military camps in the Guildford district, where she was often referred to as "the wigwam girl." Her male associate was the Canadian soldier Private August Sangret in the nearby Jasper Camp at Witley. On 12 October, three detectives went to Jasper Camp, questioned August Sangret as to his knowledge of Joan Wolfe and took him to the police station where he made a long statement which lasted until 16 October, "probably the lengthiest ever written in a murder case."[1] The substance of it was that he had picked up the girl on 17 July 1942 in a public house in Godalming, and that this meeting was the beginning of their liaison. At the end of July the girl was some days in hospital from which she wrote to him that she was pregnant and that they would have to get married. She returned to the camp and Sangret promised to marry her. He built for her a little hut of branches, leaves, and twigs and when their hideout was discovered by the Provost, he built a second shack or wigwam for her. Later on the couple spent the nights in a pavilion which belonged to a cricket club, and which was in a poor condition.

According to his statement, Sangret had last seen her when they parted at 6 A.M. on the morning of Monday, 14 September. When he returned to the camp, he told two other soldiers that he had had a quarrel with his girl about his forthcoming leave in Glasgow at which occasion she had asked him again to say definitely when they were likely to get married. She had begged him to take her to Glasgow with him.

About the midst of October it happened that the washbasin in the military guardhouse where Sangret was temporarily detained, became bunged-up. On 27 November Private Brown, whose job it was to investigate the cause of the obstruction to the plumbing, discovered a blockage within the effluent pipe which drained water away from the adjacent shower bath which was out of use for about one month. Putting his arm down the pipe, Brown retrieved a knife which unusually ended in a sort of blunt hook. The knife was recognized as one which had been found by a soldier in the middle of August, stuck into the trunk of a tree besides the shack where Sangret and the girl had slept. The soldier had taken the knife and had surrendered it to the military police at the camp. This knife had been handed over to Sangret when he was in detention and presumably he had tried to get rid of it by throwing it down the drain.

On 6 December, Sangret was charged with the murder of Joan Wolfe upon which he asserted: "No, sir, I did not do it; no, sir, someone did it and I will have to take the rap."

The trial began on 24 February 1943 at the county hall, Kingston-upon-Thames, and lasted five days, It aroused no great interest, the country was at war and a lover's quarrel could scarcely be expected to arrest much notice. The witnesses for the prosecution included the mother of the girl, soldiers, and policemen. The sole witness for the defence was August Sangret himself. He admitted that there had been a quarrel and that it was his intention to get in touch with a woman he knew in Glasgow during his forthcoming leave. He denied that he was getting tired of the girl. He denied the murder and called all evidence pointing against him untrue.

The jury deliberated two and a half hours, then they returned to court and gave a verdict of guilty with a strong recommendation to mercy.

This recommendation was forwarded to the proper authorities but was not approved. An appeal was dismissed on April 13, and Sangret was "duly" executed at Wandsworth Jail on the 29 April 1943.

With a certain naïveté, the introduction to "The Trial of August Sangret" ends with the conclusion that some uncertainties remained unanswered but that they were relatively unimportant. The so-called "Wigwam Murder" would be considered the greatest detective-plus-forensic achievement of recent times. From the standpoint of the criminologist, however, this achievement is one which the English administration of justice cannot be proud of, for several reasons as follows:

In the opening speech for the prosecution, the council for the Crown gave the definition of murder. "Murder is the taking by one person of another person's life with malice aforethought. . . . Malice aforethought merely means intention. In murder you have not necessarily got to have premeditation. It is just as much murder if you strike somebody across the head with a log of wood, or stab them, by which they come to their death, if that is done on the spur of the moment, as if you administered poison to them upon a plan which might have taken weeks or months or years to perfect." [2]

In 1943, the only punishment for murder was death. A Royal Commission to study the possible limitation of the death penalty, concluded in 1953: "The outstanding defect of the law of murder is that it provides a single punishment for a crime widely varying in culpability." [3]

For instance, English courts don't know and don't acknowledge crimes of passion, for which one finds much sympathy in America and especially in France. [4] In France, it often happens that defendants are acquitted if they can influence the jury to believe that they acted in a consuming passion. [5] The English are, according to F. Tennyson Jesse, "in the main mercyfully exempt" from the crime passionnel. [6] In the practice of the English courts, homicidal attacks are called "crimes passionnels," when they are provoked by sexual jealousy or resentment. No provocation whatever can make homicide justifiable in England, but it may reduce the offence from murder to manslaughter if the attack is made immediately and the provocation is such as would deprive a reasonable person of self-control. For instance, the finding of a spouse in the act of adultery is held to be such provocation, but the courts are very reluctant to accept mere words as sufficient and provocation in nonmarital relationships is rarely accepted as sufficient. Among criminologists, there is no doubt that the crime of Ruth Ellis who shot her lover, who had deserted her, was a real crime passionnel, but according to English decisions in similar cases, she was found guilty of murder and was hanged. One can, probably, be sure that in no other country would she have been executed. In 1953, the Royal Commission recommended the abolition of the doctrine of "constructive malice" and the acceptance of provocation by words provided that provocation was sufficient to deprive a reasonable man of his self-control. [7]

Nowadays, provocation will be dealt with as a case of diminished responsibility; in this connection it is necessary to examine the English law concerning penal responsibility.

The tests of criminal responsibility are based on the M'Naghten Rules formulated in England in 1843. The House of Lords submitted, to a panel of judges, questions regarding the criminal responsibilities of persons afflicted with insane delusions. The judges' answers have been called the M'Naghten Rules. They state in essence, that in order to establish a defence of insanity, it must be shown that the accused "was labouring under such a defect of reason from disease of the mind that 1. he did not know the nature and quality of the act he was doing, or 2. did not know that it was wrong."

Since their introduction over a hundred years ago, the rules have been criticized by both lawyers and psychiatrists. For example it was stated that only the grossly demented senile or the idiot can be said to have no knowledge of right or wrong and that these persons are seldom seen in the criminal courts. The rules completely ignore the importance of emotional factors and instinctual drives in determining human behaviour.

In the last hundred years, English courts have varied in their interpretation of the M'Naghten Rules, some courts apply the rules rigidly while others interpret them very liberally in order to avoid a miscarriage of justice. The rules may be stretched until "the ordinary non legal user of the English language is aghast at the distortions and deformations and tortures to which the unfortunate words are subjected, and wonders whether it is worth-while to have a language, which can apparently be taken to mean anything the user pleases."[8]

In fact, English juries discovered many "idiots" and pressed them into the M'Naghten Rules. In 1811, in England and Wales 263, or 14.5 percent of all accused persons charged with murder, were found insane. The percentage of insane persons charged with any other offence, was only 0.1 percent.[9]

The number of murderers who were regarded insane was always high. During the seven years from 1939 to 1945 out of 474 persons tried for murder, 209 (44 percent) were declared insane.[10]

Since insanity is a defence in English criminal law, the burden of proof of his irresponsibility lies on the defendant, and the evidence is confined to the statements of expert witnesses called by the parties. On the Continent, the prisoner's responsibility is an ingredient of his guilt. The court, therefore, before finding him guilty, must be satisfied that any doubt as to his responsibility has been cleared.

One of the most interesting defences was brought forward in 1959 by Podola who had killed a policeman in London. Podola claimed to have lost his memory and therefore being unable to defend himself and unfit to plead. Podola did not escape the death penalty. A similar defence, however, had been partially acknowledged in 1945 in Scotland in the case of Russel and had led to a less severe sentence because of the special circumstances.[11]

The Criminal Law in Scotland, for over a hundred years, knows the doctrine of diminished responsibility which has worked to the satisfaction of lawyers, psychiatrists, and the public. It enables the Scottish courts to take account of lesser forms of mental abnormality and to reduce the crime from murder to culpable homicide. During 49 years in the first half of our century, there were in Scotland 590 cases of murder, and in only 23 of these cases, was there an execution.[12]

The Homicide Act of 1957 introduced into English law the concept of diminished responsibility, "perhaps the most welcome contribution to English criminal law."[13] The diminished responsibility defence may be successful when the accused "was suffering from such abnormality of mind (whether arising from a condition of arrested or retarded development of mind or any inherent causes or inducted by disease or injury) as substantially impaired his mental responsibility for his acts or omissions." This defence may lead to a verdict of manslaughter and the sentence is left to the judge's discretion.[14]

Furthermore, the rigidity of the English law of murder can be mitigated by the Royal Prerogative of Mercy, but there were those who criticized the use of the prerogative in the large number of cases where it was applied. For instance, the Archbishop of Canterbury felt that it was wrong to pronounce the sentence of death and then, in about half the cases, not carry it out.[15]

In very few cases, the Home Office ordered the mental examination of prisoners under sentence of death and their transfer to a state asylum. From 1901 to 1922, out of a total of 585 convicted murderers, 13 or 2.2 percent were dealt with in this way. "In their practical effect these provisions compensate in some measure for the rigid conservatism of the Common Law concerning criminal responsibility."[16]

Holtzendorff refers to the materials of the Capital Punishment Commission of 1865 and the attached list of executions and pardons. According to his opinion the list shows that foreigners convicted in England for murder have only little chance to be pardoned.[17]

The weaknesses of the English criminal law system are aggravated by the principle of English criminal procedure that insanity and diminished responsibility are defences which have to be raised by the accused in person or on his behalf with his consent, and that they cannot be raised at all if the accused pleads innocence, especially mistaken identity. "This attitude of the law is unreasonable; it is difficult to understand why the defence should not have the right to argue that the accused was innocent of the act, but if the court should regard him as guilty of the facts of the offence, the plea would be changed to one of insanity or diminished responsibility."[18] In the case of the so-called A6 Murderer, James Hanratty, after his execution it was pointed out that the case had shown various circumstances which strongly indicated abnormality of mind, but that none of those defences could be raised in court because Hanratty had to the last maintained that he had not been the killer.[19]

For this reason, that means in regard to that technicality of criminal procedure, it was—to say at least—unfair from the police to ask the illiterate Indian soldier August Sangret for the whereabouts of Joan Wolfe and to take statements without telling him that she was dead and that her body was found. By this way of asking, Sangret was almost irresistibly induced to answer that he did not know anything and, afterwards, consequently to deny to have killed her. The Chief Inspector of Scotland Yard, Edward Greeno, told the court, as witness, that he took the first and second statement from Sangret without cautioning him, and that no officer from his regiment was present when the statements were taken. He was finally cautioned when he was charged with the murder of his girl friend. By this somewhat doubtful procedure, Sangret was barred from raising the defence of not being responsible. We do not know if this result was the expressive purpose of the Chief Inspector of Scotland Yard.

In the witness box Sangret denied everything, even undeniable and unimportant details. This is typical for a certain kind of defendants and no absolute proof of guilt.

In the whole, Sangret was, without very serious doubts, guilty; the hook-ended knife sealed his fate. The medical expert told the jury that the stab wounds could very well have been inflicted by this knife, and could not have been inflicted with any ordinary knife. On cross-examination the expert answered: "I have tried a number of knives and other things into these wounds and nothing fits with anything like the remarkable accuracy of this knife."[20]

After this evidence being given, one cannot blame judge and jury for condemning August Sangret, but I personally, being a judge for 20 years, would not have taken the responsibility either to convict the defendant to death or to execute him.

In the past, English like American juries have done much to avoid the stern consequences of the inflexible criminal law. It seems that the deterrent of the gallows affected the jury more than the criminal. The juries went on strike, as Koestler expresses it. They made it a rule, when a theft of goods worth 40 shillings was a capital offence, to assess the value of the goods at 39 shillings. And when, in 1827, the capital offence was raised to five pounds, the juries raised their assessment to four pounds 29 shillings. In a similar way, present-day juries bring in verdicts of "guilty, but insane" in cases where, according to medical evidence, and the judge's direction, the accused must be regarded as sane before the law. "Sometimes they succeed in saving a soul, sometimes not. Much depends on their courage and determination in disregarding a severe judge's instruction." [21]

In the case of August Sangret, they did not succeed, but apparently they did not feel well in pronouncing the verdict of guilty. Since this verdict must be unanimous, there was no juror who was so stubborn to refuse to deliver Sangret to the hangman. One only gave the recommendation of mercy, probably without much hope. It is the dangerous privilege of a jury to pronounce a verdict without being obliged to give the reasons for it; so nobody knows if the laymen really understood the problems of the case.

It is only a speculation that a better and more energetic defender so strongly could have influenced the jury as to bring in another verdict in the case of August Sangret. Apparently, the defender Linton Theodore Thorp (1884–1950) did not belong to the famous trial lawyers known for their successes, which for instance Lord Birkett described in his book *Six Great Advocates*. For many years Thorp was judge in the Native Courts in Egypt and British Delegate to the Judicial Commission in Constantinople. Later on, he was Recorder, Chairman of the Essex Quarter Sessions and Chancellor of the Diocese at Chelmsford. He wrote a book about the law of moneylending.

Probably, Thorp was a court-appointed barrister because Sangret had no money. Like in many other countries the fees paid to the defence under the Poor Prisoners Defence Act in England are "shockingly small." [22] Therefore, the best trial lawyers cannot accept this task and we know of many cases in which a man's financial means can and could influence his chances of being convicted or even suffering capital punishment.

Thorp could and should have protested against the way in which police took the three-day statement without cautioning Sangret, and, perhaps by this mean, the defender could have opened the way to bring in the defence of provocation, if he could have persuaded Sangret to tell the story of the quarrelling, making a good impression to the jury and avoiding unnecessary lies. But it is a criminological experience that many defendants cannot be counselled to their advantage and that they unconsciously destroy themselves.

The Rt. Hon. Sir Malcolm MacNaghten was born in 1869, at the time of the trial he was 74 years of age. He has been described as a kindly and courteous personality and a human judge, remembered by the bar with affection. "Although making no great mark, he made few mistakes." [23] Much of his work dealt with Inland Revenue problems.

English judges generally have a high reputation, especially in other countries. In England, in recent years, they were often criticized, for instance by Koestler. "From Coke to Stephen and beyond, they all show the same curious trend of inhumanity because, though posing as experts, they knew little of human nature and the motives of crime. Victims of their professional deformity, ignorant of the forces of heredity and social environment, hostile to any social or psychological explanation, the criminal was for them nothing but a bundle of depravity who cannot be redeemed and must be destroyed." [24] "The main obstacle to any reform of the outdated M'Naghten Rules are again the judges." [25] In 1924, the Lord Chief Justice stated in the House of Lords that 10 out of 12 judges when asked for their opinion were strongly opposed to a statutory extension of the M'Naghten Rules. [26] When a defence of insanity is set up in a murder trial, "there is likely to be a suspicion in the minds of judge and jury that mental disease has been trumped up for the purposes of the defence." [27]

After the introduction of the notion of diminished responsibility in 1957, the judges appeared to have been reluctant to give much assistance to juries by way of guidance or interpretation of the scope and meaning of this provision. The Chief Justice Lord Goddard, known for his conservatism, said, when Parliament had defined what is to amount to diminished responsibility, "it is not for the judges to redefine or attempt to define the definition." [28]

Concerning the summing up of the judges, Koestler refers to Ensor, one of the outstanding English writers on law who has said: "It is very easy for a bad judge, especially in a jury case, to defeat justice by the crassest stupidity or partisanship, without perpetrating any technical misdirection of the jury or explicit twist of the law of which an Appeal Court could take cognizance." [29]

In our case, it is doubtful if it was fair to the prisoner to give the jury the reconstructed skull and to allow them to take it with them into the jury room, "for the first time in a murder trial it is believed." [30]

Another comment may be added, made by Victor Gollancz. He wrote: "I recently heard a man being sentenced to five years' imprisonment, after pleading for mercy. How can I convey to you a sense of the wickedness that grimaced in the court at that moment? It was not so much a question of the sentence itself, which may have been necessitated, in the Judge's opinion, by the duties of his office: it was his demeanour—the contempt in his voice, the taking for granted of his own integrity and the other's worthlessness, the externality, the lack of fellow-feeling, the relation as between machines and not persons, the accent he gave the word 'punishment,' the nod of curt dismissal with which he finished and passed on—it was this that seems to put out the sun and freeze the world into starkness." [31]

In the case of August Sangret, the judge gave some examples of his ignorance of human nature and criminological experiences: it was wrong for instance to say that the circumstances of the crime suggested the work of a powerful man swept by a sudden and violent passion. "This did not accord with the action of a stranger but rather of one who was on terms of close acquaintance if not indeed intimacy. Sangret fulfilled these qualifications." [32] According to criminological experiences, a complete stranger to the victim, a sex maniac, can slay the victim with even more cruelty and passion.

The judge's summing up to the jury was somewhat unconcerned. It could have been the same in a case of theft or robbery and it completely neglected the personality of the prisoner.

We don't know much about August Sangret. He was of mixed American Indian and French colonial stock. He belonged to the Cree community which is related to the Blackfoot tribe. As nomads the Cree lived in wigwams and were noted to resort to cannibalism in times of hardship. August Sangret was illiterate, even his spoken English was imperfect. He had to get others to write letters for him. During the war, in the uniformed services, racial admixtures often presented serious disciplinary problems, especially when ill-educated recruits were transported overseas, so that they found themselves for the first time masters of such incredible delights as hard liquor, cash in plenty, and complaisant women on all sides. Indian half-breed troops did not lack courage, but they were troublesome and liable to get out of hand during inactive periods of campaigning.

During his stay in England, Sangret used to get letters every week from a woman in Halifax, Canada, and from another woman who lived in Saskatchewan. In Scotland, he knew a woman in Glasgow whom he wanted to see during his next leave. Apparently, he had a hand with women.

Sangret had been convicted four times before; among for other offences he was punished for threatening to shoot a woman in a "triangle case" and for a violent assault.

The personality of the victim is even more interesting. Critchley comments: "She seems to have been endowed with an almost duplex character, having been wayward and depraved and yet at the same time refined, serious and devote." Joan Wolfe came from a broken home, her father had committed suicide, her mother married again. She was born in Germany and was educated in a convent where she learnt fluent French. When 16-and-a-half years old she left home and kept only in sporadic touch with her family. She flitted from one job to another, and later from one soldier to another. She was, however, not a prostitute, she was always loyal to the soldier with whom she was associated. Obviously, she held Sangret in true affection and the letters which were available, "are touching in their sincerity and unselfishness." [33] Joan Wolfe was a Roman Catholic and ostensibly pious or at least religious. The combination of religion and promiscuity is by no means an unusual phenomenon. The close affinity between sexual and religious emotions is well known among criminologists. Boldberg has devoted his book *The Sacred Fire, The Story of Sex and Religion"* to this topic.

There is no doubt that the murder was "the work of a powerful man swept by a sudden and violent passion." The victim was stabbed "viciously many times;" the judge in his summing up referred to the crime "committed under the influence of wholly uncontrolled savage passion." The wounds showed "the extreme and savage violence with which the girl was attacked." [34] Sangret had admitted that there had been a quarrel between the lovers, but we only can guess which was the cause. Did perhaps Sangret doubt if Joan Wolfe was pregnant and if he was responsible for it? On 17 July they had first met, the same night they had sexual relations. Nine days later, Joan proclaimed that she was pregnant by Sangret. These dates are, to say the least of it, interesting. Apparently, Joan had seriously hoped to get married "very soon," as she wrote him. And she had pressed him many times in this direction. She dreamed about the future and she had written on the wall of the cricket pavilion "Mrs. A. S. Sangret." Perhaps she was disappointed in her expectation and perhaps this disappointment had led her to a verbal provocation like, "You dirty illiterate Indian!" The answer could have been a murder prompted by consuming passion, sudden hate, and senseless fury, that means a crime passionnel.

Critchley asked why Sangret returned to the scene of the murder,[35] but this happens more often than the layman anticipates. And Critchley asks furthermore, why Sangret did not bury the body more deeply. The best answer is not because of excess of cunning or of superstition or because Sangret was crazy with drink, the probable answer is stupidity. One of the faults most often committed by criminologists is to overestimate human intelligence, planning, and foresight.

Sellin showed how culture conflicts arose, especially when the Indian became subject to the white man's law and what happened when legal norms were imposed upon a group previously ignorant of them.[36] Sangret was at least half Indian. One of the instructors said in court that it takes a lot to upset an Indian chap. The prosecutor believed to have found evidence proving the guilt of Sangret because, during his first statement, he did not ask the inspector where Joan had been found, if she was dead, and how she died. "Those are the sort of questions, I should have thought, if you were honestly in love with the girl, and were shocked to discover that she had been found, you would have been asking the Inspector?"[37] Apparently, the prosecutor did not know how Indians react in such a situation. Besides this, criminologists know that nothing is more difficult than to display the exact amount of post-murderous grief which is not leading to suspicion. According to von Hentig, "the psychological problem of post-murderous grief is full of perplexities. A tremendous variety of reactions is met."[38]

August Sangret was convicted for murder and "duly" executed in England in a time in which modern criminology and the study of the personality of the offender were in the beginning while the law of murder was rigid and unflexible. The author of this contribution has long wished that August Sangret had been stationed in a military camp in Scotland instead of one in England. His fate, perhaps, would have been the following one: Taking into account his diminished responsibility, he would have been convicted to a limited term of imprisonment—postponed till the end of the war—and would have been transferred to an especially tough and rough combat unit, charged with dangerous missions. The American Devil's Brigade deliberately assembled a group of men who shared the common denominator of past, present, or potential hardness. One of these "ideal" fighters, for instance, was a murderer.[39] In this unit, Sangret probably would have been of more use to his country than in the hands of the English hangman.

12

The "Second Life": A Cross-Cultural View of Peer Subcultures in Correctional Institutions in Poland and the United States

MARIA LOS and PALMER ANDERSON

We will present some preliminary generalizations from our observations of informal inmate subcultures within correctional institutions in Poland and the United States. Observational phenomenon having to do with the manner in which inmate roles are played out within the prison and juvenile corrections milieu will be noted. We are interested first in the interactions that take place within the institutional confines, but also in how the macroculture influences those modes of interaction within this "total institutional setting."[1] While we intend to draw out a number of generalizations as well as advance some propositions for examination, it is our intention that this paper should be read more as a notation for further thought than as a finished analytical document.

STUDIES IN POLAND

Stanislaw Jedlewski presented an image of the "second life" in a correctional institution for juveniles substantially as follows: The strong elite (*londyn*) under the command of a very powerful leader terrorizes the rest of the boys (*getto*). The leader is more experienced than the rest of the boys; he teaches them how to steal and how to evade the police and other authority figures, but he treats them as his slaves and servants. Jedlewski found this leader to be in actual command of the institution.[2]

More recently, students of sociology at the University of Warsaw, under the direction of Adam Podgorecki were involved in extended research within the correctional treatment setting in Poland.[3] They were interested in looking at informal inmate structures and modes of interaction within sets of interrelationships in both the juvenile and adult milieu. We will outline some of the principal findings of their research along with the conclusions drawn by the researchers. The results of these newer studies are not consistent with the picture presented by Jedlewski. It is very probable that some changes inside the institutional structures took place during this period.

Institutions for boys in Poland are of middle size, generally from one to two hundred inmates.[4] They are, to an extent, treatment oriented; however, treatment consists almost entirely of giving the wards an opportunity of learning a trade or vocation. The questions of reform and improvement of situation in the juvenile and penal corrections fields are discussed among Polish scholars and practitioners and are considered to be very important issues. However, the most advanced ideas, for example, the "open model" of corrections, are seldom implemented in the correctional facilities.

Juvenile institutions usually have a relatively well-equipped functional school within the institution. Generally, there is not much physical resemblance between a corrections house and an adult prison, but treatment houses for juveniles present even less of a penal appearance and atmosphere. Some juvenile institutions have a fence or high wall surrounding their designated territory and inmates in the correctional type institutions must wear standard uniforms and keep their hair cropped short, in the usual instance.

The students researching in Poland under the direction of Podgorecki discovered that they could delineate a very sharp division of inmates into two clearly dichotomized, basic categories which in juvenile argot and local terminology are called *ludzie* (people) in plural form (*czlowiek*—man, in the singular) as the dominant "caste," and *frajerzy* (suckers, *cad*, slaves, or *slumsy*) referring to the subordinate "caste." The people were found to have their special language and a highly indigenous set of magic customs and taboos. Suckers are not permitted to communicate with people in the normal course of daily events and they are never supposed to use the code of the people in communicating with each other.

In Polish institutions the "people" form an extremely cohesive and solitary group, having their own rigidly defined values that are extended

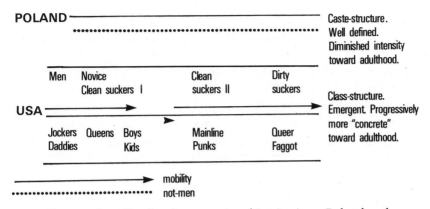

Fig. 18. Stratification in correctional institutions, Poland and
the United States

to all other people only. A "man" will never denounce his fellow to the
authorities even under circumstances of extreme threat. However, the
norms of people are valid only in relationship to other people. They can,
and usually do, break their normative reference in relations with "not-
people." In fact, it is a sign of pride and knowledgeability for them to be
able to do this. Being able to treat "suckers" differentially in all respects
is an indication of higher position and superior category for the man.

Normally, suckers are not permitted to speak to the man. Nor can
they legitimately touch him or his property. The sucker knows better
than to put his hands on a man's kitchen utensils, food, cigarettes, or
personal possessions. Suckers are universally regarded as "dirty" and
a man can become contaminated merely by illegitimate contact with
suckers.

In Polish inmate life, it is the role of the sucker to serve the man in
any way requested. He is constrained to obey orders put to him by the
man. A principal role of the sucker is to serve as a sexual object for the
use of the man to receive sexual gratification. It is important to note that
the sucker is never considered to be a sexual partner in any co-equal
sense. As far as the man is concerned, gratification is a one-way relationship. The man can never take the passive side in these relationships and
if he is ever constrained to do so, for whatever reason, he can no longer
be a man, for he loses his status with his fellows.

As a general rule, when one gets the sucker label, he keeps it forever. Generally, there is no mobility between sucker status and man status. Only in the case where one might fall into the slave category for a
slight reason, i.e., for eating from a dish touched by a sucker, can some

special ceremonial cleansing rite be operationalized to restore status. Cleansing is not ever possible however, in the case of being used as a woman in the sexual act, as well as in the case of "stooling off" a man to the authorities. Most importantly, when an inmate is transferred to another institution or is set free, he is still labelled according to his prevailing position in the social structure of the institution from which he departed. A fairly accurate statement about the statuses might be: Act like a man, always a man; once a sucker, always a sucker.

In some Polish institutions there appears to be a mild gradation inside these two basic categories, and the inner divisions are gradated differentially in different institutions. However, the general delineations of people and suckers are universal in Polish institutions. It is necessary to add that all divisions are more distinct in juvenile institutions than in adult prisons, and that these phenomena are far less observable (that is to say that relationships are much more equalitarian) in female penal populations than among male subcultures.

Polish Juvenile Homes

Now that we have presented a general picture of the "second life" in Polish correctional facilities, we will outline some basic differences in development from the juvenile to the adult level.

The most important part of social life in the correctional institutions for boys is *grypserka* (the secret code), which consists of special language and rules pertaining to social interaction among people on one hand and suckers on the other. Rules concern mainly the "curses," the "rituals," the "oaths," and the "spying" (denouncing or informing). The rules are particularly important in determining and perpetuating the social division: "people" and "suckers," and are very much adhered to in determining the status of a new boy coming to the institution.

The "novice" has to admit that he is a sucker if he was a sucker in a previous institutional hierarchy. If he attempts to conceal this fact the people soon learn about it anyway by writing coded letters to that institution and sending them to boys whom they know. It appears that elaborate information networks ("the grapevine") function to furnish this and other information to the people. Suckers do not have access to this communication system. The consequences of concealing one's sucker identity are dire. Usually the boy is flogged and sexually raped. The cheated people "clean themselves" ritually if they had had any contact with him when they thought he was a man.

If the new inmate was a man in a previous institutional experience, he cannot merely claim his identity and assume the privileges of "manhood." He must say, "ask the other people," and he must give names of other inmates in institutions or "on the streets" who can certify his status. The "novice" who has friends among the people in the institution is in the best situation and may avoid the trial by ordeal.

If the new novice is not experienced, he has one or two weeks to learn the special code, the curses, the rituals, and the oaths. During this time his status is in limbo but he is specially protected by the people. After this period of limbo, the novice is put to trial. Special procedures are connected with this period. Attempts are made to frighten him, fool him; he is teased, beaten, and cajoled. If attempts to make him wash another man's socks or play the passive role in sexual relationships are successful, the new inmate is forever a sucker. There are many ways that a man becomes sucker (downward mobility) and we will summarize them briefly:

1. Informing, spying, denouncing on the people.
2. Any passive role in homosexual relations.
3. Being victim of a rape or being forced to wash a man's socks.
4. Forbidden contact with dirt. Often connected with toilet rites.
5. Shaking hands with a sucker or defending one in any interaction.
6. Eating from a sucker's dish, using his towel, etc.
7. Breaking one's word to other men.
8. Not answering to a curse. Using curses toward a man or toward himself.

There is little possible upward mobility in the system. Mobility from category of sucker to the category of people is rarely possible. Only in that rare cases where a man becomes a sucker for a very questionable reason and was liked and defended by a man or the people is upward mobility possible. In the light offenses where there may have been a questionable relegation to the sucker status in the first place, there are special magic ceremonies permitting the individual to regain man status. These ceremonies differ, and depend on the reasons for the man becoming a sucker. Suckers may never ask to re-become a man. All in the group must make this decision unanimously. Sometimes a person is taken back into the people group on three or four weeks probation. However, we would reiterate that upward mobility is most difficult.[5]

Sometimes there are, among the people, a subgroup called *gitmeni* (git-people). They are more experienced than other people, and have some criminal connections on the outside. Attributes that can be imputed to them are brave, clever, and charismatic. In some juvenile houses the suckers are divided into three categories: the clean sucker, with possibilities of becoming a man (very small group); the clean sucker who cannot become a man because he was caught informing staff, but has no homosexual inclinations and has resisted or avoided rape; and the dirty sucker, who is the passive homosexual and can never become a man.[6]

Thus, the inmate subculture in Polish juvenile correctional institutions appears to be irrational to the outside observer. Magic customs and ceremonies take on meaning only in context with the institutional realities. The subculture is fatalistic and deterministic. For example, it is taken for granted that many boys are born to be suckers, while others are predestinated to be people. As we shall see, the juvenile correctional structure is more inclusive and monocultural than is the adult prison subculture.

Polish Prison Subcultures

In prison, the subcultural divisions are more complex. We must take at least five factors into consideration in order to outline the differences.

1. Age—there are both juveniles and adults incarcerated in prison.

2. Prestige—this is more distinct among juveniles, Hierarchies, similar to those in juvenile institutions, exist. However, other status systems parallel the people-suckers system. We should mention that, whereas nobody can stay out of the man-sucker structure in juvenile institutions, the prison subculture presents more flexibility in Poland, permitting a number of status systems to flourish independently within the same institutional structure. As we shall point out again below, this existence of relatively independent subcultural systems within the same institution is to a degree one significant point of difference between Polish prisons and those in the United States.

3. The existence of major cleavages in social and cultural backgrounds of the inmates from town and countryside. The "man from the town" has little in common with the "cad" from the countryside or village.

4. Type of offense may be more important in Poland than in the U.S. prisons for determining status role within the subculture. In Poland, the thieves constitute the elite group, after which follow the "bandits" and "hooligans." Sexual offenders are not taken into account at all, they do not count. It is significant to note that homosexuality is not considered a crime in Poland.

5. The frequency and length of stay (term) have an effect on the position of the inmates.

The intake ritual in Polish prisons is important for our consideration. We are more specifically interested in looking at the formal intake ritual to do with the new member's integration into the various subcultural groups. In Poland, the novice is put on trial for at least three months. This period may be adjusted downward if (1) the novice becomes popular among inmates and is accepted soon after his arrival; (2) the new member has friends in "high places" among the inmate population; (3) he is well acquainted with the customs and codes used in the subculture; (4) if he is strong, as a personality and/or physically; (5) if a composition of a given cell or area is changing and new members must be received.

Thus, they will select a novice on trial and get him assigned to their group rather than permit the administration to assign someone randomly to their group.

Thus, we maintain that the informal intake procedure is more relevant in determining the new member's status and role within the subculture. As we shall elaborate below, the informal system has more meaning for all inmate groups, than does the formal admission and orientation routine. In addition, the informal system, wherever we find it, depends on and reinforces the new member's former statuses rather than erases them. In prison, more than in juvenile corrections, a life-style of roles played out before entry is respected in terms of subcultural positioning. Very clearly, the inner stratification of Polish prisons is not produced directly by the penal structure in isolation because elements of the people-suckers system are absent among such groups as white-collar prisoners. In the United States, one finds the people-suckers subculture most clearly representative among the state-raised youth.[7]

In the subcultural categories or statuses among the younger Polish prison inmates the investigator finds some similarities with subcultural members in American prisons. For example, the *urka*, an inmate of the very highest prestige, has usually graduated from being a "git-man" in the juvenile institution. The urka is highly respected on the streets within the outside criminal milieu and receives instant acceptance within the penal subculture when he is taken in. The urka is usually from the thief culture and the American counterpart is sufficiently described in Irwin's analysis of the "regular," which includes "right guy," "good head," "solid con," "people," "folks," "all right."[8] The urka can be counted on to "deliver the goods" when called on to come to the aid of regulars. He is definitely not a "hoosier" or a "grifter" because he has more "class" and exhibits "style" and finesse in his sense of timing, his ability to "make connections," "get things done," and "con the turkey." The people form a broad mass of acceptable "persons," more or less regulars in Irwin's usage. The *cwel* appears to be the counterpart of the "mainline homosexual" in American prisons. He has no class or status, no power base, and is truly an outsider buffed about by the whim and fancy of the other members of the subculture. The clean sucker in Polish juvenile institutions resembles the relatively harmless "stoolie," "fink," or "the man's man" in American prisons. Because his talebearing is not as serious or harmful as is the "rat's" (one who informs on potential prison breaks and large "pruno" catches) he is more or less consigned to an amorphous limbo within the inmate system. When juvenile offenders grow into convicts, they learn to sort out the "rats" from the "storytellers," thus they grow away from mere symbolism and ritual toward the practical and utilitarian.

In any event, there are a number of similarities in these roles across international cultural boundaries. As we move to a consideration of the American penal structure, comparisons will become more evident.

STUDIES IN THE UNITED STATES

MacLand, Oregon, and Creston, California, are typical "schools for boys" or "schools of industry" in the Western United States. Boys have been committed to these institutions for a variety of reasons ranging from mala prohibitum acts such as repeated runaway, to criminal law violations, i.e., "armed robbery and assault, with intent to kill." In Oregon, boys are committed to MacLand by the various juvenile courts in the state, while in Creston intake is authorized by the California Youth Authority.

Stateside and Midline Oregon are maximum security, custody-oriented penal institutions.[9] In Stateside are older and more seasoned cons, along with those convicts considered dangerous. Midline, while a maximum security facility, is the "young men's prison," a facility for first offenders under 26 years of age. Although we have said that these institutions are of the maximum security, custody-oriented type, we must make clear that staff is generally committed to a treatment program.

If we modify the terminology of "men" to include "jockers," "wolves," and "daddies" and alter the term "sucker" to include "boy," "punk," "queen," and "queer," there are some remarkable similarities in the above description of Polish correctional subcultures with those in the United States.[10] However, we would note a number of rather important differences concerning the observable data, which imply that categories are not, at any level, nearly as clear-cut in American institutions as they appear to be in their Polish counterparts.

For example, the category of "not-people" or suckers appears to have strong asexual as well as sexual denotations in the Polish model. (See figure 18 and text above). One can determine the existence of asexual roles within the parallel category in American institutions. However, in terms of how these roles get acted out, it appears that there are stronger sexual "intonations," both in American prisons and juvenile institutions. Moreover, it would appear that the developmental processes are substantially reversed. That is, the importance of sexual role dimensions (highly symbolic) is most significantly noted at the juvenile level in Polish institutions and decreases in importance. It could be argued, although Irwin and others appear to believe not, that sexual roles among prisoners in American institutions are learned over time, and become more important as they become more utilitarian. Therefore, although symbolic meaning is attached to sexual roles at the juvenile level of institutionalization, role identities, in the case of individual members, take on permanent form and meaning in early adulthood. We will follow this thought below.

U.S. Juvenile Institutions

In the typical boys industrial school of 200 or more population, power-status hierarchies develop. There appear to be two types of leaders. The "brute force" leader attains his position and gathers his men around him in the usual way. He solicits favors by threats or innuendo and takes what he wants from lesser peers. Lesser peers are often forced to perform various homosexual acts, and thus are relegated to a position of low regard. It may be true that this is one very functional method for determining status.

The "Duke" figure is a very prominent member of the boy's school scene. Dukes get along best whenever the institutional structure is closed, secure, custody oriented. Surrounding the Duke is a devoted clique of "strong boys" who form the prime influential group within the unit or cottage. Duke and his strong boys determine who gets what, when, and where. The devotion of the strong boys to the Duke appears to be highly correlated with his inputs on dimensions of strength, meanness, and cunning. Lesser Dukes are always waiting on the edges of the clique, ready to assume power as the occasion permits. The strong boys

Criminology and Justice

are aggressive and domineering, set the informal rules, establish precedent, and outline "territory." The boys in the "weak group" are punished severely for not abiding by the rules laid down, not following precedent, and for infringing on territory as outlined by the Duke and his boys. Boys may start in either group and there appears to be mobility on both upward and downward dimensions. Boys fall into the weak group for (1) being "kissy" (kiss asses) and ingratiating themselves with the officials; (2) being a "fink," a "rat," or a "talebearer"; (3) getting tagged as a "messup," with connotations of being "outlaw" [11] and getting the group in trouble with the "bulls"; (4) being a chicken, or unwilling to fight or face challenges, which signifies lack of manhood to Duke and the "strong boys." The kid who becomes a "pacifist" out of principle almost certainly finds himself in limbo between the strong and the weak. A strange position indeed. He has a hard time justifying himself before the "Duke" and he is generally a cut above the "weak boys"; (5) perhaps the surest way to lose status with the Duke and his boys is to be found out "heating" on a drug score.

As with nondelinquent groups, social power is associated with a variety of talents.[12] However, the Duke and his boys maintain their position primarily from adept physical aggression. Unlike the not-people of Polish institutions, the weak boys are not—with the exception of a few obvious cases—considered innately or permanently weak. They are not suckers by definition, and challenges from those consigned to that status are forthcoming and must be met.

The second type of leader in the juvenile "joint" is the charismatic leader. He is something like the regular or "right guy" in American prison life,[13] and similar to the urka in Polish adult institutions. He holds groups in his power through their emotional attachment to him. In juvenile surroundings, however, his hold is very shaky. The charismatic leader is right guy to both the authorities and the inmates and his position is tenuous at the juvenile level for two reasons. Not only is he constantly under judgment of both peers and administrators, but the immaturity of his peers usually precludes their full acceptance of the possibility of this role. Practically speaking, the charismatic leader never seems to have the power base enjoyed by the Duke. Interestingly enough, we would assert, the positions reverse in adult prisons. The Duke's role is unambiguous at the juvenile level where issues are joined by force and power, but all Dukes are viewed as being reformatory residuals by most prison inmates. Dukes are good to have around when muscle is needed but they bring on too much heat. On the contrary, charisma has little symbolic value for youngsters and the charismatic leader is always viewed with suspicion in the juvenile institution, but he is generally seen as a right guy in prison so long as he "keeps his skirts clean," "plays it cool," and "foxes the man."

U.S. Prison Subculture

About 40 percent of the inmates in a maximum security penal institution like Stateside do not fall anywhere in the universe represented by figure 18. This is because roughly 20 percent are "gleaning."[14] That is to say, they are engrossed in bettering themselves through college programs, Great Books courses, therapy groups, etc., and another 20 percent are considered so incompetent, "fruity," crazy, or degenerate as to be out of it altogether. It should be noted that jockers and their boys, "daddies" and their "kids" are often engaged in a relatively asexual relationship, so that one couldn't gather all the relevant data pertinent to an assessment of this set of relationships merely by counting sexual actus reas, or observing fondling, arm linkage, or the like.

In American prisons the sucker category is largly undescriptive without a lot of qualification. Let us consider the subcategories in figure 18, above. The queen actually has relatively high status in many prisons even when compared with all other members of the inmate subculture. They are considered, by many inmates, to be attractive "females," in same manner as the pre-liberated woman in our society. As long as "she" retains a semblance of beauty and charm, the "queen" is highly regarded. Jockers fight over their queens—this is when the "shivs," pipes, and table legs are liable to come out of storage—and they are considered prize possessions. But, more importantly, jockers are often as completely in love as in the traditional man-woman relationship. The queen is generally always treated kindly by "her" jocker except when the losers fall out. Then, the queen will often undergo derogation by being treated as "queer." To the extent that the jocker in this relationship has power, or "squeeze" his out-queen will suffer derogation at the hands of all. Queers are disdained both in prison and on the "bricks." They are presumed to be innately inferior in the moral sense and are never accorded anything remotely resembling equal status with other members of the inmate social order. Stories are common, in prison, of "making it in every way possible" with queers. No inmate with any "class" forms a permanent alliance with a queer. They are, at best, sexual objects to be used as a last resort when a "clean young boy" or a "righteous queen" is not available.

The "mainline punk" or "commissary punk" is a label generally reserved for the young novice who is "testing his buns." Many young men are persuaded upon entry into the inmate system to assume the feminine role for survival. Not only do they benefit materially from this exchange by payment in cigarettes, they usually are offered various degrees of protection from random and relatively vicious assaults by depraved inmates. In fact, by accepting the protection from a jocker the young punk often undergoes the rite of passage and becomes a boy. Usually if a young punk doesn't soon become a protected boy, he will degenerate in status to a queer. Therefore, punks actively seek alliance with potential daddies or jockers to gain a relatively secure niche in the social structure. A young boy measures his self-worth by the esteem others have for his jocker or daddy. In a very real sense a boy is an apprentice, learning to be a convict and an effective criminal. His teacher is his jocker, and bonds of loyalty, friendship, and trust grow up between them that far supersede the sexual relationship. Boys often grow up to become jockers themselves. This graduation is epitomized in the joking relationship by such asides among the inmates as "once a smart young bottom dog, eventually a smart old top dog." At times in the American penal structure, the inmate will be boy or kid in one relationship and jocker in another, simultaneously. These relationships obtain most often in correctional institutions for young offenders where "proper" inmate behavior is being learned. This marginal status in sexuality, as evidenced by ambivalent behaviors, appears to be merely part of the nature of marginality which epitomizes the process of becoming a convict.

When the young inmate actor continues to play the role of a mainline or commissary punk, he takes on the identity of the whore. He is regarded with varying levels of disdain or approval depending on how one views the prostitute role; however, his role is strictly a utilitarian one from his own perspective. The punk "puts out" for "five packs of butts" in a straightforward commercial deal. Probably, he was sexually attacked early on in training school and learned from hard knocks that he might as well get remunerated for what others could and would take, in any event. Again the punk sometimes becomes a boy or a queen if he is attractive and intelligent enough. Often, however, he maintains his punk status because he lacks the initiative and ability to get ahead. Occasionally the punk degenerates into a queer; however, queers are seen by inmates as true degenerates who will perform any act at any time, any place, for free or not.

As a generalization from the above observations we infer that higher rates of mobility among role sets occur in the American instance. Derogation of individuals in "inferior" status categories is less prominent in American corrections subculture.

"Second lives" in correctional and treatment institutions in Poland and the United States have much in common. This finding is not surprising, as the structural and functional characteristics of these institutions are, to an extent, similar in both countries. We could argue that it is a result of criminal or antilegal subcultures, relatively independent of their social and political systems in the larger society. These similar patterns might also be caused by such common factors as isolation, closed penal systems or corrections structures, and the deprivation of heterosexual relations. However, within the context of the larger similarities, we did find a number of discrete, significant differences.

The theoretical socio-psychological interpretation of the "second life" in Polish institutions, by Adam Podgorecki seems to adequately explain some of the general rules and mores of the American peer subculture described above.[15] He concentrated his explanation on the significance of the needs of rewards in social interactions with other people as well as the needs of domination of the weak by the strong. According to his view, the pain connected with isolation in the penal milieux is fully as important for the inmate as are the psychological pains caused by the process of social determination which makes him a member of a closed social group. This frustrating situation causes aggression directed toward the representatives of the correctional institution. The obvious difficulties inherent in demonstrating overt aggression toward staff tends to use these aggressions to be transferred toward peers. But it is neither possible nor convenient to continue the aggression in a random and senseless manner—everybody against everybody. This situation causes only pain for all members of the group. It brings about a reintegration of the group divisions being ordered according to some code. In this new situation some persons get only punishments, and other people get only rewards. Some persons learn to treat others not as goals or values in themselves, but as means to achieve their own person goals or to satisfy their needs. The only possibility of satisfying the needs and aspiration of the dominant inmate group is for them to transfer their perception of other members into the status of things or objects. This occurs especially in those situations where deprivation of things (goods) occurs in a systematic way. These attempts to reintegrate the inmates' personality by depriving the others of their dignity are caused by the fear of the destruction of one's own integrity. This hypothesis is consistent with our finding in Poland: the more integrated the personality, especially among the older inmates, the weaker the structure of "the hidden, second life."

However, this appears not to be the case in American institutions for adults. It is very possible that the rules and meaning of informal structures of inmate society in Poland and the United States are quite different in the sense that in Poland they are more symbolic and connected with the valuation of the whole person (ego), while in the United States, inmate cultures seem to express to more pragmatic and practical aspects of role play among individuals. So, it appears to be understandable that, in the U.S., the older inmate, who has a highly developed practical point of view, places a higher value on the structure of roles and their distribution within the system. As an example, we shall examine the perceptual differences of homosexuality, and the different way these roles get operationalized, in Polish and American inmate subcultures.

The homosexualists are perceived and valued differently, one country to the other. In Poland, the passive partner in homosexual relationship has very low prestige; in fact he has no prestige. Under a number of circumstances the homosexual's ascribed prestige in American subculture is not low at all. For example, refer to our discussion of the queen and boy status categories above. We showed that the queen is often highly regarded and that upward mobility among the rank of the boys is not only possible, but sometimes is systematic. Therefore, it appears that homosexual prostitution is often valued in American subcultures from a pragmatic point of view, while in Poland it is a negation of honor and dignity among men which has always been very highly valued in Polish tradition. (In Poland it is always considered better to be dignified, although without money, than to be rich at the cost of honor.) So if a boy is forced by the situation to be a sexual object for other boys, he doesn't want to make the situation worse, in a moral sense, by claiming any material gratification. Most American boys, finding themselves in this situation would sooner or later rationalize: "the situation is bad, but I can benefit by it and at least try to improve my material situation."

According to Podgorecki the need of domination is one of the most distinct needs in every social group.[16] It is expressed in different ways in different social structures. In isolated peer groups where no kind of economical dependence, as well as no difference of social roles can be observed, the domination of some people over the others must be provided for by some kind of mysterious and magic signs of prestige. As outlined above, this was discovered to be the case in Polish juvenile institutions. The role of magic and ritual elements is not so obvious in the United States, neither are the various divisions so clear-cut. It may be that economic relationships and dependencies are much stronger in American institutions and are generally considered to be the more important social dimensions.

The more specific psychological interpretation was given by J. Kurczewski who described the "second life" and its rules as a function of the sexual needs of inmates which are very strong in the conditions of forced isolation, and especially among the growing boys in juvenile institutions.[17] (His analysis of their slang, customs, and magic spells indicated that the sphere of sexuality is one of the greatest importance for them.) But they know that the only normal kind of sexual relationships is the heterosexual type. So they try to avoid the feeling of guilt and abnormality by the way of self-sexuality and of sexual intercourse with persons whom they define as non-people. These individuals can be treated instrumentally without any bad feeling of humiliation or guilt. The kind of dichotomical structure in the isolated, unisexual groups is forced by the stronger and more physical younsters and is used by them as the ideal way of avoiding the moral stress caused by their participation in dirty, forbidden acts. Kurczewski's analysis has a great deal of utility in explaining the dichotomical structure of juvenile institutions in Poland. However, the acceptance of partner-like homosexual relationships on a number of levels—jocker-queen, daddy-boy, etc.—in American inmate subculture demonstrates a major point of difference and tends to lead us in the direction of a more socioeconomic analysis.

Our analysis leads us to suggest that the inmates' needs for rewards and confirmation of their own significance is very strong and natural. In everyday life people try to compete and cooperate with others on many different levels, and if they are not successful in one field they make attempts to be appreciated on other dimensions. The rewards offered to inmates by the formal structure of correctional institutions are rather scarce and not regarded as very important by most in the population. They cannot expect many significant rewards from impersonal relationships inside the informal structure because of their own external reference point as well as the lack of a high degree of positive competition among the inmates. In this situation the system of rewards grows up around the negative phenomenon of the degradation of others. The artificial hierarchy inside the isolated group supplies the need for higher status for the authors of this hierarchy. Even though the people know that their social position is low, they realize that there is a category of not-people who are much lower socially and compared to them, they can see themselves as real men. In Poland, the brutality and mysteriousness with which the people guard their position against the suckers are due to the fact that this hierarchy is the only dimension of social status available to them, and are also due, we suspect, to their perception of the lack of any essential basic validity in this hierarchy (its fully artificial character). In this kind of "negative" structure, the only source of reward lies in administering punishment to the weak, and the only possibility of achieving higher status is found in pushing down other individuals.

A macrostructural explanation of the caste-like structure of Polish juvenile institutions as compared with the class-type structure in the U.S. may have the most explanatory power. The relatively similar social and economical backgrounds of Polish offenders, together with the relatively undifferentiated social structure in Poland, with its lack of ethnic minorities, does not provide the inmates with objective criteria with which to build a highly stratified society within the institutional subculture. Therefore, they tend to develop very artificial, simple, clear-cut structural systems that are functional for satisfying their needs in isolation. These structural systems are maintained by the use of special magic and symbolic ceremonial methods of communication and domination—the strong over the weak.

The American society is, to a much higher degree, differentiated along ethnic, economic, and cultural dimensions. This differentiation appears to predict that the inmates will build their informal structures on a more rational experimental base. Thus, the society furnishes the boys with objective, socially established criteria, as well as patterns of interaction, generalized from a broader class structure. The temporary isolated community of the institution tends to reproduce the complex structure of the society outside the walls; and its character reflects the prejudices, evaluations, and stereotypes internalized earlier. Only the change in the sexual life in isolation instigates a system of substitute roles peculiar to the inmate communities, yet, not fully divorced from the broader societal patterns (such as the use of female names to indicate role).

In this context we can better understand those significant differences in stratification within inmate subcultures in the two countries. In the Polish case, inmate subcultures manifest an artificial symbolism relatively divorced from the larger social order. However, in the adult case, the broader life experiences and a higher ethical referent contribute to a diminishing of the symbolic structure and lead to a lessened intensity of the dichotomous, sexually oriented, inmate social structure.

In the American case, it appears that the incrementing significance of rational and pragmatic attitudes and behaviors, consistent with individual maturation, tend to develop within the inmate subculture a social system not highly differentiated from the larger social structure, or, at least, a system relatively undifferentiated from selected elements of the macroculture. The higher incidence of mobility between polar roles in American penal subcultures is indicative of a pragmatism relatively unknown in Polish society.

13

Crime and Delinquency Research in Selected European Countries

EUGENE DOLESCHAL

EDITOR'S COMMENT: *The statements made by Doleschal about the primary directions of European criminological research have retained their validity during the past decade. Much of the continental research on crime is still highly legalistic and concerned with the cases of individual offenders or special groups of criminals. Though increasing research has been done on such larger social problems as migration and crime, the research of most European countries continues to be quite pragmatic and not that applicable outside of the researcher's country.*

This paper reviews European research on crime and delinquency reported in the literature since 1963. The purpose of this review is to describe the current state of crime and delinquency research in Europe, to identify the topics on which research is being conducted, and to record comments and conclusions of European criminologists regarding the value of European research. Primarily, we wish to highlight the value European research may have to the American student of crime and delinquency.

Studies or descriptions of research projects in progress are examined for Austria, Belgium, Czechoslovakia, Denmark, France, East and West Germany, Italy, Poland, Sweden, Switzerland, and Yugoslavia. Because it is so progressive and so far advanced, Scandinavian criminology is discussed in a separate chapter and is not considered together with other European efforts.

It is not within the scope of this paper to evaluate research methods or results; but the findings of comparative surveys and the opinions of several European experts are noted.

The most important English language reference tool giving a comprehensive account of European crime and delinquency literature is *Abstracts of Penology and Criminology* (formerly *Excerpta Criminologica*), published by the Criminologica Foundation in Amsterdam, Holland, since 1960. The journal offers a virtually complete inventory of all significant research and general criminological literature published throughout Europe. Abstracts are arranged in major subject categories and subdivided into smaller classes of subjects. An annual cumulative subject and author index and serials guide make this abstracting service one of the world's best.

Current (i.e., ongoing and not completed) criminological research projects in member states of the Council of Europe are periodically reported and published by the European Committee on Crime Problems in Strasbourg, France, under the title *International Exchange of Information on Current Criminological Research Projects in Member States*. Arranged by country, the projects are cross-indexed by type of research project, and a progress report on previously reported projects is given in each issue.

Periodically, the European Committee on Crime Problems calls a conference of European directors of criminological research institutes and publishes the proceedings of these meetings. The documents constitute comprehensive reference tools for all subjects in the field of crime which occupy European researchers, often providing previously unpublished bibliographies on certain subjects. Reviews of research or of program activities and reviews of the current state of criminology or correction in member states are the committee's main contributions to the literature.

Reports of some of the more significant research studies conducted by Scandinavian criminologists are currently being translated under the auspices of the Scandinavian Research Council for Criminology and published by Tavistock Publications, London. Two volumes have already appeared, and a third volume, scheduled for publication in late 1970, presents a general discussion of Scandinavian criminological research by Nils Christie, Director of the Institute of Criminology of Oslo, Norway, and updates an earlier review published in 1965 in the *International Review of Criminal Policy* (no. 23).

COMPARISON OF AMERICAN AND EUROPEAN RESEARCH METHODS

In the United States a typical research project in crime and delinquency employs a rigid research design to discover new data, demonstrate a specific fact, or test a general hypothesis. The emphasis is on a methodology whereby subjects are exposed to a particular treatment in a systematic way in order to ascertain the effects of that treatment. Ideally, the procedure involves two or more randomly selected groups of subjects, only one of which receives the treatment under inquiry. Thus, a before-after measurement of both the experimental group and the control group is available, and the data are subjected to comparative statistical analysis.

Studies of this type are rare in European research, outside of the Scandinavian countries. A 1967 listing of European projects submitted to and reported by the Council of Europe in Strasbourg shows only one study which conforms to the research design described above.[1] The most frequent methodology used in European projects is a descriptive analysis of all available statistics and information on a given topic; the aim of the typical European study is to give a "detailed statistical description," presenting the kind of data most frequently found in annual reports of American correctional agencies.

In reporting research in a professional journal, the American researcher typically states the purpose of his study, the hypotheses tested, the methodology followed, and the characteristics of the population studies; he will then devote the bulk of this report to findings and conclusions. In the conclusions he will establish which findings are statistically significant and which are not; ultimately, he will attempt to interpret the findings, discuss various interpretation possibilities, and state whether the hypotheses were proved or disproved.

The European researcher, on the other hand, is likely to examine the historical background of the problem being studied or to review past literature on the subject. Thus a study of female thieves is introduced by a general description of the female body and its biological processes, character peculiarities of women, and female behavior characteristics.[2]

The European researcher may examine all available statistical data from various vantage points, without utilizing sociometric instruments (such as Minnesota Multiphasic Personality Inventory, California Personality Inventory, etc.). A European study is rarely designed to yield findings of statistical significance. Conclusions and recommendations are more likely to be arrived at by reason, logic, or speculation.

Europeans on European Research

A 1963 survey conducted by the Council of Europe regarding the effectiveness of delinquency prevention programs in European countries found that no rigorously scientific evaluative research had been or was being undertaken.[3] Nils Christie, in a 1966 review of major research in delinquency prevention in Europe, states flatly that "no major study which fulfills any minimum standard of sophistication has hitherto been published."[4]

Experts who review their own countries' research efforts echo the Council of Europe's findings. A German criminologist, in comparing the status of criminology in Germany with that of the United States, concludes that criminology in Germany is a maze of opinions, programs, and speculative points of view rather than a dynamically developing science. He finds that it is possible to critically examine specific questions in American criminology whereas German criminology is still preoccupied with fundamentals.[5]

Another criminologist charges that dilettantism has taken the place of true scholarship. He argues that pure statistical observations, which constitute the majority of European studies, are not enough and that the criminologist must be prepared to evaluate his data and find the significant conclusions contained therein.[6]

Certain European criminologists prefer to subdivide criminology into sociological and clinical criminology.[7] While conceding that there is indeed a wide gap between what has been achieved by American sociological criminology and what has been achieved in Europe, they believe that European criminology can look back on substantial achievements in the study of the biological, medical, and psycho-dynamic components of crime and call for the integration of the two major criminological approaches.[8]

Another German author believes that if the fight against crime is to become more effective, all persons in the field must have special training which will take into careful account the research of foreign countries, especially the United States. German criminology, he believes, will have to intensify its efforts and make more contributions to empirical research. Centrally coordinated, systematic research efforts will have to be made to equal the quality of research abroad.[9]

In 1969, Franco Ferracutti, one of Italy's best-known criminologists, coauthored a survey on all monographs and articles published in standard Italian criminological journals from 1965 to early 1969. In all, 560 articles were examined and classified by subject and type of article. The vast majority of published articles was found to have been concerned with general criminology (379, or 68 percent); 24 percent were general discussions without a well-defined subject; 29 percent were concerned with juvenile delinquency; 36 percent with treatment and correctional systems; 42 percent were interdisciplinary studies or discussions; 11 percent were classified as psychiatric; 11 percent as psychological and 7 percent as sociological; 11 percent were concerned with the causes of crime and delinquency; 10 percent with criminal phenomenology; 9 percent with diagnosis and classification; and 6 percent were case studies. The most infrequent articles concerned research methodology (2 percent), articles describing action programs (1 percent), and cross-cultural studies (0.5 percent).

The authors found the scarcity of sociological and cross-cultural studies particularly deplorable and emphasized the overpowering influence of the psychological, psychiatric, medical, and legal disciplines on Italian criminology. They explained that Italian criminology had come to a standstill during a quarter of a century of fascism and did not begin to develop again until after the end of World War II.[10]

Gerhard Mueller, in a 1969 article reviewing criminological research internationally, found that only the U.S., Canada, and some of the nations of Western Europe (but not Germany and France), currently offer any significant training for research and research-oriented personnel in criminal justice.[11]

The Scandinavian countries have been able to achieve close coordination of their research efforts, and in 1961 established the Scandinavian Research Council for that purpose. Continent-wide coordination, as opposed to national cooperation, appears impossible at the present time. This fact is brought out in a report to the United Nations, authored by the Council of Europe.[12]

While some criminologists appear impatient with the Europeans' preoccupation with fundamentals, others insist that the first step in any research effort should be one of reflection and formulation of a theoretical basis upon which to approach the topic.[13] Some contend that the behavioral sciences have failed to explain the causes of crime and delinquency; they are distrustful of statistical methods, and suggest that the current chaos in criminology can be overcome only with the help of sound philosophical reflection.[14]

The preference for a more traditional approach is also voiced by an Italian writer who, in commenting on the reinstitution of the teaching of criminal anthropology at the University of Turin, concludes that, with certain modifications, the "illustrious tradition and theory of Cesare Lombroso is still valid today."[15]

That prominent theorists of past centuries continue to be regarded as basic to criminological research is evidenced by the large number of articles about them which continue to appear in European crime and delinquency literature. The implications of articles discussing such pioneers as the Italians Cesare Beccaria and Cesare Lombroso, the German Franz von List, and the Frenchman Gabriel Tarde are that the old writers still have a lot to teach us and that their theories should be reexamined.

A good example of this type of article is a French study of Tarde's methodology (originally published in 1886). Although the author concedes that Tarde solved few problems and offered premature conclusions, he nevertheless believes that Tarde's theories have not lost their relevance.[16]

TYPES OF RESEARCH

The comments of European criminologists indicate some of the weaknesses and strengths of European crime and delinquency research. With few, but notable, exceptions the student of crime and delinquency should not expect to find, in European research, controlled and experimental studies using rigid designs and sociometric methods.

When historical, theoretical, or doctrinal reference is sought, the serious student cannot afford to ignore such European crime and delinquency writings as a study of Beccaria's treatise on crime and punishment[17] or a study of opinion on the death penalty during the Age of Englightenment.[18] Nor can he afford to ignore the many studies analyzing the effects of a particular law and which may have implications for contemplated legislation in the United States. This may be a study of a new law using psychological tests of maturity for offenders 18 to 20 years old to determine whether they should be handled in juvenile or adult court;[19] or it may be a major project examining the administration of justice in an entire country.[20]

For a study of crime in Europe the student must turn to European literature. For example, he must refer to a French study when attempting to examine crime trends in France,[21] when looking for a survey of the public image and the self-image of the French police officer,[22] when attempting to compare the characteristics of American juvenile auto thieves with their French counterparts,[23] or when attempting to study the causes of juvenile delinquency in France.[24]

Thus, the student will find studies of crime patterns among foreign workers in West Germany[25] or Switzerland,[26] a one-of-its-kind study of the impact of communism on the crime patterns of a Polish town,[27] an attempt to replicate Leslie Wilkins' delinquent generations study with Polish children,[28] a study of the attitudes of Italian delinquents toward courts and justice,[29] or the crime patterns of rural migrants to the big cities of Italy.[30]

For a study of the role of the expert witness in court, the student of crime and delinquency may turn to a European study describing the current status of the expert witness and, in addition, tracing this tradition from Greek to Roman times.[31]

Because of the considerable achievements of European countries in biology, medicine, and psychiatry, it is not surprising that many of these methods and concepts have spilled over into "clinical criminology." Europe's long tradition in clinical criminology continues to be reflected in the literature; because Europe's clinical and diagnostic research is second to none, it should be regarded as a rich resource.

The European clinician's preference, however, seems to be for the study of the rare and unusual. Thus, an unexpectedly large number of studies are found on unusual types of offenders who form but a tiny fraction of the total offender population. For example, not only are several studies of arsonists reported in the European literature each year, but special subtypes of this class of offender are studied separately, e.g., only arsonists who committed a series of arsons[32] or only those whose motives were of a sexual nature.[33]

While studies of suicide abound in America, studies of "extended suicides," i.e., the killing of dependent children followed by suicide, are quite rare. A European study will carry the subdivision even further by studying only those cases of extended suicide in which the parent succeeds in killing his children but fails in the attempt to kill himself.[34]

A random selection of these types of studies will give the reader a general idea of the wealth of material that exists on the rare class of offender, on unusual treatments, and on the unusual crime cause or motivation.

"Possibilities of suicide prevention," an interesting study of the pre-suicidal syndrome, from an Austrian psychiatric clinic, found that the syndrome displays the following characteristics: (1) a progressive narrowing of the patient's life, in which depression leads to monotonous experiences, uniformly negative; (2) inhibited aggression in which the act directed against the self is also motivated by feelings of aggression toward specific persons in the patient's environment, and as such may be regarded as prevented homicide; (3) suicidal fantasies and thoughts leading to an ever increasing preoccupation with suicide.[35]

The findings of a Belgian study, "The role of leisure in the etiology of juvenile delinquency," which show that the role of increased leisure in juvenile delinquency is inseparable from problems of education, mental hygiene, and social integration, casts doubt over the simply restrictive measures that are sometimes used to combat delinquency.[36] In Brussels, "A study of suicide by children and adolescents" was made using court records for factual data, and psychiatric hospital cases for in-depth study.[37] It was also discovered in Belgium, in "A study of families who have lost parental rights due to court contact," that the assistance of a social worker prior to court contact was of major assistance in enabling a family to retain parental rights.[38] A Belgian study, entitled "Criminological aspects of installment buying," examined fraud, embezzlement, breach of confidence, and usury in installment buying and attempted to identify a typology of offenders, both buyers and sellers. The statistics were gathered in an effort to provide the basis for a social policy on such buying.[39]

A Danish study on "Un-operated phimosis and its possible relation to sexual deviation and sexual criminality" indicates that patients with this disease were overrepresented in a group of sex offenders and that the blockage, from phimosis, of a normal sexual outlet might have been a contributing cause of sexual aberration.[40] "Some investigations on the effects of pornographic pictures" have been undertaken in Denmark, using materials confiscated in an institution for sex offenders to determine if there are differences in these materials. So far, clinical work with sex offenders has indicated that these persons are strikingly uninterested in the usual heterosexual pornographic pictures and that even in sexually normal persons the range of interest is limited.[41]

A French study, "Criminogenic cerebral injuries," indicates that the connection between brain damage and criminal conduct depends on the seriousness of the cerebral defect, the area of the brain affected, and the personality and value concepts of the person affected.[42] A "Comparative study of psycho-motivity with the aid of a battery of instrumental tests applied to a population of delinquents, a population of mentally ill, and a population of normals" showed that the psycho-motivity of the delinquent group was inferior to the normal group, but superior to the pathological group.[43] Another French study, "The false problem of simulation or the theatrical relation," has pointed out the distinction between hysterical and simulated illnesses in the prison setting; simulated illnesses are a symptom of the general transformation of human relations under the impact of prison life.[44]

In a French study, "Painting studio in an observation center for juvenile delinquents—Study of the theme: 'A family surprised by a thunderstorm in the forest,'" the choice of colors and symbols was found to be related to different types of emotional disturbance and to seriousness of delinquent acts.[45]

In a study of the characteristics of the populations involved in 31 cases of group rape in Paris, "Sociological aspect of group rape," the age curve of the offenders indicated one age peak at 19 years, and two peaks at 14 and 17 years. The victims came from broken homes far more often than the defendants.[46] In "Residential overcrowding and criminality," statistics on population density and overcrowding in Paris were correlated with those on criminality, revealing that there is no apparent relationship between density of population and criminality, but that there is a clear correlation between overcrowded housing and criminality.[47]

A study entitled "Illegal acquisition of state subsidies" involved a search of court records to determine the causes and extent of abuses and embezzlement of government farm subsidies in Germany. The kinds of sentences given by the courts were noted.[48] A German legal study on "Borderline secret societies" examines those provisions of the West German Draft Code of 1962 that govern political offenses, particularly treason. The most important innovation in the code is that a person, in order to be subject to punishment, must have willfully or knowingly endeavored to overthrow the government, and not simply have held membership in an association whose existence, purpose, or constitution is kept secret from state authorities.[49]

"Fines in the future criminal code" proposes for Germany, which already uses fines for many penal sanctions, a system of day-fines based on the following formula: the offender's daily net income, minus the amount needed for daily necessities (already determined by the Federal Social Aid Law), equals the amount of the day-fine.[50]

In another article from Germany, two cases of "Homicide due to 'hate-love'" are described.[51] "A study of group sex offenses by juveniles in Germany" is a detailed investigation of group rape.[52] Also under way is a "Study of the problems which arise when a parent is in prison."[53] In "Homosexuality and suicide" it was found that the percentage of homosexuals who are seriously considering suicide is far greater than among the general population. Group therapy with suicidal homosexuals sought to create in them an understanding of their inner conflicts and an insight into their problems and the causes of their suicidal tendencies.[54] German studies over a 27-year period in *Personality Change in Detention: The Effects of Penalties and Measures* indicated that there is an urgent need for expertly trained correctional staff and appropriate treatment of offenders in order to initiate positive developmental processes in the inmates.[55]

One German study, "Personality changes in the sex offender," focused on the effects of imprisonment on homosexuals, and found that imprisonment had no noticeable effect on personality.[56] "Changes in the subconscious; the dream world of the prisoner" reports that inmates' dreams about the criminal offenses are rare, and that the injury to the prisoner as a social person was felt by him more intensely than guilt about the violation of ethical norms.[57] "The flamethrower attack in Cologne-Volkhoven" is the case of a paranoiac man who committed multiple homicides with a flamethrower; the study found no concrete reason for the act.[58] In *The Killing of the Intimate Partner*, a study which used representative case material, it was found that the killer of a lover is normally in a position of dependence and submissiveness; the killer of a marriage partner has many of the same characteristics as the killer of a lover and may see himself as isolated from and confronted with a united front of family, friends, and neighbors; the killer of a casual partner, however, is usually provoked, and his efforts to escape an embarrassing situation may result in the homicide.[59] Another interesting German study describes "Murder weapons in homosexual situations," used by males against their homosexual partners.[60]

Although it has been hypothesized that there was a decline in Nazi Germany, "Significant decrease of juvenile delinquency prior to World War II?" shows that the statistical decline of juvenile adjudications between 1933 and 1945 was due to a policy of prosecution suspensions, and that the concept of juvenile delinquency during the period 1933–1945 was entirely different from the one prevailing during civilized times.[61] The case of the killing of a woman by her brother-in-law is examined in "Murder in revenge."[62] Three cases are examined in a study entitled "Suicides by means of rectal application of soporifics."[63]

"Political offenders," an eight-year study of 200 persons who committed treason, found that almost all of them were from lower- to middle-class families, and 50 percent were motivated by financial reasons. Of 300 persons who committed other offenses against the country's safety, most were from lower-class backgrounds, 93 percent were communists, and 75 percent had acted out of conviction.[64]

"A case of the crime of passion in Italy" studied a 37-year-old southern Italian woman who murdered her young lover. Findings were that the murder was justified in her own mind by the system of values and morality prevailing in her region. This finding was corroborated in a comparison between Japanese and Italian crimes of passion, where it was noted that the Japanese woman, who from ancient times has been instructed to be obedient to her husband or lover and not to take revenge for offended honor, usually chooses suicide over the killing of the lover.[65]

"Moral perception in a study of prison inmates," using 116 non-psychopathic offenders in various Italian institutions, gained information on the guilt feelings of various categories of offenders. Those guilty of taking a human life had a precise concept of the seriousness of their offense, but considered that they had acted with just reason; individuals committed for minor offenses deemed their punishment to be just and deserved.[66] Another Italian study, "The dynamics of aggressiveness in a group of offenders," measured the effects of a motion picture (Mondo Cane) on aggressive tendencies of murderers. It was found that reactions depend upon the kind of emotional participation of each subject to the picture—hostility increases if the subject's participation shows no external manifestations, and decreases if it does.[67]

A Yugoslavian study, "Prefrontal leucotomy in delinquents who are habitual swallowers of metal objects," showed that the leucotomies in the three cases studied corrected this habit and improved the patients' personalities without harmful aftereffects.[68]

Developments Since 1969

The latest edition of the Council of Europe's listing of current research projects shows a trend toward more sociological studies and the employment of more sophisticated methodology.[69] However, the bulk of the studies are still classified as psychological, psychiatric, socio-psychological, or "descriptive analysis." The type of studies in demand by American students of crime (controlled, follow-up studies, and those examining the effectiveness of treatments) are still scarce, and most of these are Scandinavian.

An example of a project that promises to supply useful data to American researchers is a Swedish follow-up study which will investigate and attempt to determine which characteristics best equip youthful offenders to acquire vocational skills in correctional institutions and to what extent youngsters are carrying on corresponding trades in the free community. American longitudinal studies of the effectiveness of vocational training have invariably produced negative results in respect to the rehabilitative value of vocational training as well as the ability of ex-offenders to market the skills learned in the institution.

Swedish correctional institutions are providing vocational training closely corresponding to actual skills required in the labor market; they enjoy the support of employers and unions; and the acceptance of the ex-offender by the general public is reputed to be one of the most favorable in the world.

In spite of the trend toward sociological studies, the attraction of European researchers to the clinical approach and the more exotic aspects of crime remains undiminished. Such subjects as the XYY syndrome,[70] the personality development of castrated sex offenders,[71] group rape,[72] homicide during latent schizophrenia,[73] or the effect of brain damage on crime[74] continue to abound in the criminological literature of Europe.

A valuable, although informal, survey from Germany in 1969 concerns the attitudes of probation officers toward the supervision of probationers of the opposite sex. The insights gained from this poll have relevance to probation management and the recent emphasis on matching officers with offenders for maximum effectiveness.[75]

A study of interest to students of juvenile criminal gangs is reported in an East German journal which notes that part of the code of the typical East German gang is the wearing of "Western clothes," a preference for "beat culture," and an ideological rejection of the East German Democratic Republic.[76] Rehabilitative efforts toward conformity to socially acceptable norms are different indeed in that country.

This review of studies in crime and delinquency in the countries mentioned above, and of comments by European criminologists, has shown that, by their own admission (with the exception of studies in the

Netherlands and Scandinavia), researchers are behind their American colleagues in the use of rigorous scientific methods. The strength of research in those countries lies in clinical, legal, and historical studies. Crime and delinquency literature there is a rich resource of materials on the rare or unusual type of offender, the unusual crime cause or motivation, and unusual offender treatment.

The Netherlands

One noteworthy exception to the generally unsatisfactory state of criminology in Europe is research in the Netherlands, a country with a long tradition in criminology. An English language article by G. Mueller presents a brief review of some of the more prominent Dutch studies and their implications and influence on American research.[77] Mueller describes important research studies on perjury, criminal abuse of credit, and experimental studies attempting to evaluate the effectiveness of correctional camps for juveniles in comparison to traditional institutions. An interesting theory emerging from the "Utrecht School" of criminology is the idea of "shell formation" in the recidivist: each new contact with the police, the courts, and the correctional agency leads to a hardening of this shell, resulting in ever increasing isolation of the offender from society. At the "Leiden School" of criminology it is argued that the time has come to look into the shell formation in the criminal law (that is, its relative invulnerability to change) and into the attitudes of legislators and the public which they represent.[78] The Leiden School has thus joined the new trend in emphasizing the role played by society in the study of crime.

Scandinavia

While American criminology is viewed as being almost completely sociological in approach and continental European criminology as being primarily legal and medical in its outlook, Scandinavian criminology practices an interdisciplinary approach.

Trends in research in Scandinavian countries parallel, in many ways, recent trends in the United States, and methodological capabilities of the Scandinavians are second to none in sophistication, skill in execution, and boldness. Scandinavian researchers have become weary of dead-end research and have discarded research approaches when they were found to be fruitless. Scandinavians are addressing themselves to frontier issues in criminology.

It is now common knowledge among most students of crime that the officially designated criminal is the final product of a long process of selection. Based on this recognition, Scandinavian research in the 1960s has shifted its focus from the study of the causes of crime (and statistical descriptions of crime and criminals) to crime control systems. A great deal of criminological data has been usefully applied for the latter purpose.

Nils Christie, perhaps the best known of Scandinavia's criminologists, believes that the lawbreaker must be seen and considered in relation to the total social structure.[79] Christie relates that Denmark, Norway, Finland, and Sweden have made long, serious attempts to coordinate their criminal statistics. In spite of their cultural, linguistic, and administrative similarities, these attempts have had very little success; subtle differences in the criminal selection process of each country, in attitudes of law enforcement agents, and a multitude of additional factors were found to result in final statistical products that could not be usefully compared among countries.

Even though their criminal statistics are regarded as the finest in the world, Scandinavian researchers tend to distrust them because they are viewed more as a process of social selection than an actual indicator of crime and criminals. In Scandinavia, the criminologist himself assumes the work of criminal registration and generates the raw data for his study. Research is based on self-reports and other similar techniques which are well suited for acquiring elementary data on the prevalence of specific types of behavior. In comparative research, the most promising techniques are viewed by the Scandinavians to be those which are limited to narrowly defined social systems, such as schools and correctional institutions, which can be studied in their totality.[80]

Studies of offender characteristics, offense categories, or psychiatric or psychological studies of the causes of crime, so predominant in continental research, have been severely criticized by the Scandinavians. They argue that studies of this type produce meager results that are of little value for decision-making in the criminal justice system.

Inkeri Anttila, director of the Institute of Criminology of Helsinki, Finland, states unequivocally that the entire concept of the cause of crime is obsolete: "As a matter of fact, the whole concept of the causes of crime should be abandoned if one accepts the sociological view of crime as a necessary and indispensable element of any viable society."[81]

Patrick Törnudd, one of Scandinavia's foremost criminologists, calls the search for causes of crime the dead end of criminology because it approaches the question of crime the way medical science would investigate the causes of disease. He considers this method inappropriate and inapplicable to criminology. It ignores, Tornudd argues, the decisive part played by society and social values in defining the nature of criminal behavior, in identifying criminals, in selecting those that will be punished, and in deciding the severity of that punishment.[82]

As society becomes more and more complex, Tornudd believes, the variety of value judgments will multiply, and more and more behavior will be identified as criminal. Research, therefore, should stop searching for causes and concentrate on (1) changes in the trends of crime, and (2) the selection process by which various acts are labeled criminal and various individuals singled out as criminals to be punished. In this way, criminological research can be made more practical by addressing itself to the prevailing social attitudes that define criminal behavior.

Research of this nature is in full swing throughout the Scandinavian countries and, in spite of the substantial cultural and social differences, many essential findings conform to those of parallel studies in the United States.

A 1955 study of white-collar offenders known to police in Helsinki examined the relationship of the socioeconomic status of the suspect on the decisions of the police, the prosecutor, and the judge.[83] Like many American studies on this relationship the study found, not surprisingly, that persons belonging to the higher socioeconomic group had significantly greater chances of having their cases adjusted informally by the police, of not being subjected to prosecution even if referred to the courts, and of not being sentenced. Only 26 percent of the higher socioeconomic group went through the entire judicial procedure to the final stage of sentencing. As interpreted by the researcher, results showed that upper-class persons have more experienced and skillful defense attorneys and that prosecutors and judges, themselves belonging to the higher social strata, can more easily identify with defendants from the same social strata. In spite of the differences between Finnish and American society, and in spite of the complicating problem of racial prejudice in the United States, these results have a familiar ring to students of American crime and delinquency and identify social status as one of the prime variables in the selection of the criminal.

Through a combination of favorable circumstances, Scandinavian researchers are in the enviable position of seeing many of their findings and recommendations translated into their nation's criminal policy. In the United States the voice of the researcher may be heard in the legislature like that of any other citizen, but important legislation is rarely based on criminological findings. More often than not, it is the result of a clamor for harsher penalties. Capital punishment serves as a good example. While it was widely known by the late 1940s and 1950s that capital punishment does not serve as a deterrent to murder, the death penalty continues to linger on in the majority of state criminal codes and continues to be defended on the grounds of the deterrence fallacy. In Scandinavian countries, as in most of Europe, capital punishment was abolished shortly after World War II, and the issue has been a closed one since. The United Kingdom stands out as the lone exception, having finally abolished capital punishment only recently.

A classic example of a direct application of research findings to criminal policy can be seen in a large-scale Finnish experiment with alcoholic offenders.[84] Six medium-sized Finnish towns were used in this comparative study; intoxicated persons continued to be arrested, but the average prosecution percentage was reduced from 40–50 percent to 9–24 percent of all arrests. A comparison of drunkenness arrests in the three experimental towns and the three control towns showed no differences over a three-year period. The risk of arrest and the risk of a fine were used to measure the preventive effect on the individual offender. The risk of the fine was found to have a negligible effect.

Up to the time of the experiment, 15 to 20 percent of Finland's prison inmates had been imprisoned because of failure to pay fines for public intoxication. They were a great burden to the police, the criminal courts, and the correctional system. On the basis of the experiment the researcher recommended that fines for drunkenness be abolished and the public drunk no longer treated as a criminal. The study was completed in 1967, and less than two years later the recommendations were put into effect. Finland thereby became the first country to have diverted the public drunk out of the criminal justice system.[85]

Substantial interest in the issue of unknown or unrecorded crime is evident in many Scandinavian studies. This research was inspired by Norwegian criminologists and has been useful for decision-making in criminal policy. The realization that only a small percentage of crimes lead to detection and punishment has increased concern for equality before the law and "equality within the law" and has stimulated efforts to repeal sanctions against certain acts which are not viewed as crimes by a major segment of the population.[86]

A number of studies have directly attempted to analyze the public sense of justice. In a recent study a representative sample of the Finnish population was asked to indicate the proper punishment in 11 test cases and the results were compared with the corresponding answers of trial judges.[87] The variance among the judges was quite large although it was only one-fifth to one-tenth the variance among the general population. Other studies have attempted to measure the development of the sense of justice among children and the perception of equality within the legal system.[88]

Several recent criminological projects in Scandinavia have dealt with cost-effectiveness and the relationship between the systems of social control and recidivism. A comparison of open penal institutions (so-called labor colonies without walls or guards, in which inmates receive labor market wages) with traditional prisons has shown that recidivism among the populations of the two types of institutions was about the same. As prisons are more expensive and discipline-oriented, the re-searcher recommended that open institutions be used more extensively.[89]

An investigation of the effect of a Finnish law increasing penalties for automobile theft was concluded in 1969 and is another example of Scandinavian attempts to examine and manipulate penalties for preventive purposes. This particular study was inconclusive in that it was not possible to determine the deterrent effect of increased penalties on the incidence of automobile theft. It was observed that the new law had a definite effect on the crime of automobile theft, but the researchers were unable to state with certainty whether the impact was temporary, whether it should be attributed to the harsher penalty, the increased use of pretrial detention, or the publicity accompanying the law.[90]

The phenomenon of secondary effects of legal punishments has also been the object of much interest. It was realized that very little is known about the loss of employment, expulsion from school, and disruption of family life and career caused by arrest and conviction.

The uses of the official records of crime are the subject of a study in Finland expected to be completed shortly.[91]

While many of these examples of research were conducted by institutes of criminology attached to universities or (in Finland) part of the Ministry of Justice, other research is done by or on behalf of national correction departments and is designed to help provide solutions to immediate problems in correction. During one fiscal year the Correctional Administration of Sweden reports having conducted several psychological studies on inmates in Swedish institutions. Among the findings was the discovery of no important differences between the general intelligence of inmates and that of a corresponding group of civilians. A study of narcotics offenders in Swedish institutions found that one of the basic differences between Swedish addicts and nonaddicts was the addicts' dissatisfaction with their social relationships. A study of escapees found a correlation between youth and long imprisonment, and a strong predisposition to escape. Several experiments in treatment were initiated: a program of three-week vacations for long-term inmates, with no obligation to work and with the possibility of the company of a close friend or relative, had very good results and will probably become a permanent part of Swedish corrections. A far-reaching effort to preserve family ties was the subject of an experiment in another institution in which accommodations were made available to long-term inmates and their families. These experiments are expected to stimulate forms of correctional treatment radically different from traditional ones.[92]

The trend toward increasingly more humanitarian correctional treatment, toward diversion of certain offenders out of the criminal justice system, and the diversion of others from a more drastic type of punishment to a more libertarian alternative is unmistakable throughout Scandinavia. At the same time it is also evident that there is an increased skepticism toward all kinds of "treatment," and institutional treatment in particular, among many Scandinavian criminologists. A heightened awareness of the human and civil rights of the individual has led to the recognition of the fact that the mere labeling of a measure as "treatment" or therapy does not make it more humane than labeling it "punishment."[93] One of the questions that Scandinavian research is asking is to what extent prison penalties can be replaced by penalties merely affecting the standard of living.

The goal of the new criminology, according to one Scandinavian criminologist, should be to discover methods by which society can lessen the cost and the suffering brought about by crime and the effort to control crime. The problems relevant to Scandinavian criminologists today are how this cost can be reduced by changing the criminal law, by changing the behavior of the agents of the law, and by educating the public sense of justice.[94]

NOTES
SOURCES OF ARTICLES
INDEX

NOTES

INTRODUCTION

1. Wolf Middendorf, "The Case of August Sangret," *International Annals of Criminology* 12 (1973): 61.

2. John C. Meyer, Jr., "Methodological Issues in Comparative Criminal Justice Research," *Criminology* 10 (1972): 298.

3. Josine Junger-Tas, "Some Issues and Problems in Cross-Cultural Research in Criminology," (Paper presented at the American Society of Criminology, Dallas, Texas, November 1978), p. 2.

4. See as examples, Hermann Mannheim, *Comparative Criminology* (London: Routledge & Kegan Paul, 1965), vols. 1 and 2; essays in Dae H. Chang, ed., *Criminology: A Cross-Cultural Perspective* (Durham, North Carolina: Carolina Academic Press, 1975); and Lois B. De Fleur, "Delinquent Gangs in Cross-Cultural Perspective: The Case of Cordoba," *Journal of Research in Crime and Delinquency* 4 (1967): 132–41.

5. Paul C. Friday, "Problems in Comparative Criminology: Comments on the Feasibility and Implications of Research," *International Journal of Criminology and Penology* 1 (1973): 153.

6. Ibid., pp. 152–53.

7. Marvin E. Wolfgang, "International Criminal Statistics: A Proposal," *Journal of Criminal Law and Criminology* 58 (1967): 65.

8. Friday, p. 156.

9. Wolfgang, p. 65.

10. Ibid.

11. Ted Robert Gurr, *Rogues, Rebels and Reformers:A Political History of Urban Crime and Conflict* (Beverly Hills, Calif.: Sage, 1976); and Ted Robert Gurr, Peter N. Grabosky, and Robert C. Hula, *The Politics of Crime and Conflict: A Comparative History of Four Cities* (Beverly Hills, Calif.: Sage, 1977).

CHAPTER I. AMERICAN WOMEN AND CRIME

1. Lady Barbara Wooten, "A Magistrate in Search of the Causes of Crime," *Crime and the Criminal Law* (1963): 6–8.

2. Rose Giallombardo, *Society of Women: A Study of a Women's Prison* (New York: John Wiley, 1966), p. 7.

3. Sheldon Glueck and Eleanor Glueck, *Five Hundred Delinquent Women* (New York: Knopf, 1934), p. 96.

4. Daniel A. Green, "The Dark Side of Women's Liberation: Crime Takes a Female Turn," *National Observer* (September 1974):2.

5. Ibid.

6. For a more detailed discussion of how the indeterminate sentence is applied

to women, see Linda Temen, "Discriminatory Sentencing of Women Offenders," *Criminal Law Review* 11 (Winter 1973): 355.

7. R. R. Arditi et al., "The Sexual Segregation of American Prisoners," *Yale Law Journal* 82 (November–May 1973): 1266.

8. It may appear that this discussion uses arrest statistics as proxies for describing crime rates among men and women without regard for the hazards of doing so. While the hazards are recognized, unfortunately there are no other data prior to these statistics that provide information about the characteristics of the suspect as well as the offense he or she is believed to have committed. Criminologists usually prefer to use statistics for determining crime rates that are computed on the basis of crimes known to the police, but those statistics do not identify the suspect in any way. It is also recognized that the proportions of arrests vary considerably from one type of offense to another. Arrest rates are more accurate proxies for behavior in violent types of crimes than they are for crimes against property.

9. The type II offenses referred to (embezzlement and fraud, forgery and counterfeiting, offenses against family and children, narcotic drug laws, prostitution, and organized vice) have been included because there has been a change in the arrest pattern for women or because they are offenses for which arrest rates for women are consistently high.

10. I. Murder: Any act performed with the purpose of taking human life, no matter under what circumstances. This definition excludes manslaughter and abortion, but not infanticide.

II. Sex offenses: Each country uses the definition of its own laws for determining whether or not an act is a sex crime; rape and trafficking in women are also included.

III. Larceny: Any act of intentionally and unlawfully removing property belonging to another person. This category includes such a wide variety of offenses that it was subdivided into A, Major larceny: robbery with dangerous aggravating cirumstances (for example, armed robbery, burglary, housebreaking); B, Minor larceny: all other kinds of larceny (for example, theft, receiving stolen goods)

IV. Fraud: Any act of gaining unlawful possession of another person's property other than by larceny. This category includes embezzlement, misappropriation, forgery, false pretenses, trickery, deliberate misrepresentation, swindle in general.

V. Counterfeit currency offenses: This includes any violation in connection with manufacture, issuing, altering, smuggling, or traffic in counterfeit currency.

VI. Drug offenses: This category covers any violation involving illicit manufacture of, traffic in, transportation of, and use of narcotic drugs.

11. The state of California maintains the most comprehensive crime and judicial statistics in the 50 states.

12. They obtained a 10 percent random sample of 1967 offenses and arrest reports from the following cities: Atlanta, Boston, Chicago, Cleveland, Dallas, Detroit, Los Angeles, Miami, Minneapolis, New Orleans, New York, Philadelphia, Saint Louis, San Francisco, Seattle, and Washington.

CHAPTER 2. AFFLUENCE AND ADOLESCENT CRIME

1. United Nations Secretariat, *Second United Nations Congress on the Prevention of Crime and the Treatment of Offenders* (New York: Department of Economic and Social Affairs, 1960), pp. 8–18.

2. In 1964, the number of registered automobiles in Japan was 6,775,971, about 47 times as many as were registered in 1945. The number of traffic deaths in Tokyo was 1,050, about 9.8 per 100,000 population and about 9.9 per 10,000

registered automobiles. The latter rate is much higher than for large cities in the United States. *Summary of the White Paper on Crime* (Tokyo: Training and Research Institute, Ministry of Justice, March 1966), p. 6.

3. "Crime rate" refers to the number of persons investigated by the Japanese police for a penal code violation per thousand persons of the base population.

4. *Summary of the White Paper on Crime,* 1966, p. 18.

5. The interviews were conducted in Japanese with the help of a skilled interpreter, Masahiko Kikuchi, during March and April of 1964. The opportunity to visit the training school and interview inmates was graciously provided by the Correction Bureau of the Ministry of Justice and in particular by Director Osawa, Mr. Kakuichiro Ogino, and Mr. Akira Tanigawa.

6. Children born in Israel had a delinquency rate in 1960 of 5.6 per thousand of juvenile court age. Children born in Europe or America had exactly the same rate. But children born in Asia had a delinquency rate of 11.4 per thousand in the base population and children born in Africa a rate of 17.6 per thousand. *Statistical Abstract of Israel,* 1963 (Jerusalem; Central Bureau of Statistics, 1963), p. 688.

7. The interview was conducted in Hebrew with the help of Israeli colleague, Aryeh Leissner. The opportunity to visit a reformatory and interview prisoners was graciously provided by Dr. Zvi Hermon, Scientific Director, Prison Service of Israel.

8. "Post-War Juvenile Delinquency in Sweden" (Mimeographed) (Stockholm: Department of Justice and the Swedish Institute, July 1960), p. 19.

9. Robert Wallace, "Where's the Party—Let's Crash It!" *Life* 55 (1963): 62–67.

10. "Post-War Juvenile Delinquency in Sweden," p. 20.

11. In 1965 there were 486,000 auto thefts reported in the United States, 51 percent more than in 1960 and more than double the percentage increase in automobile registrations. Sixty-two percent of the persons arrested for auto theft were under 25. *Uniform Crime Reports of the United States,* 1965 (Washington, D. C.: U. S. Government Printing Office, 1966), pp. 17–18.

12. *Post-War Juvenile Delinquency in Sweden,* p. 14.

13. This interview was conducted in English in a reception center for young offenders near Uppsala, Sweden, in 1960. In addition to studying English in school, as all Swedes do, the prisoner has been a merchant seaman and had visited English-speaking countries. The opportunity to visit a reception center and interview inmates was graciously provided by Thorsten Erikson, Director-General, Swedish National Prisons Board.

14. "Lappen" is a nickname meaning Laplander. At the age of 6, he spent six months in Lapland with his maternal grandparents when his mother was too sick to take care of him. When he returned to Stockholm, his friends noticed a trace of a Lapland accent and dubbed him "Lappen." "I liked that name because not everyone knew my real name. If someone told it to the police, they might not catch me."

15. In 1890, women constituted 15.8 percent of the white civilian labor force; in 1957, they constituted 34.1 percent. In 1890, divorced, separated, and widowed women constituted 28.6 percent of working women; in 1957, these categories constituted 40.4 percent of working women. U.S. Bureau of Census, *Historical Statistics of the United States, Colonial Times to 1957* (Washington, D. C.: U. S. Government Printing Office, 1960), p. 72.

16. In Sweden, unmarried mothers not only receive allowances for their children. They are visited regularly by social workers who attempt to give some of the guidance that a husband-father might provide. Children from broken families, nevertheless, have a higher delinquency rate than children from intact families. The supportive institution is not fully successful.

17. Mark Abrams, *The Teenage Consumer* (London: London Press Exchange, 1960).

18. Jackson Toby, "Educational Maladjustment as a Predisposing Factor in Criminal Careers: A Comparative Study of Ethnic Groups," (Ph.D. diss., Harvard University, 1950).

19. Jackson Toby, "The American College Student: A Candidate for Socialization," *American Association of University Professors Bulletin* 43 (1957): 319–22.

20. U. S. Office of Education, *Equality of Educational Opportunity* (Washington, D. C.: U. S. Government Printing Office, 1966).

21. Richard A. Cloward, "Illegitimate Means, Anomie and Deviant Behavior," *American Sociological Review* 24 (1959): 164–76.

22. Nelson Algren, "Remembering Richard Wright," *The Nation* 192 (January 28, 1961): 85.

CHAPTER 3. YOUTH CRIME IN POST-INDUSTRIAL
SOCIETIES

1. M. B. Clinard, "Urbanization and Crime," in *Criminology: A Book of Readings*, ed. C. B. Vedder (New York: Dryden, 1953): 238–46.

2. C. R. Shaw and H. D. McKay, *Juvenile Delinquency in Urban Areas* (Chicago: University of Chicago Press, 1969).

3. R. K. Merton, *Social Theory and Social Structure* (New York: Free Press, 1960).

4. W. B. Miller, "Lower Class Culture as a Generating Milieu of Gang Delinquency," *Journal of Social Issues* 14 (1958): 5–19; A. K. Cohen, *Delinquent Boys: The Culture of the Gang* (New York: Free Press, 1955).

5. Sheldon Glueck and Eleanor Glueck, *Unraveling Juvenile Delinquency* (New York: Commonwealth Fund, 1950).

6. F. Thrasher, *The Gang* (Chicago: University of Chicago Press, 1936); L. Yablonsky, *The Violent Gang* (New York: Macmillan, 1962).

7. E. H. Sutherland and D. R. Cressey, *Criminology* (Philadelphia: J. P. Lippincott, 1974).

8. D. Matza, *Delinquency and Drift* (New York: John Wiley, 1964).

9. S. Briar and I. Piliavin, "Delinquency, Situational Inducements, and Commitment to Conformity," *Social Problems* 13 (1965): 35–45; T. Hirschi, *Causes of Delinquency*, (Berkeley: University of California Press, 1969).

10. W. Reckless et al. "The Good Boy in a High Delinquency Area," *Journal of Criminal Law and Criminology* 48 (1957): 18–25.

11. Hirschi.

12. G. Marwell and J. Hage, "The Organization of Role Relationships: A Systematic Description," *American Sociological Review* 35 (1970): 884–900.

13. D. Bell, *The Coming of Post-Industrial Society: A Venture in Social Forecasting* (New York: Basic Books, 1973).

14. H. A. Bloch and A. Niederhoffer, *The Gang: A Study of Adolescent Behavior* (New York: Philosophical Library, 1958).

15. D. Downes, *The Delinquent Solution* (New York: Free Press, 1966), p. 263.

16. W. Wattenberg, "Review of Trends," in *Social Deviancy Among Youth*, ed. W. Wattenberg (Chicago: University of Chicago Press, 1966), p. 9.

17. D. Glaser, *Adult Crime and Social Policy* (Englewood Cliffs, N.J.: Prentice Hall, 1972), p. 9.

18. J. Coleman, *Adolescent Society* (New York: Free Press, 1961), p. 3.

19. E. Z. Friedenberg, *The Vanishing Adolescent* (New York: Dell, 1959), p. 9.

20. Paul C. Friday, "Differential Opportunity and Differential Association in Sweden: a Study of Youth Crime," (Ph.D. diss., University of Wisconsin, 1970).

21. Hirschi.

22. Sutherland and Cressey.

23. Friday.

24. M. J. Hindelang, "Causes of Delinquency: A Partial Replication and Extension," *Social Problems* 20 (1973): 471–87.

25. Reckless et al.

26. G. Homans, *The Human Group* (New York: Harcourt Brace, 1950).

27. H. Rodman and P. Grams, "Juvenile Delinquency and the Family: a Review and Discussion," in U.S. Task Force Report: *Juvenile Delinquency and Youth Crime* (Washington, D. C.: U. S. Government Printing Office, 1967): 181–221.

28. Edmund W. Vaz and John Casparis, "A Comparative Study of Youth Culture and Delinquency: Upper Class Canadian and Swiss Boys," *International Journal of Comparative Sociology* 12 (1971): 1–23.

29. M. Kobal, "Delinquent Juveniles from Two Different Cultures," *Revija za Kriminalistiko in Kriminologijo* 4(1965).

30. M. B. Clinard and D. J. Abbott, *Crime in Developing Countries* (New York: John Wiley, 1973).

31. "Zivujenske razmere delinkventne vladinc," Institut za Kriminologiji pri Pravni facultet Univerze v Ljubljana (n.d).

32. J. Feldhusen, J. Thurston, and J. Benning, "A Longitudinal Study of Delinquency and Other Aspects of Children's Behavior," *International Journal of Criminology and Penology* 1 (1973): 341–51.

33. E. Durkheim, *Education and Sociology* (New York: Free Press, 1963), p. 67.

34. Glaser.

35. E. Durkheim, *On Morality and Society* (Chicago: University of Chicago Press, 1973), p. 134.

36. E. Durkheim, *The Division of Labor* (New York: Free Press, 1933).

37. G. Marwell, "Adolescent Powerlessness and Delinquency," *Social Problems* 14 (1966): 35–47.

38. A. Mosciskier, "Delinquency in Regions under Intensified Industrialization and the Relation between the Dynamics of Delinquency and the Dynamics of Socioeconomic Processes (1958–1960 and 1964–1968)," *Archives of Criminology* 4 (1969): 223–28.

39. C. W. Kiefer, "The Psychological Interdependence of Family, School and Bureaucracy in Japan," *American Anthropologist* 72 (1970): 66–75.

40. Reckless et al.

41. H. Maccoby, "The Differential Political Activity of Participants in a Voluntary Association," *American Sociological Review* 23 (1958): 524–32.

42. Clinard.

43. L. H. Rogler, "Neighborhoods and Slums in Latin America," *Journal of Inter-American Studies* 9 (1967): 507–38.

44. Clinard and Abbott.

45. L. Karacki and J. Toby, "The Uncommitted Adolescent: Candidate for Gang Socialization," *Social Inquiry* 32 (1962): 203–15.

46. Friday.

47. J. F. Short and F. L. Strodtbeck, *Group Processes and Gang Delinquency* (Chicago: University of Chicago Press, 1965).

48. Paul C. Friday, "Research on Youth Crime in Sweden: Some Problems in Methodology," *Scandinavian Studies* 46 (1974): 20–30.

49. Hirschi.
50. Hindelang.

CHAPTER 4. A COMPARATIVE STUDY OF YOUTH CULTURE
AND DELINQUENCY: UPPER MIDDLE-CLASS CANADIAN AND
SWISS BOYS

1. R. Cavah and J. T. Cavan, *Delinquency and Crime: Cross-Cultural Perspectives* (New York: J. B. Lippincott, 1968).

2. James Coleman, *The Adolescent Society* (Glencoe: Free Press, 1961); Jessie Bernard, "Teen-Age Culture: An Overview," *Annals of the American Academy of Political and Social Science* 338 (1961): 1–12; Edmund W. Vaz, "Delinquency and the Youth Culture: Upper and Middle-Class Boys," *Journal of Criminal Law, Criminology and Police Science* 60 (1969): 33–46.

3. Edmund W. Vaz, "Middle-Class Adolescents: Self-Reported Delinquency and Youth Culture Activities," *Canadian Review of Sociology and Anthropology* 2 (1965): 52–70.

4. This was accomplished with the help of two German adolescents newly arrived in Canada who were familiar with the "style of life" of German and Swiss teenagers. Also one of the authors is Swiss born and was educated in German.

5. One example of Graubunden's tradition and conservative milieu is seen in the results of the 1963 elections to the Canton council. The Socialist and Communist candidates together polled 6.2 percent of the vote, while in Switzerland generally they polled 28.8 percent, and in the industrial city of Basel they polled 36.2 percent. See Roger Girod, "Milieux Politiques et Classes Sociales en Suisses," *Cahiers Internationaux de Sociologie* 39 (1965): 51.

6. *Eidgenossisches Statistisches Amt, Eidgenossische Volkszahlung vom I. Dezember 1960, 1964,* for data on Switzerland and Graubunden. *Die Wirtschaftliche Entwicklung der Stadt Chur, Separatadruck einer Botschaft des Stadtprasidenten an den Stadtrat von Chur vom 16. Juli, 1964,* for data on Chur.

7. In the absence of a validated index of social position for Switzerland, we expanded into eight categories a sixfold classification of occupations, developed by Girod and Tofigh on the basis of income, education, and occupation data. See Firouz Tofigh and Roger Girod, "Family Background and Income, Social Career and Social Mobility of Young Males of Working-Class Origin—A Geneva Survey," *Acta Sociologia* 9 (1965): 94–109. Compare also Maurice Erard, "Esquisse d'une Sociologie des Classes Sociales en Suisse," *Cahiers Internationaux de Sociologie* 39 (1965): 3–28. Our "upper class" is very similar to the top two categories in the Geneva study. Girod and Tofigh include managers and owners of big business, top level private and civil service executives, and professions requiring university degrees in their highest category, "professions and management." Their second highest category, "technicians and staff," includes technical, administrative, and professional staff of middle rank. They separate this level from the category "white collar workers without special responsibilities," which corresponds to our clerical and sales group, and find a mean income differential of 580 Swiss francs between these two levels. The types of occupations in our categories are, for example: (a) unskilled: janitor, bellhop, casual laborer, (b) semiskilled: truck driver, postman, waiter, (c) skilled: plumber, tool and die maker, electrician, (d) farmers, (e) petty shopkeepers, and artisans running their own small shops or businesses such as master plumber, master baker, master mechanic; the generic term for this group is *Gewerbe,* (f) clerical and sales: white collar salaried employees are known generically as *Angestellte* and have to be categorized by level of education and responsibility, (g)

pharmacist, hotel manager, minister, and *Hohere Beamte* which is a civil service category and includes, for example, teachers in the Kantonsschule, (h) architect, physician, lawyer, factory owner, university professor, university-degree engineer. That these are meaningful social categories in the Swiss context is evidenced also when voting statistics are analyzed by social class. See Girod, 29–54.

8. Bernard Blishen, "The Construction and Use of an Occupational Class Scale," *Canadian Journal of Economics and Political Science* 24 (1958): 519–31.

9. Frederick Elkin, *The Family in Canada*, (Ottawa: Vanier Institute of the Family, 1968); and Norman Ryder, "Components of Canadian Population Growth," *Population Index* 20 (1954): 71–79.

10. E. W. Heise, ed., *New Horizons for Canada's Children* (Toronto: University of Toronto Press, 1961), pp. 18–29.

11. For an overview, see Jessie Bernard, "Teen-Age Culture: An Overview," *Annals of the American Academy of Political and Social Science* 338 (1961): 1–12; Vaz, "Middle-Class Adolescents"; and John Seeley, R. Alexander, and E. W. Loosley, eds., *Crestwood Heights* (New York: Basic Books, 1956).

12. Seeley, Alexander, and Loosley.

13. Joseph Scott and Edmund W. Vaz, "A Perspective of Middle-Class Delinquency," *Canadian Journal of Economics and Political Science* 29 (1963): 324–35.

14. Bernard.

15. See *Task Force Report: Juvenile Delinquency and Youth Crime* (Washington, D. C.: U. S. Government Printing Office, 1967), table IA, p. 134.

16. Forty-four percent of our total Swiss "sample" grew up in rural areas. The Kantonsschule in Chur has many rural students who come to study as early as age 13. They live in boarding houses and often commute home on weekends; others commute daily from nearby villages. Another indication of strong rural influence is provided in Graubunden's first school census taken in 1967. It was found that 21.8 percent of the student body attending the Kantonsschule and related types of college preparatory schools were the sons and daughters of farmers, *Neue Bundner Zeitung*, 1968, p. 3.

17. One-quarter of our total "sample" of Swiss boys attends church every Sunday; one-third attends two or three times a month. Although church attendance, especially among Protestants, is low the church remains an important institution and the minister or priest a significant person in the community. It is considered essential, even among the nonchurched, that children be properly baptized and confirmed, and that one be married and buried by the church.

18. In 1964, approximately the time of our two studies, the divorce rate per 100,000 population was 30.3 for Graubunden, but 82.8 for all of Switzerland. *Statistisches Jahrbuch der Schweiz*, 1966, p. 65.

19. A picture of the traditional family patterns existing in Graubunden's rural areas as recently as 20 years ago is described in Hans Casparis, "Social and Religious Patterns among College Youth in a Swiss Mountain Society" (unpublished manuscript, 1946). These patterns include a consanguineal-extended family with separate living arrangements in the same house for the grandparents, a strict sexual division of labor with clearly defined spheres of authority for husband and wife, and an early and careful distinction in childrearing practices for boys and girls. A comparison with urban cases revealed that these patterns underwent modification with urbanization. We have found no further research in Switzerland to assess the extent of these changes. A recent study comparing families in Washington, D. C., with those in the industrial city of Turin found that Italian parental values are somewhat more adult-centered while American ones are more child-centered. See Leonard Pearlin and Melvin I. Kohn, "Social Class, Occupation and Parental Values: A

Cross National Study," *American Sociological Review* 31 (1966): 478.

20. See *Task Force Report: Juvenile Delinquency and Youth Crime*, table 4, p. 141.

21. These boys provide more than their share of membership in "delinquent gangs" coming to the attention of the police. The more "traditional" areas such as Graubunden figure only rarely in these accounts; 17 of the gangs were reported for Zurich, 11 for other large cities and only 3 for rural areas. See Sylvia Staub, *Ursachen und Erscheinungsformen bei der Bildung Jugendlicher Banden* (Zurich: Schulthess, 1965).

22. *Schulordnung für die Bundner Kantonsschule in Chur*, 1953; *Diszinplinarordnung für Schulflichtige Jugend der Stadt Chur*, 1946; *Verordnung betreffend die Lichtspiel theater*, 1930.

23. Jackson Toby, "Affluences and Adolescent Crime," in *Task Force Report: Juvenile Delinquency and Youth Crime* (Washington, D. C.: U. S. Government Printing Office, 1967), p. 143.

24. Vaz, "Middle-Class Adolescents."

25. Coleman.

26. We are indebted to James Coleman's work for some of our items.

27. Vaz, "Middle-Class Adolescents." This is not to suggest a youth conspiracy against academic excellence. Some studies have found that the most popular students are those who rate high academically and socially: See Ralph Turner, *The Social Context of Ambition* (San Francisco: Chandler, 1964).

28. Seeley, Alexander, and Loosley.

29. The Swiss version of the questionnaire is presented in this paper.

30. Some of these practices also exist among Swiss boys, not so much as a prerequisite for group membership, but rather as a sign that one is approaching adulthood. Older boys seldom drink before a "big" date or dance since liquor is usually served at such affairs.

31. Organized opportunities for youth to engage in "wholesome" recreation including high school dances, "formals," church "socials," parties, etc.

32. It may be that Canadian boys are responding to our question mainly in terms of drinking, while Swiss boys may be stating their attitudes towards "necking."

33. Items included four response categories: four or more times, three or more times, once or twice, and never.

34. Vaz, "Middle-Class Adolescents"; Howard Myerhoff and Barbara Myerhoff, "Field Observations of Middle-Class Gangs," *Social Forces* 42 (1964): 328–36.

CHAPTER 5. HOMICIDE IN 110 NATIONS: THE
DEVELOPMENT OF THE COMPARATIVE CRIME DATA FILE

1. Some important exceptions are the following works: M. Straus and J. Straus, "Suicide, Homicide and Social Structure in Ceylon," *American Journal of Sociology* 58 (1953): 461–69; V. Verkko, "Survey of Current Practice in Criminal Statistics," *Transactions of the Westermark Society* (1956): 5–33; Marvin E. Wolfgang, "International Crime Statistics: A Proposal," *Journal of Criminal Law and Criminology and Police Science* 58 (1967): 65–69; Marvin Wolfgang and Franco Ferracuti, *The Subculture of Violence* (New York: Tavistock, 1967); M. B. Clinard and D. J. Abbott, *Crime and Developing Countries: A Comparative Perspective* (New York: Wiley, 1973); G. Newman, *Comparative Deviance: Perception and Law in Six Cultures (New York: Elsevier, 1976); Ted Robert Gurr, Peter N. Grabosky, and Robert*

C. Hula, *The Politics of Crime and Conflict: A Comparative History of Four Cities* (Beverly Hills, Calif.: Sage, 1977).

2. Thorsten Sellin and Marvin E. Wolfgang, *The Measurement of Delinquency* (New York: Wiley, 1964); Hermann Mannheim, *Comparative Criminology* (London: Rutledge & Kegan Paul, 1965); D. J. Mulvihill and M. M. Tumin, *Crimes of Violence*, vols. 11, 12, 13 (Washington, D. C.: U. S. Government Printing Office, 1969); and Marvin E. Wolfgang, "International Crime Statistics."

3. Peter Sorokin, *Contemporary Sociology Theories* (New York: Harper, 1928), pp. 340–44.

4. An important exception was the early study of Thorsten Sellin, "Is Murder Increasing in Europe?" *Annals of the American Academy of Political and Social Science*, 126 (1926): 29–34. Sellin compared the post-WWI homicide rate changes in five belligerent nations and four nonbelligerent nations.

5. Hermann Mannheim, *War and Crime* (London: Watts, 1941).

6. Dane Archer and Rosemary Gartner, "Violent Acts and Violent Times: A Comparative Approach to Postwar Homicide Rates," *American Sociological Review* 41 (1976): 937–63.

7. Marvin E. Wolfgang, "Urban Crime," in *The Metropolitan Enigma*, ed. J. Q. Wilson (Cambridge, Mass.: Harvard University Press, 1968) pp. 245–81.

8. The few exceptions have generated considerable interest precisely because they have not found general increase in crime rates with populations growth; e.g. R. Lane, "Urbanization and Criminal Violence in the 19th Century: Massachusetts as a Test Case," in *Violence in America: Historical and Comparative Perspective*, ed. Hugh Davis Graham and Ted Robert Gurr (Washington, D. C.: U. S. Government Printing Office, 1969), pp. 359–70.

9. J. P. Gibbs, *Crime, Punishment and Deterrence* (New York: Elsevier, 1975).

10. Andrew F. Henry and James F. Short, Jr., *Suicide and Homicide: Some Economic, Sociological and Psychological Aspects of Aggression* (New York: Free Press, 1954).

11. A well-known exception is the work of Sir Leon Radzinowicz—e.g. "Economic Pressures," in *Crime and Justice: The Criminal in Society* ed. L. Radzinowicz and Marvin E. Wolfgang (New York: Basic Books, 1971), pp. 420–42.

12. For example, M. H. Brenner, *Mental Illness and the Economy* (Cambridge, Mass.: Harvard University Press, 1973).

13. Archer and Gartner.

14. In addition, we are working on a number of analyses internal to the CCDF data set itself. For example, we are using the time series in the file to learn whether the trends of various offenses are collinear, or whether there are factors of offenses which vary together over time. Finally, we are using the CCDF to try to resolve a number of methodological issues—one of which is discussed below.

15. Archer and Gartner.

16. The classic and recent literature on urban rates of crime and violence are reviewed in some detail in Dane Archer et al., "Cities and Homicide a New Look at an Old Paradox," in *Comparative Studies in Sociology*, vol. 1 ed. R. Tomasson (Greenwich, Conn.: JAI Press, 1977). Only the central themes of this literature are indicated here.

17. Mannheim, *Comparative Criminology*, p. 545.

18. Emile Durkheim, *The Division of Labor in Society*, trans. by G. Simpson (New York: Free Press, 1933), p. 350.

19. L. Wirth, "Urbanism as a Way of Life," *American Journal of Sociology* 46 (1940): 743–55.

20. This cross-sectional question has been addressed using some data from

other nations by Mannheim, *Comparative Criminology*; D. Szabo, *Crimes et Villes* (Louvain: Université Catholique, 1960); H. Tarniquet "Crime in the Rapidly Industrializing Urban Environment," *Revue Internationale de Criminologie et de Police Technique* 22 (1968): 49–58.

21. Marvin E. Wolfgang, "Urban Crime," and M. B. Clinard, *Sociology of Deviant Behavior* (New York: Holt, Rinehart and Winston, 1974).

22. Archer et al.

23. R. Lane and E. Powell, "Crime as a Function of Anomie," *Journal of Criminal Law, Criminology and Police Science* 57 (1966): 161–71; T. Ferdinard, "The Criminal Patterns of Boston since 1849," *American Journal of Sociology* 73 (1967): 84–99.

24. An important recent work in this area is by Gurr, Grabosky, and Hula, *The Politics of Crime and Conflict*. These authors studied "common" crimes (offenses against persons and property combined) in four international cities and found a decreasing trend in this aggregate index until 1930 and an increase after. Again, these results run counter to any expectations that offense rates should increase systematically with urban population growth.

25. A. Q. Lodhi and C. Tilly, "Urbanization, Crime and Collective Violence in 19th Century France," *American Journal of Sociology* 79 (1973): 296–318.

26. Although it is tempting to try to make direct homicide rate comparisons across the international cities and across the nations shown in table 13, such comparisons are hazardous without a careful inspection of the CCDF from which these data are drawn. Although the same indicator (e.g., offenses known) was used within each pair in table 13, not all pairs used the same indicator. In addition, national idiosyncracies in homicide classification and definition make cross-national comparisons of absolute homicide rates far from uncomplicated.

27. Alternate explanations are not difficult to find. In terms of the Durkheim-Wirth hypothesis discussed earlier, for example, it might be that major cities involve a weakening of kinship and community ties in developed societies but not in developing nations. Perhaps developing societies have lower rates of mobility, or perhaps people moving to cities in developing societies move with intact families rather than alone. Developed societies might also have greater controls over rural homicides— e.g., decentralized law enforcement which reduces blood feuds, marauding gangs, etc.

28. Two of the very few cities to decline in population or show discontinuous growth are Belfast and Glasgow.

29. A plausible interpretation for the narrowing of this gap after 1960 is suggested by the exceptional cases in table 13. After roughly 1960, developing nations are increasingly represented in the CCDF, and table 13 suggests that developing nations may not have the same relationship between city size and homicide as is found in developed nations.

CHAPTER 6. CONTEMPORARY CRIME IN HISTORICAL PERSPECTIVE: A COMPARATIVE STUDY OF LONDON, STOCKHOLM AND SYDNEY

1. A detailed North American statement of this point of view is Clayton A. Hartjen, *Crime and Criminalization* (New York: Praeger, 1974). Others are Austin Turk, *Criminality and Legal Order* (Skokie, Ill.: Rand-McNally, 1969); Richard Quinney, *The Social Reality of Crime* (Boston: Little, Brown, 1970); and idem, *Critique of Legal Order* (Boston: Little, Brown, 1974). Critical European analyses are provided by Herman Bianchi, Mario Simondi, and Ian Taylor, eds., *Deviance in*

Europe: Papers from the European Group for the Study of Deviance and Social Control (London: Wiley, 1975); Ian Taylor, Paul Walton, and Jock Young, *The New Criminology: For a Social Theory of Deviance* (London: Routledge & Kegan Paul, 1973).

2. For a more extensive discussion of definitions, see Ted Robert Gurr, *Rogues, Rebels and Reformers: A Political History of Urban Crime and Conflict* (Beverly Hills, Calif.: Sage, 1976), chaps. 1 and 2.

3. There has been little comparative historical research on crime. We know of some 20 quantitative studies of the changing incidence of crime in English-speaking societies, only 4 of which span as much as a century, and none of which examines more than one society. The principal American contributions, all dealing with Boston, are Theodore N. Ferdinand, "The Criminal Patterns of Boston since 1849," *American Journal of Sociology* 73 (1967): 688–98; Roger Lane, *Policing the City: Boston, 1822–1885* (Cambridge, Mass.: Harvard University Press, 1967); and Sam Bass Warner, *Crime and Criminal Statistics in Boston* (Cambridge, Mass.: Harvard University Press, 1934). An exception to the singular fascination with Boston is Elwin H. Powell, *The Design of Discord: Studies of Anomie* (New York: Oxford University Press, 1970), pt. 2, which focuses on the history of crime in Buffalo, New York. Two major studies of England are V. A. C. Gatrell and T. B. Hadden, "Criminal Statistics and Their Interpretation," in *Nineteenth Century Society: Essays in the Use of Quantitative Methods for the Study of Social Data*, ed. E. A. Wrigley (Cambridge: At the University Press, 1972), pp. 336–96; and J. M. Beattie, "The Pattern of Crime in England 1660–1800," *Past and Present* 62 (1974): 47–92.

4. Daniel Bell, "The Myth of Crime Waves," in his *The End of Ideology* (New York: Free Press, 1960), p. 157. A more recent North American critique is Donald Mulvihill and Melvin Tumin, "American Criminal Statistics: An Explanation and Appraisal," in *Crimes of Violence* (Washington, D. C.: National Commission on the Causes and Prevention of Violence, 1969), vol. 11. For general commentary on the sources, uses, and limitations of criminal statistics, with special reference to Britain, see Hermann Mannheim, *Comparative Criminology* (Boston: Houghton Mifflin, 1965), chap. 5, and especially Nigel Walker, *Crime, Courts and Figures: An Introduction to Criminal Statistics* (Harmondsworth, England: Penguin, 1971). The adequacy of contemporary Australian data on crime is discussed in Paul Wilson and J. Brown, *Crime and the Community* (St. Lucia: University of Queensland Press, 1973).

5. See the case studies in Ted Robert Gurr, Peter N. Grabosky, and Robert C. Hula, *The Politics of Crime and Conflict: A Comparative History of Four Cities* (Beverly Hills, Calif.: Sage, 1977).

6. Many of the components of these composite crime indicators are separately analyzed in Gurr, Grabosky, and Hula, pts. 2–4, and almost all of them prove to have similar trends. The most significant exception is burglary in London, which increased throughout the nineteenth and early twentieth centuries.

7. These are representative correlations (Pearson r's) between alternative indicators of disorder: Stockholm, 1865–1963, thefts known versus convictions, r = .89; London, 1893–1931, arrests for all indictable offenses versus convictions on trial, r = .84; New South Wales, 1914–1970, arrests for crimes of aggression versus convictions, r = .75; arrests for acquisitive crimes versus convictions, r = .89.

8. For a more detailed analysis of crime in London, see Gurr, Grabosky, and Hula, pt. 2.

9. For a more detailed analysis of crime in Stockholm, see ibid., pt. 3.

10. For a more detailed analysis of crime in Sydney and New South Wales, see Ibid., pt. 4.

11. The following procedure was used to determine the common trends: For each city, the moving 10-year average for convictions was recorded for every fifth year for which data were available for 1830, 1835, 1840, and so forth. The lowest rate in each series was set equal to 1.0 and the other rates expressed as a ratio of that. In London, for example, the lowest average conviction rate recorded for indictable murders and assaults between 1820 and 1930 was 1.36 per 100,000 in 1930, while the highest was 12.5 in 1845. The 1930 ratio was set at 1.0; the 1845 ratio, therefore, was 12.5/1.36 = 9.2. The procedure was repeated for the trend in indictable thefts, and for both kinds of convictions in New South Wales (higher court convictions) and Stockholm (all convictions). Since all the series have a common minimum of 1.0, they can be plotted on the same graph. The graph covers only the period for which at least four ratios were available. New South Wales is excluded before 1850 because of its exceptionally high rates during the convict era; if they were included, the 1830's average would exceed 10. The vertical bars represent the range of variation around the mean. In 1880, for example, the highest ratio score was 4.8 (aggressive crimes in Stockholm), the lowest was 2.0 (theft in New South Wales), the average of six ratios was 3.2. Neither kind of offense and no one city has a consistently higher or lower rate of decline.

12. Trends in "victimless" crimes and political offenses in the three cities are analyzed in Gurr, Grabosky, and Hula. In some instances they parallel the trends in common crime; in others, not. It should be noted that the most frequent occasion for arrests in all the cities in the nineteenth and early twentieth centuries was not "common crime" but drunkenness, while in the mid-twentieth century traffic violations have pride of place.

13. For a comparative analysis of changing legal boundaries of crime see Gurr, *Rogues, Rebels and Reformers*, pt. 2, chap. 3.

14. For a comparative discussion of the evolution of modern policing systems in the three cities, and more detailed evidence on the impact of changes in policing on crime rates, see ibid., pt. 2, chap. 4.

15. For a complete discussion of judicial and penal policies in the three cities, see ibid., pt. 2, chap. 5.

16. See Gatrell and Hadden, "Criminal Statistics and their Interpretation."

17. See Abdul Q. Lodhi and Charles Tilly, "Urbanization, Crime and Collective Violence in Nineteenth Century France," *American Journal of Sociology* 79 (1973): 296–318.

18. On Boston, see the references in note 3, above. Data on Chicago are reported in Wesley G. Skogan, *Chicago Since 1840: A Time-Series Data Handbook* (Urbana: Institute of Government and Public Affairs, University of Illinois, 1975).

19. Ted Robert Gurr, "Crime Trends in Modern Democracies since 1945," *International Annals of Criminology* 16 (1977): 41–86. The rates of increase have been lowest in the German-speaking countries. Japan offers a marked contrast to the Western experience: its rates of common crime have declined steadily and substantially since the early 1950s.

20. Leon Radzinowicz, "Changing Attitudes towards Crime and the Devices Used to Combat It," *Proceedings of the Royal Institution of Great Britain* 37 (1958–59): 29–53.

CHAPTER 7. THE MODERNIZATION OF CRIME IN GERMANY
AND FRANCE, 1830–1913

1. Samples of reevaluation of the city may be found in Philip M. Hauser and Leo F. Schnore, eds., *The Study of Urbanization*, (New York: Wiley, 1967); and in

Paul K. Hatt and Albert J. Reiss, Jr., eds., *Cities and Society: The Revised Reader in Urban Sociology*, (New York: Free Press, 1967).

2. For criminal violence see, for example, Andrew F. Henry and James F. Short, Jr., *Suicide and Homicide: Some Economic, Sociological and Psychological Aspects of Aggression* (New York: Free Press, 1968), pp. 90–91; George B. Vold, "Crime in City and Country Areas," *Annals of the American Academy of Political and Social Science* 217 (1941): 38–45; and Karl O. Christiansen, "Industrialization and Urbanization in Relation to Crime and Juvenile Delinquency," *International Review of Criminal Policy* 16 (1960): 7–8. Recent work on collective violence is summarized by George Rudé, *Debate on Europe 1815–1850* (New York: Harper & Row, 1972), pp. 80–87.

3. This discussion is extracted from the author's unpublished Ph.D. dissertation, a broader study of crime entitled, "Patterns of Crime in Nineteenth-Century Germany and France: A Comparative Study" (Ph.D. diss., Rutgers University, 1974) and his *Crime and Development of Modern Society: Patterns of Criminality in Nineteenth Century Germany and France* (London: Croom Helm, 1976).

4. The nineteenth century is defined here as the period from about 1830 to 1913 both because of the availability of sources for this period and because it spans the classic period of the industrial revolution in these countries.

5. V. A. C. Gatrell and T. B. Hadden, "Criminal Statistics and Their Interpretation," in *Nineteenth Century Society: Essays in the Use of Quantitative Methods for the Study of Social Data*, ed. E. A. Wrigley (Cambridge: At the University Press, 1972), pp. 336–96, have written an important recent study which has recognized the significance of the crime phenomenon.

6. A valuable though slightly dated discussion of FBI crime figures is by Fred P. Graham, "A Contemporary History of American Crime," in *Violence in America: Historical and Comparative Perspectives*, ed. Hugh Davis Graham and Ted Robert Gurr, (Washington, D. C.: U. S. Government Printing Office, 1969), pp. 371–85.

7. An example of the literature dealing with these problems is Thorsten Sellin and Marvin E. Wolfgang, *The Measurement of Delinquency*, (Montclair, N.J.: Patterson Smith, 1964).

8. While the total number of complaints and reports to French police nearly doubled between 1857 and 1900, the number of policemen empowered to receive them increased by only 41 percent. Whereas in 1857 there was one agent for every 360 persons, in 1900 there was one agent for every 470 (based on crime records in the *Compte général de l'administration de la justice criminelle en France,*1857, Table XCCIV, pp. 211–28, and 1900, Table XLVI, pp. 106–7.

9. In France, for instance, rates of persons tried for theft rose 60 percent between 1830–1839 and 1900–1909 while rates or reports to public prosecutors rose 230 percent. Indices of persons tried and of persons convicted in Germany 1882–1912 show a similar divergence. Sources are cited in notes 11–12 below.

10. Published annually in the Staats-Anzeiger für Württemberg (1849ff).

11. Indices are based upon statistics of persons tried found in annual volumes of *Compte général* and in the annual *Kriminalstatistik* volumes of the *Statistik des deutschen Reichs*. Rates have been calculated per 100,000 punishable persons. Persons under the age of 10 or 12, who presumably commit few crimes and, even if they did, would rarely appear in court, have been left out of the population figures.

12. Raw statistics come from the *Compte général*. Reports dropped because no offense was found to have occurred were eliminated from this index.

13. Again, the source is the *Compte général*. Due to the unavailability of age-specific demographic data, rates for the selected case studies are per 100,000 inhabitants.

14. Raw crime statistics are taken from the published administrative reports (*Verwaltungsberichte*) and/or *Statistische Jahrbucher* for these cities. In addition, archival material is available for Bochum, 1879–1904 (Stadtarchiv Bochum MSS, Zeitungsberichte), for Düsseldorf ("Zeitungsberichte," Stadtarchiv Düsseldorf MSS, Aktenbanden III 4588–4603), and Duisburg ("Verbrechen und Vergeben," Stadtarchiv Duisburg MSS Polizeiakten 301/172).

15. Crime statistics come from the *Staats-Anzeiger*, 1890–1913; from "Autogaben und Leistungen der Polizeistatistik," *Allgemeines Statistisches Archiv*, IX Heft 2/3 (Munich, 1915), p. 375; and from "Konigliches Landjagercorps: Übersicht über die Festnahmen und Anzeigen," 1900–1913, Hauptstaatsarchiv Stuttgart MSS, E151cII no. 429.

16. For purposes of comparability, the category of theft here includes a number of related crimes such as receiving or burglary which involve the taking of property.

17. Due to the small numbers involved, the role of homicide in this ratio is, of course, negligible.

18. Correlations between the TVR and proportions of the population in crime-prone age, sex, and marital groups were all low ($r = \pm .06$ to $.18$), indicating that the correlation between TVR and city cannot be explained away on the basis of high percentages of such groups in the city. Note that Pearson correlations assume a linear relationship; judging by figure 8, the correlation would be stronger if nonlinear correlational methods were used. The proportion of the variance in a dependent variable which can be "mathematically explained" (this does not necessarily imply or prove causative relationship) by the variance in an independent variable $= r^2$.

19. Unless otherwise noted, French national figures are based on prosecutor reports rather than persons tried.

20. *Statistik des deutschen Reichs*, N. F. 45, pp. II.17–18. Cf. Hans Hermann Burchardt, *Kriminalitat in Stadt und Land* (Berlin: Abhandlungen des Kriminalistischen Instituts an der Universitat Berlin, 1936), pp. 139–140.

21. The highest correlation in this group ($r = .28$) was with the proportion of males aged 10–30 in the population.

22. See note 19 as well as *Statistik des deutschen Reich*, N. F. 23,p. II.22, and Burchardt, *Kriminalitat*, p. 142.

23. Rates of homicide dropped 9 percent in France between 1831–1839 and 1900–1909, while in the German Reich they dropped 25 percent between 1882–1889 and 1900–1909.

24. See, for instance, Henry and Short, *Suicide and Homicide*, pp. 90–91.

25. The literature on the frustration-aggression hypothesis is voluminous. A useful bibliography of relevant material is provided by Ted Robert Gurr, *Why Men Rebel* (Princeton, N.J.: Princeton University Press, 1971), pp. 369–407. The idea of substitute objects of aggression is discussed by Lewis Coser, *The Functions of Social Conflict* (New York: Free Press, 1964), p. 40.

26. E. J. Hobsbawm, *Primitive Rebels: Studies in Archaic Forms of Social Movement in the 19th and 20th Centuries* (New York: Norton, 1965).

CHAPTER 8. URBANIZATION AND CRIME: THE SOVIET CASE
IN CROSS-CULTURAL PERSPECTIVE

1. A. S. Shliapochnikov, "O sozdanii edinovo ucheta prestupnosti," *Sovetskoe gosudarstvo i pravo* 9 (1965): 105.

2. Mervyn Matthews, *Class and Society in Soviet Russia* (New York: Walker, 1972), pp. 53–54.

3. Ibid., p. 54.

4. Ibid., p. 53.

5. M. N. Gernet, *Prestupnost' i samoubiistv vo vremia voiny i posle nee* (Moscow: Tsentralńoe Statisticheskoe Upravienie, 1927), p. 160.

6. Leon Lipson and Valery Chalidze, eds., *Papers on Soviet Law* 1 (1977): 185.

7. Ibid., p. 186.

8. Ibid.

9. M. M. Babaev, "Demograficheskie protessy i problemy terrotial'nykh razlichii prestupnosti," *Voprosy bor'by s prestupnostiu* 21 (1974): 9.

10. M. M. Babaev, "Kriminologicheskie issledovaniia problem migratsiia naseleniia," *Sovetskoe gosudartsvo i pravo* 3 (1968): 86.

11. Ibid., pp. 86–87.

12. Ibid., p. 87.

13. Fahad Al-Thakeb, "Crime Trends in Kuwait," International Criminological Symposium, Stockholm, Sweden 1978. Franco Ferracuti, "European Migration and Crime," in *Crime and Culture* (New York: Wiley, 1968), pp. 189–219.

14. Thorsten Sellin, *Culture, Conflict and Crime* (New York: Social Science Research Council, 1938), pp. 63–70.

15. M. M. Babaev and Iu. M. Antonian, "Sotsial'naia sreda i lichnost' prestupnikov migrantov i postoiannykh zhitelei," *Voprosy bor'by s prestupnostiu* 22 (1975): 5.

16. M. B. Clinard and D. J. Abbott, *Crime in Developing Countries* (New York: John Wiley, 1973), p. 119.

17. Babaev, "Kriminologicheskie issledovaniia problem migratsiia naseleniia," p. 89.

18. Ibid., p. 88.

19. Ibid., pp. 88–89.

20. Clinard and Abbott, pp. 117–19.

21. Babaev and Antonian, p. 12.

22. Ibid., p. 16.

23. Ibid., p. 13; Clinard and Abbott, pp. 124–26.

24. Babaev and Antonian, p. 13; Clinard and Abbott, p. 127.

25. Clinard and Abbott, p. 120.

26. Babaev and Antonian, pp. 16–17.

27. A. F. Sokolov, "Urbanizatsiia i nekotorye vorposy bor'by s prestupnost'iu," *Sbornik uchenykh trudov Sverdlovsk* 28(1973): 150.

28. *Sourcebook of Criminal Justice Statistics—1977*, (Washington, D. C.: U. S. Government Printing Office, 1978), pp. 314, 402.

29. M. M. Babaev, "Kriminologicheskaia otsenka sotsial'no-ekonomicheskikh i demograficheskikh faktorov," *Sovetskoe gosudartsvo i pravo* 6 (1972): 98.

30. See Louise I. Shelley "Crime in Moscow in 1923 and 1968" and "The Current Dynamics of Soviet Criminality and the Constitutional Response." Mimeographed.

31. O. V. Derviz, "Rabota ili ucheba vne mesta postoiannovo zhitel'stva—odin iz faktorov prestupnosti nesovershennoletnikh," *Prestupnost i ee preduprezhdenie* (Leningrad: Izd. Leningradskogo Universiteta), p. 67.

32. Ibid., pp. 65–66.

CHAPTER 9. UNITED NATIONS CRIME SURVEY 1977

1. This section also includes information provided in the responses to a questionnaire addressed to Member States on 14 May 1975 in pursuance of Economic and Social Council Resolution 663 C (XXIV) of 31 July 1957 and General Assembly Resolution 3144 B(XXVIII) of 14 December 1973 in which the Assembly re-

quested the Secretary-General, in preparing the report on the situation of crime prevention and control, to take particularly into account the current application of the Standard Minimum Rules for the Treatment of Prisoners (see *First United Nations Congress on the Prevention of Crime and the Treatment of Offenders: Report by the Secretariat*) and to make suggestions about the measures needed to ensure their most effective implementation.

2. It is almost impossible to draw up a definitive and universal list of crimes, as the cultural values and legal traditions and system of countries vary so much. There is, however, a common core of acts defined as criminal in practically all countries: these can be classified under the headings of "crimes against the person" (intentional homicide, assault, sexual offences, kidnapping, and robbery), "crimes against property" (theft and fraud), and "crimes involving drugs of various kinds" (illegal trafficking in drugs, abuse of drugs by consumption, and abuse of alcohol). Robbery is a difficult crime to classify, as it is an offence against both person and property, but as the person can eventually remain injured by the act, it is here classified as an offence against the person.

3. It should be noted in this connexion that, while 64 countries responded, only 50 provided data which could be used in statistical analysis. Other replies were not sufficiently detailed, or arrived too late for inclusion in the computer analysis. However, they were taken into account in presenting the qualitative analysis and regional review.

4. The methods used were statistical techniques of correlation coefficients and multiple regression.

5. A wide variety of sources were used, but data were drawn specifically from issues of the United Nations *Statistical Yearbook*, the *UNESCO Statistical Yearbook*, the *World Health Statistics Annual*, the International Labour Office's *Year Book of Labour Statistics*, and the United Nations *Demographic Yearbook*.

6. For this region, however, it has been possible to use replies to an earlier vote verbale of the Secretary-General of 10 July 1974 and information stemming from the regional preparatory meeting of experts on the prevention of crime and the treatment of offenders.

CHAPTER 10. A CROSS-CULTURAL STUDY OF CORRELATES OF CRIME

1. Sophia M. Robison *Juvenile Delinquency: Its Nature and Control* (New York: Holt, 1960).

2. J. W. M. Whiting, "The Cross Cultural Method," in *Handbook of Social Psychology*, ed. Tedby G. Lindzey (Cambridge, Mass.: Addison-Wesley, 1954), pp. 523–31.

3. The 48 societies included in this study are as follows: Africa—Ashanti, Azande, Bena, Chagga, Dahomeans, Lovedu, Mbundu, Thonga; Asia—Andamanese, Baiga, Chenchu, Chukchee, Lepcha, Muria, Tanala, Yakut; North America—Cheyenne, Comanche, Flatheads, Hopi, Jamaicans (Rocky Roaders), Kaska, Kwakiutl, Navaho, Papago, Tepoztlan, Western Apache; South America—Aymara, Cuna, Jivaro, Siriono, Yagua; Oceania—Arapesh, Balinese, Buka (Kurtachi), Ifaluk, Kwoma, Lau Fijians (Kambara), Lesu, Manus, Maori, Pukapukans, Samoans, Tikopia, Trobrianders, Trukese, Ulithians, Vanua Levu (Nakoroka). All information was obtained from ethnographic studies available in the literature or in the Human Relations Area Files. Ratings were, so far as possible, of the aboriginal practices of the group in order to reduce the influence of acculturation.

4. T. Parsons, *Essays in Sociological Theory* (Glencoe, Illinois: Free Press, 1954), pp. 304–05.

5. W. B. Miller, "Lower Class Culture as a Generating Milieu of Gang Delinquency," *Journal of Social Issues* 14 (1958): 5–19.

6. J. W. M. Whiting, R. Kluckhohn, and A. Anthony, "The Function of Male Initiation Ceremonies at Puberty," in *Readings in Social Psychology*, 3rd ed., ed. by Eleanor E. Maccoby, T. Newcomb, and E. L. Hartley (New York: Holt, 1958), pp. 359–70.

7. The whole problem of the mechanism whereby identification occurs has been omitted from this study. In all theories it would appear that identification with the father would be in some degree a function of the father.

8. J. W. M. Whiting, "Sorcery, Sin and Superego: A Cross-Cultural Study of Some Mechanisms of Social Control," in *Nebraska Symposium on Motivation: 1959*, ed. M. R. Jones (Lincoln: University of Nebraska Press, 1959), pp. 174–95.

9. G. P. Murdock, "World Ethnographic Sample," *American Anthropologist* 59 (1957): 664–87.

10. L. N. Robins and Patricia O'Neal, "Mortality, Mobility and Crime: Problem Children Thirty Years Later," *American Sociological Review* 23 (1958): 162–71.

11. Sheldon Glueck and Eleanor Glueck, *Unraveling Juvenile Delinquency* (New York: Commonwealth Fund, 1950).

12. J. H. Rohrer and M. S. Edmondson, eds., *Eighth Generation: Cultures and Personalities of New Orleans Negroes* (New York: Harper & Row, 1960).

13. A. Davis and J. Dollard, *Children of Bondage* (Washington: American Council on Education, 1941).

14. Rohrer and Edmondson, pp. 162–63.

15. Herbert Barry III, Margaret K. Bacon, and Irvin L. Child, "A Cross-Cultural Survey of Some Sex Differences in Socialization," *Journal of Abnormal and Social Psychology* 55 (1957): 327–32.

16. W. Healy and A. F. Bronner, *New Light on Delinquency and its Treatment* (New Haven, Conn.: Yale University Press, 1936).

17. Glueck and Glueck.

18. O. Fenichel, *The Psychoanalytic Theory of Neurosis* (New York: Norton, 1945), pp. 370–71.

19. Both variables are taken from Murdock. Our manner of treating his data is described in Barry, Child, and Bacon, "Relation of Child Training to Subsistence Economy," *American Anthropologist* 61 (1959): 51–63.

20. J. W. M. Whiting and I. L. Child, *Child Training and Personality* (New Haven, Conn.: Yale University Press, 1953).

21. Whiting, Kluckhohn, and Anthony, pp. 359–70.

22. The variable of mother-child sleeping might be considered to favor feminine identification. In that event, the fact that it shows correlations in the positive direction with both types of crime tends toward confirmation of the findings in our earlier section on correlates of crime in general.

23. Whiting, "Sorcery, Sin and Superego," pp. 174–95.

CHAPTER 11. THE CASE OF AUGUST SANGRET

1. MacDonald Critchley, *The Trial of August Sangret*, Notable British Trial Series, vol. 83 (Edinburgh, Scotland: William Hodge, 1959), p. vi.

2. Ibid., p. 4.

3. W. C. Tuttle, *The Crusade Against Capital Punishment in Great Britain* (London: Stevens & Sons, 1961), p. 87.

4. W. Middendorf, *Die Gewaltkriminalitat in den U.S.A.* (Berlin: Walter de Gruyter, 1970), p. 75.

5. V. Holtzendorff, *Das Verbrechen des Mordes und die Todesstrafe*, Criminal-politische und psychologische Untersuchungen, Berlin 1875, (Frankfurt: Nachdruck des Verlages Ferdinand Keip, 1970), p. 268.

6. F. T. Jesse, *Comments on Cain* (New York: Collier, 1964), p. 24.

7. Tuttle, p. 87.

8. John M. MacDonald, *The Murderer and his Victim* (Springfield, Ill.: Charles C. Thomas, 1961), pp. 315–17.

9. Holtzendorff, p. 376.

10. Sir Norwood East, *Society and the Criminal* (London: His Majesty's Stationery Office, 1949), p. 270.

11. Rupert Furneaux, *Guenther Podola* (London: Stevens & Sons, 1960), pp. 318–19.

12. A Koestler, *Reflections on Hanging* (London: Victor Gollancz, 1956), pp. 82–83.

13. Tuttle, p. 153.

14. MacDonald, p. 319.

15. Tuttle, p. 87.

16. M. Grunhut, *Penal Reform, A Comparative Study* (Oxford: Clarendon Press, 1948), p. 437.

17. Holtzendorff, p. 367.

18. H. Mannheim, *Comparative Criminology* (London: Routledge & Kegan Paul, 1965), p. 346.

19. Cooper Blom, *The A6 Murder, Regina vs. James Hanratty, The Semblance of Truth* (Harmondsworth, England: Penguin, 1963); Jean Justice, *Murder vs. Murder* (Paris: Olympia Press, 1964).

20. Critchley, p. 127.

21. Koestler, pp. 56 and 81.

22. Ibid., p. 133.

23. Critchley, p. xi.

24. Koestler, pp. 46-47.

25. Ibid., p. 82.

26. Grunhut, p. 434.

27. George Godwin, *Criminal Man* (New York: George Braziller, 1957), p. 185.

28. Tuttle, p. 154.

29. Koestler, p. 124.

30. Critchley, p. xiii.

31. V. Gollancz, *My Dear Timothy* (London: Victor Gollancz, 1952), p. 377.

32. Critchley, p. xvi.

33. Ibid., pp. xviii–xix.

34. Ibid., pp. xvi, xxx, 221, and 227.

35. Ibid., p. xxxi.

36. Thorsten Sellin, *Culture, Conflict and Crime* (New York: Social Science Research Council, 1938), p. 64.

37. Critchley, p. 193.

38. v. Hentig, "Return to the Scene of the Crime," in *Essays in Criminal Science*, vol. 1, ed. G. O. W. Mueller (New York: New York University Press, 1961), p. 373.

39. Walton Adelman, *The Devil's Brigade* (Philadelphia: Bantam, 1967), p. 46.

CHAPTER 12. THE SECOND LIFE: A CROSS-CULTURAL VIEW
OF PEER SUBCULTURES IN CORRECTIONAL INSTITUTIONS

1. E. Goffman, *Asylums* (Garden City, N.Y.: Anchor Books, 1961).

2. S. Jedlewski, *Nieletni w zakladach poprawczych* (Warsaw, 1962).

3. The studies on which this part of the paper is based were carried out in 1969–1971 in several Polish institutions, both juvenile and adult, by students of Professor Adam Podgorecki. The members of the research team were S. Malkowski, A. Pilonow, M. Rydz, J. Wasilewski, B. Zielinska, and the consultants, M. Los and J. Kurczewski. The study was an integral part of the research group on social norms and pathology of social life at the University of Warsaw, Institute of Sociology. The results of this research were published in the quarterly *Etyka*, no. 8, (1971); and some findings are also presented in M. Los, "Prawo i wiezi spoleczne," in *Pravo w Spoleczenstwie*, ed. J. Kurczewski (Warsaw: Panstwowe Wydawn Naukowe, 1975), and A. Podgorecki, *Zarys socjologii prawa* (Warsaw: Panstwowe Wydawn Ictowo Naukowe, 1971).

4. Specific mention of particular institutions was not made in the Polish studies we have cited above.

5. The above generalizations are based to a large extent on the very profound studies carried out by Stanislaw Malkowski in two correctional institutions. His method was observation and interview. These studies are confirmed by other research findings [*Etyka*, no. 8 (1971)].

6. The findings of A. Pilonow and J. Wasilewski [*Etyka*, no. 8 (1971)].

7. J. Irwin, *The Felon* (Englewood Cliffs, N.J.: Prentice Hall, 1970).

8. Ibid., p. 83.

9. Mr. Anderson was a member of the inmate subculture of "Stateside" for over 10 years. He has visited the prison on several occasions since his release.

10. We recommend the following literature for general background: G. Sykes, *The Society of Captives* (Princeton, N.J.: Princeton University Press, 1958); H. Polsky, "Social Structure in A Juvenile Institution"; and P. Garbedian, "Social Roles and Processes in the Prison Community," in *The Sociology of Punishment and Corrections*, ed. N. Johnston, (New York: J. Wiley, 1970); Irwin, *The Felon*; R. Minton, *Inside Prison U. S. A.* (New York: Random House, 1971); and L. Hazelrigg, ed., *Prison within Society* (Garden City, N.Y.: Anchor Books, 1969). Much of the material below is written from the direct observations of Mr. Anderson who for 14 years was an inmate of juvenile and adult institutions in three states.

11. Sykes.

12. S. Rosen et al., "Perceived Sources of Social Power," *Journal of Abnormal Social Psychology* 62 (1961).

13. Irwin.

14. Irwin, p. 76.

15. Podgorecki.

16. Podgorecki.

17. J. Kurczewski, "Bluzg, grypserka, drugie zycie—proba hipotezy interpretacyjnej" (An address before the conference organized at the Institute of Sociology, Warsaw University, April 25, 1970).

CHAPTER 13. CRIME AND DELINQUENCY RESEARCH IN
SELECTED EUROPEAN COUNTRIES

1. Council of Europe, European Committee on Crime Problems *International Exchange of Information on Current Criminological Research Projects in Member States*, vol. 14 (Strasbourg, 1967), project 296.

2. Albert Ochmann, *Diebstahlsdelikte von Frauen und ihre Ursachen* (Hamburg: Kriminalistik Verlag, 1965).

3. Council of Europe, European Committee on Crime Problems, *The Effectiveness of Current Programmes for the Prevention of Juvenile Delinquency* (Strasbourg, 1963).

4. Nils Christie, "Research into Methods of Crime Prevention," *International Social Science Journal* 18 (1966): 140.

5. Fritz Sack, "Zum Stand der Kriminologie-dargestellt an zwei Publikationen," *Kolner Zeitschrift für Kriminologie* 18 (1966): 355–65.

6. Thomas Wurtenburger, "German Criminology and Anglo-American Research," in *Criminology in Transition: Essays in Honor of Hermann Mannheim*, ed. Tadeusz Grygier, Howard Jones, and John C. Spencer, (London: Tavistock, 1964), pp. 197–209.

7. Franco Ferracuti and Marvin Wolfgang, "L'integrazione della criminologia," *Quaderni di Criminologia Clinica* 7 (1965): 155–92; 7 (1965): 275–306.

8. Thomas Wurtenberger, "Das Menschenbild unserer Zeit und die Kriminalitat als sozial-kulturelles Phänomen," *Bewahrungshilfe* 13 (1966): 3–16.

9. Hans Joachim Schneider, "Entwicklungstendenzen auslandisher und internationaler Kriminologie," *Juristenzeitung* 11/12 (1966): 369–81.

10. Franco Ferracuti and Maria Christina Giannini, "Tendence prevalenti della ricerca criminologica in Italia negli ultimi cinque anni," *Quaderni di Criminologia Clinica* 11 (1969): 423–32.

11. Gerhard Mueller, "The Function of Criminology in Criminal Justice Administration," *Abstracts of Criminology and Penology* 9 (1969): 577–90.

12. Council of Europe, Criminological Division, *Criminological Research and the Council of Europe* (Strasbourg, 1965).

13. See for example, J. J. Desmarez, "Contribution à l'étude de la méthodologique médicolégale, medico-sociologique et criminologique," *Revue de Droit Pénal et de Criminologie* 45 (1965): 787–932.

14. Wolf Middendorf, "Die Ursachen der Jugendkriminalitat," *Vortäge in Landeskriminalpolizeiamt Niedersachen* 1 (1964): 77–94.

15. M. Borbos Portigliatti, "Tradizione e attualita dell' antropologia criminale," *Quaderni di Criminologia Clinica* 8 (1966): 3–15.

16. M. Raymond Boudon, "La statistique psychologique de Tarde," *International Annals of Criminology* 2 (1964): 342–57.

17. Paul Savey-Casal, "Le deuxième centénaire de traité des délits et des peines," *Revue de Science Criminelle et de Droit Pénal Comparé* 19 (1964): 497–507.

18. Jean Imbert, "La peine de mort et l'opinion au XVII siècle," *Revue de Science Criminelle et de Droit Pénal Comparé* 19 (1964): 509–25.

19. Anne-Eva Brauneck, "Die Jungendlichenreife nach Art. 165 JGG," *Zeitschrift für die gesamte Strafrechtswissenchaft* 77 (1965): 209–19.

20. Renato Treves, "Una ricerca sociologica sull' adminstrazione della guistizia in Italia," *Rivista di Diritto Processuale* 20 (1964): 1025.

21. Jean Pinatel, "L'évolution de la criminalité en France," *Revue de Science Criminelle et de Droit Pénal Comparé*, 21 (1966): 392–98.

22. Jean Susin, "Élements d'une analyse sociologique de la police à travers son image dans l'opinion publique," *Revue de Science Criminelle et de Droit Pénal Comparé* 20 (1965): 916–24.

23. Centre de Formation et de Recherche de l'Éducation Surveillée, *Vols et Voleurs de véhicules à moteur* (Paris: Vaucresson, Edition Cujas, 1965).

24. Roger Mucchielle, *Comments ils devient délinquants* (Paris: Les Editions Sociales Francaises, 1965).

25. Bernard Wehner, "Gastarbeiterkriminalitat—auch ein Schlagwort?" *Kriminalistik* 20 (1966): 175–76.

26. Jean Graven, "Le problème des travailleurs étrangers delinquants en Suisse," *Revue Internationale de Criminologie et de Police Téchnique* 19 (1965): 265–90.

27. Witold Swida, "Einfluss der Veranderung der Gesellschaftsordnung und Bevölkerungsumschichtung auf die Kriminalität in Polen," *Zeitschrift für die gesamte Strafrechtswissenschaft* 77 (1965): 346–58.

28. Jerzy Jasinski, "Delinquent Generations in Poland," *British Journal of Criminology* 6 (1966): 170–82.

29. Maria Ivaldi, "Il minore e il magistrato," *Esperienze di Rieducazione* 12 (1965): 27–54.

30. Ennio Pontrelli, "Immigrazione, dissocialita e disaddattamento minorile," *Esperienze di Rieducazione* 14 (1965): 29–38.

31. Walter Hepner, *Richter und Sachverständiger*, (Hamburg: Kriminalistik Verlag, 1966).

32. Georg Helmer, "Serienbrandstifter," *Archiv für Kriminologie* 136 (1965): 39–55; 106–16; 156–64.

33. Hans von Hentig, "Der Pyropath," *Zeitschrift für die gesamte Strafrechtswissenschaft* 76 (1964): 238–49.

34. W. Witter and R. Luthe, "Die Strafrechtlichte Verantwortlichkeit beim ertweiterten Suicid," *Monatsschrift für Kriminologie und Strafrechtscreform* 49 (1966): 97–113.

35. Erwin Ringel, "Möglichkeiten der Selbsmordverhütung," *Kriminalistik* 19 (1965): 521–26.

36. A. Racine, "Rôle des loisirs dans l'étiologie de la délinquance juvénile," in *Loisirs et délinquance juvenile*, ed. Centre d'Étude de la Délinquance Juvénile (Brussels:, 1966), pp. 41–45.

37. Centre d'Étude de la Délinquance Juvénile, Bruxelles, "A Study of Suicide by Children and Adolescents," *International Bibliography on Crime and Delinquency* 3 (1965): 195.

38. Belgian Ministry of Justice, "A Study of Families Who Have Lost Parental Rights due to Court Contact," *International Bibliography on Crime and Delinquency* 3 (1966): 182.

39. Council of Europe, *International Exchange of Information on Current Criminological Research*, vol. 14, project 250.

40. Ibid., project 255.

41. Ibid., project 256.

42. Franz Petersohn, "Les lésions cérébrales criminogènes," *International Annals of Criminology* 2 (1964): 373–89.

43. P. R. Bize and M. Duguet, "Étude comparative de la psychomotricité à l'aide d'une batterie de tests instrumentaux appliqués à une population de délinquants, une population pathologique et des population normales," *Annales de Vaucresson* 2 (1964): 3–56.

44. Jacques Hochmann, "Le faux problémé de la simulation où la relation théâtrale," in *La Relation Clinique en Milieu Penitentiare* (Paris: Masson, 1964), pp. 19–38.

45. Simone Gruner and Marie Therese Mazerol, "Atélier de peinture dans un centre d'observation pour jeunes délinquants. Étude sur un thème: une famille sur-

prise par l'orage en forêt, *Annales de Vaucresson* 2 (1965): 191–231.

46. Paul Crespy, "L'aspect sociologique du viol commis en reúnion," *Revue de Science Criminelle et de Droit Pénal Comparé* 20 (1965): 837–66.

47. V. V. Stanciu, "Les incidences de l'entessement dans le logement sur la criminalité," *Études Internationales de Psycho-Sociologie Criminelle* 9–10 (1965): 17–27.

48. Council of Europe, *International Exchange of Information on Current Criminological Research*, vol. 14, project 264.

49. Heribert Waider, "Grenzbereiche der Geheimbundelei, "Zeitschrift für die gesamte Strafrechtswissenschaft 77 (1966): 579–633.

50. Heinz Zipf, "Zur Ausgestaltung der Geldstrafe im kommenden Recht," *Zeitschrift für die gesamte Strafrechswissenschaft* 77 (1966): 526–62.

51. Karl Leonhard, "Mord aus Hassliebe," *Monatsschrift für Kriminologie und Strafrechtsreform* 49 (1967): 9–17.

52. Berlin Landesjungendamt, "A Study of Group Sex Offenses by Juveniles in Germany," *International Bibliography on Crime and Delinquency* 3 (1965): 158.

53. Johannes Guttenberg University, Germany, "Study of the Problems Which Arise when a Parent Is in Prison," *International Bibliography on Crime and Delinquency* 3 (1965): 192.

54. Hans-Joachim Van Schumann, *Homosexualität und Selbstmord*, (Hamburg: Kriminalistik Verlag, 1965).

55. A. Ohm, *Personlichkeitswandlungen unter Freiheitsentzug. Auswirkungen von Strafen und Massnahman* (Berlin: Walter de Gruyter, 1964).

56. Ibid., pp. 97–133.

57. Ibid., pp. 135–61.

58. Karl Kiehne, "Das Flammenwerferattentat in Köln-Volkhaven," *Archiv für Kriminologie* 136 (1965): 67–75.

59. Wilfried Rasch, *Totung des Intimpartners* (Stuttgart: Enke Verlag, 1964).

60. Hans von Hentig, "Mordwaffen in der homophilen Sphäre," *Archiv für Kriminologie* 135 (1965): 122–29.

61. Franz Marcus, "Enheblicher Ruckgang der Jugendkriminalitat vor dem zweiten Weltkrieg?" *Monatsschrift für Kriminologie und Strafrechtsreform* 48 (1964): 298–99.

62. Herbert Kosyra, "Mord aus Rache," *Archiv für Kriminologie*, 134 (1964): 148–50.

63. W. Maresch, "Selbstmorde durch rektale Applikation von Schlafmittein," *Archiv für Kriminologie*, 134 (1964): 172–77.

64. Clemens Amelunxen, *"Politische Strafater"* (Hamburg: Verlag Kriminalistik, 1964).

65. Aldo Semerari et al., "A Case of the Crime of Passion in Italy," *Acta Criminologiae et Medicinae Legalis Japonica* 32 (1966): 41–51.

66. F. Mattarazzo, "La vigilanza moral attraverso una inchiesta presso ospitia di instituti di privenzione e di pena," *Rassegna di Studi Penitenziari* 15 (1965): 167–86.

67. L. Aucona and M. Fontanesi, "La dinamica della aggressivita in un gruppo di criminali," *Quaderni di Criminologia Clinica* 7 (1965).

68. Milos Kobal, "Prefontal Leucotomy in Delinquents Who Are Habitual Swallowers of Metal Objects," *International Annals of Criminology* 2 (1965): 341–46.

69. Council of Europe, *International Exchange of Information on Current Criminological Research Projects in Member States*, vol. 8 (Strasbourg, 1969).

70. Ibid., project 399.

71. S. Binder, "Zur seelichen Entwicklung zurechnungsunfaehiger Sexual verbrecher nach der Kastration," *Monatsschrift für Kriminologie und Strafrachtsreform* 52 (1969): 73–83.

72. Council of Europe, *International Exchange of Information on Current Criminological Research*, vol. 8, project 400.

73. R. Luthe "Über Totungsdelikte bei Latenter Schizophrenie," *Monatsschrift für Kriminologie und Strafrechtsreform* 52 (1969): 91–109.

74. Clarita Dames, "Die Kriminogene Bedeutüng hirnorganischer Schaden oder Storungen," *Vorträge in Landeskriminalpolizeiamt Niedersachen* 5 (1968): 26–37.

75. G. Wunder, "Zur Situation der Bewahrungshelfer: Allgemeiner zur Arbeitssituation der Bewahrungshelferinnen," *Bewahrungshelfer* 16 (1969): 91–107.

76. Gunther Kraupl, "Der Einfluss sozial fehlentwickelter Jugendlicher auf die Enstehung, Entwicklung, Struktur und Funktion krimineller Gruppen 14–25 jahriger," *Staat und Recht* 18 (1968): 63–76.

77. Gerhard Mueller, "The Function of Criminology in Criminal Justice Administration," *Abstracts of Criminology and Penology* 9 (1969): 577–90.

78. Ibid., p. 582.

79. Nils Christie, "Comparative Criminology," *Canadian Journal of Corrections* 12 (1970): 40–46.

80. Ibid.

81. Inkeri Anttila, "Criminological Research in Finland," in *Seventh Conference of Directors of Criminological Research Institutes* ed. Council of Europe (Strasbourg: 1969), p. 3.

82. Patrik Törnudd, "Search for Causes—The Cul-de-Sac of Criminology," *Sosiologia* 3 (1969).

83. Paavo Usitalo, *White Collar Crimes and Status Selectivity in the Law Enforcement System* (Helsinki: Institute of Sociology, 1969).

84. Patrik Törnudd, "Fylleribote som kriminalpolitisky problem," *Alkoholpolitik* 1 (1967).

85. Patrik Törnudd, "Search for Causes," p. 2.

86. Ibid., p. 2.

87. Klaus Mäkela, "Public Sense of Justice and Judicial Practice," *Acta Sociologica* 10 (1966).

88. Patrik Törnudd, "Search for Causes," p. 2.

89. Paavo Usitalo, *Vankila ja työsürtola rangaistuksens* (Helsinki: 1968).

90. Patrik Törnudd, "Search for Causes," p. 2.

91. Ibid., p. 2.

92. Sweden Correctional Administration, *Kriminalvarden 1968* (Stockholm: 1969).

93. Patrik Törnudd, "Search for Causes," p. 2.

94. Ibid., p. 3.

SOURCES OF ARTICLES

1. Reprinted from the *Annals of the American Academy of Political and Social Science* 423 (January 1976): 31–46.
2. Reprinted from *Task Force Report: Juvenile Delinquency and Youth Crime*, Report on Juvenile Justice and Consultants' Papers, Task Force on Juvenile Delinquency—The President's Commission on Law Enforcement and Administration of Justice. (Washington, D.C.: U.S. Government Printing Office, 1967), App. H, pp. 132–44.
3. "Youth Crime in Postindustrial Societies: An Integrated Perspective," by Paul C. Friday and Jerald Hage is reprinted from *Criminology* 14, no. 3 (November 1976): 347–68 by permission of the publisher, Sage Publications, Inc.
4. Reprinted from *International Journal of Comparative Sociology* 12 (March, 1971): 1–23.
5. Reprinted from *International Annals of Criminology* 16, nos. 1 and 2 (1977): 109–39.
6. Reprinted from *Annals of the American Academy of Political and Social Science* 434 (November 1977): 114–36.
7. Reprinted from *Journal of Social History* 8, no. 4 (1974), pp. 117–41.
8. Reprinted from Report of the Secretary-General, *Crime Prevention and Control* (September 22, 1977) pp. 3–4, 6–19, 25–32, 34.
10. Reprinted from the *Journal of Abnormal and Social Psychology* 66, no. 4, 291–300. Copyrighted 1963 by the American Psychological Association. Reprinted with permission.
11. Reprinted from *International Annals of Criminology* 12, nos. 1 and 2 (1973): 61–73.
12. Reprinted with the permission of the author from *The Polish Sociological Bulletin* 4 (1976): 47–61.
13. Originally published under the same name in the Crime and Delinquency monograph series of the Center for Studies of Crime and Delinquency, National Institute of Mental Health.

INDEX

Index

1900–1902, 135; on women and, 17; women as victims of, 14
Assault and battery, 123, 125, 134–35
Attachments, attenuated, 44, 49, 54–55
Attitudes, boys', 57, 66–72, 186
Australia, juvenile delinquency in, 172–73
Austria, arrest, larceny, and fraud statistics for, 11–12
Automobile ownership, 21
Automobile theft. *See* Theft, automobile
Authority, parental, in Japan, 22
Autonomy, adolescent, 35–36

Babeav, M. M., research of, 147, 149
Baltics, crime patterns in the, 148–49
Bank robbery. *See* Robbery, bank
Beccaria, Cesare, research of, 222
Behavior, criminal, 104–6, 112–13, 121, 175; dating, attitudes of Swiss and Canadian boys toward, 68–72; delinquent, 39, 51; deviant, 84, 119; illegal, 118; masculine, 73, 76; pathological, 83; police, 10
Belfast, homicide rates of, 94
Belgium, research projects on juvenile delinquency in, 218, 224
Bell, Daniel, 104
Bernard, Jessie, 60–61
Blishen Occupational Class Scale, 59
Bombay, India, homicide rates in, 91, 93
"Borderline secret societies," 225
Boston, Mass., homicide study for, 86, 91, 93
Boys, 63, 65, 71–76
Breaking and entering, 114
Bronner, A. F., 182
Brown, Private, 191
Buffalo, N.Y., homicide study for, 86, 91, 93
Burglary, 1, 107–8, 116
Burma, female arrest statistics for, 11, 12

Canada: April 1963 data on boys in, 57; crimes of violence and drugs compared to the United States, 11; on criminal justice personnel in, 173; family structure in, 59; level of affluence in, 21; on middle-class delinquency in, xxii–xxiii; students com-

pared with Swiss students, 61–63; youth in, xxv–xxvi, 49, 56
Cannibalism, 198
Canton Graubunden, Switzerland, 57, 61
Capital punishment, 117, 196, 232
Capital Punishment Commission of 1865, 194
Car thefts. *See* Theft, automobile
Casparis, John, 49
Caste system, in Polish juvenile institutions, 202
Chicago, Ill., study of gang activities in, 54
Child, L. L., 186
Children, 1, 175, 179, 181–82
Children of Bondage, 180
Chimpira gang (Japanese), 22–24
Christie, Nils, 219, 220, 230
Chur, Switzerland, as used in comparative study, 57
City (cities): as centers of crime and violence, 82–83; and disorder, 120; effect of population size on crime in the, 86–87; growth of, 92–95; homicide rates in, 90, 98
Civel (Polish prison term), status of, 208
Civilization, as an accomplice of crime, 42
Civil strife. *See* Crime; Disorder
Clinard, M. B., 49, 52, 84, 147–49
Coleman, J., quoted on adolescent society, 47
Collective farm workers, mobility of, 143–44
Colombo City, homicide rates for, 94
Committals, to trial per 1,000. *See* Trial, committals to, per 1,000 population
Comparative Crime Data File (CCDF), 41, 44, 81–83, 88, 91–99
Compulsive stealing. *See* Stealing
Conduct, 64–65, 112–13
Conflict, cities produce class, cultural and racial, 83
Conflicts, culture, 41, 200
Consumers, offenses against, 164
Conviction rates, 109, 113–14
Convictions: on decline of, 106–10; men and women, examinations of, 11–13; nineteenth-century decline in, 116, 117; per 1,000 population, 105–6; rates of, 109, 113–14; statis-

Index

tics during nineteenth century for, 108; for theft and violence, 111

Convicts, transportation of, 110

Correctional Administration of Sweden, 233–34

Correctional system, as means to confine crime, xxxi

Correlates, general, 177

Corruption, 154, 156

Council of Europe, 218, 219, 220, 221, 227–28

Counterfeiting, 1, 9–10

Court records, use of, 122, 126–27

Credit, criminal, abuse of, 229

Crime: academic response to, xxxiii; adolescent, xxiii, 18, 54, 55; affluence as material basis for, 21, 33, 41; assessments of, 164; comparative study of, xxv; control and prevention of, 40, 154–55, 164–65, 230; cost of, 42; defined as covert behavior, 104; detection of, through citizen complaints, 115; increased women's participation in, 16; on legal definitions of, xxvi-xxvii; as a major world problem, 154; political, 157; official data on, 105–6; organized, 173; origins of, 81; passional, 192; patterns of, 48, 128, 131; in preliterate societies, xxviii; rates of, 18, 105, 115, 123–24, 137; records, 121–22; as related to colored persons, 26; research, xxv, xxxiii, 219–20, 222–34 passim; sex motivated, 122–23, 198; and society, xx–xxi, xxiv, xxv, xxviii–xxxii; statistics, 11, 104, 121, 151; study of, xix; on the switch in economic correlates of, 138; trends in, 113–16; urban, 82–87, 141, 143; violent, 1; world, 153, 158. See also Convictions; Disorder; Juvenile delinquency and crime

Crime in Developing Countries, 147, 148

Criminal and noncriminal norms, youth exposure to, 48–49

Criminal behavior. See Behavior, criminal

Criminality: contribution by juveniles to total, 18; dynamics of, xix; and educational accomplishment, 38–39; emphasis on social and political order of

society to, xx; on explanations of, xxvii–xxviii; female, trends in, 1; impact of social forces on, xxxiii; and integration in interaction system of the community, 52; on isolation of social and familial influences, xxxii; level of, xxvi; parental status and, 40; sexual differences in, xxix; social forces shape the extent and form of, xxxiv; study of, xxi; universal explanation of, xxii; variables effect on, xxiii–xxiv

Criminal justice. See Justice, criminal

Criminal justice system. See Justice systems, criminal

Criminal phenomenology. See Phenomenology, criminal

"Criminogenic cerebral injuries" (French study), 224–25

Criminologica Foundation, Amsterdam, Holland, 218

"Criminological aspects of installment buying" (Belgian study), 224

Criminological theory, international application of, xx

Criminologists, on society and crime patterns, xxi

Criminology, comparative: based on a social explanation of crime, xx–xxi; field research in, xxii; methods and the problems associated with, xxviii–xxxiv; on the relationship between social, political, and economic conditions and crime, xix–xx; research problems of, xxiv; study of, xix–xx

Criminology, European, study of, xxvi

Criminology, world, xx

Critchley, MacDonald, 199, 200

Cultural differentiation, material basis for, 41

Culture, lower-class, and delinquency, 178

Culture, teenage. See Culture, youth

Culture, youth: among upper middle-class Canadian and Swiss boys, 56–77 passim; differential engagement in the, 66; effect of social and economic change in Canada, 59–63; phenomenon of, 41; prominence of, 60; transition from childhood to adulthood, 35–36; values, attitudes, and styles of behavior of the, 76–77

Index

male victims of, 15; 1970 through 1975 survey on, 155; rate of increase of, 162, 173; study of theft by, 219–20
Feminine identification, 177, 178, 181
Feminism, militant, 3
Ferdinand, T., study of homicide in Boston, 86
Ferracuti, Franco, study of, 146, 221
Feuds, kinship, 90
Fighting, 67–68, 72, 74, 76, 77
Finland, study based on alcoholic offenders in, 232
Firearms, illicit trade in, 157, 172. *See also* Gun control laws
Forgery, 1, 9–10, 11, 16, 108
Frajerzy (suckers, "cad," slaves or slumsy). *See* Poland, juvenile institutions
France: arson rates in, 123; court records of crime rates for, 124; crime and industrialization studied in, 131; criminal behavior study in, xxxi; effect of industrialization and urbanization on crime in, 86, 127–28, 131, 132, 136; female arrest statistics for, 11–12; increase in theft rates in, 126–35; ratio of crime decline between 1826 and the 1930s, 118
Fraud, 9–11, 16, 108–9, 157, 163
Freud, Sigmund, theory of paranoia of, 187
Friday, P. C., 47, 49, 53–54
Friedenberg, E. Z., views on youth and society, 47
Frustration: methods of dealing with, 139, 140

Gambling, and the youth of Israel, 27
Gangs, youth, 36, 43, 53, 72, 180–81. *See also* Sweden, juvenile gangs in
Germany: arson rates in, 123; automobile ownership in, 21; conviction statistics for, 134; court records of crime rates for, 124; criminal behavior study in, xxxi; criminology in, 220; rates for assault and battery increased in, 135–36; sex offenders in, 226, 228; theft-violence ratio and urbanism in, 127–28, 129–30, 132, 134
Glasgow, homicide rates for, 94
Glueck, Eleanor, 2, 179, 183
Glueck, S., 2, 179, 183

Goddard, Lord Chief Justice, 197
Gollancz, Victor (quoted), 198
Great Britain: crime in, 11–12, 19, 26, 35
Green, Daniel, 2–3
Greeno, Edward (chief inspector of Scotland Yard), 195
Grypserka (secret code), importance of, to Polish boys, 204
Gun control laws, 80

Hage, J., research study of, on post industrial societies, 45
Haltzendorff, V., opinion of, on criminal justice, 194
Hanratty, James, criminal case of, 195
Happy (Yemenite adolescent), case study of, 26–28
Harris, Emily, 17
Health, as a factor in crime, xxiii, 168
Healy, W., study by, 182
Helsinki, Finland, crime in, 94, 231
Henry, Andrew F., study of, on homicide, 80
Hijacking, 164, 171
Hindelang, M. J., study of, on crime correlates, 49, 55
Hirschi, T., study of, on juvenile delinquency, 44, 48, 54–55
Homicide: coefficients for, for Germany and France, 135; criminal, 1, 13, 15–16; culpable, 194; female arrests for, 9, 10, 17; intentional, 157–59, 161, 163, 167; lack of information for research on, 79; national data statistics on, 15; patterns of, 165; reliable indices on crimes of, 122; in rural areas, 85–86; social origins, and rates of, 79–80, 81, 82, 87; study of, xxx; United States and Great Britain data on, 78; increase of, in urban areas, 95–99; use of, as index of violence, 126; variance in rates of, 1900–1902, 135; various definitions for, 123
Homicide Act of 1957, 194
Homosexuality, 113, 206, 214, 226
Hostility, objects of, 139
Household, classifications of, 178, 179, 180
Housing, 152
House of Lords, participation of, in the case of August Sangret, 193

Index

Index

Resentment and criminal development, 192

Residence, permission for, required in the U.S.S.R., 143

Rights, defendants', expansion of, 116

Riots, 120

Rivalry, 186

Road Devils (Swedish gang), 30

Robbery: an acquisition crime, 108; bank, 123; decrease in, by countries, 157; increase of, 19, 159, 161, 163; male offenders in, 15; ratio of male-female victims in, 16; regional analysis for, 167; restrictions on persons convicted of, 144; time series rates for period 1900–1970 for, 81; women as victims of, 14; women in, 1–17

Robins, L. N., study of, on problem children, 179

Robison, Sophia M., 175

Rogler, L. H., study of criminality in Puerto Rico, 52

Rohrer, J. H., study of, on effect of matriarchal household on children, 180

Role relationships, five major patterns of, 44

Royal Commission, recommendations of, 192

Royal Marine Camp, Hankley Common, England, 189

Royal Prerogative of Mercy, 194

R.S.F.S.R., study of, on Soviet migrants and crime, 146–48

Rural life, characteristics of, 83, 139

Sack, Fritz, 220

Sacred Fire, The Story of Sex and Religion, The, 199

Sangret, August, case history of, xxxiii, 195–200

Scandinavia, criminology in countries in, xxvii, 229–34

Scandinavian Research Council for Criminology, 218, 221

Scholarship, in criminology, need for, xxiv, 61–62

School: as contributor to delinquency, 50; attendance ratio, 165; in Canada and Switzerland, 66–67; extracurricular activities of Canadian youth in, 61–62; important in socialization of the young, 59–60

Scotland, crimes in, 11, 19, 194

Scotland Yard, 195

Security, maximum, 183, 208

Seeley, John, study of, on Canadian boys, 65

Segregation, residential, 139

Self, and role relationships, 49

Self-reliance, in childhood, 182

Sellin, Thorsten, 200

Senility, 193

Separation, marital. See Divorce and separation

Sex crimes. See Crime, sex motivated

Sex differential, scale of the, 2

Sexual deviation, and phimosis, 224

Sexual experience, attitude of adolescents toward, 71

Sexual identification, 178

Short, James F., Jr., study of, on homicide, 80

Slum neighborhood. See Neighborhood, slum

Singapore, law enforcement agencies of, 169

Six Great Advocates (Birkett), 196

Smith, Adam (quoted), 83

Smuggling, 169, 171, 172

Social behavior, in the nineteenth century, xxxi

Social change, forms of, xxx, xxxi

Social class, xxiii

Social class structure, effect on youth crime, 43

Social conflict, expressions of, 139

Social control, 144, 183

Social development, crime trends in relationship to, xxxi

Social disorganization, 137, 139

Socialist society, crimes unique to, 142

Socialization, 44, 61, 177–78, 181, 183

Social movement, by women, 2

Social order, changing, xix, 35, 175

Social phenomenon, crime as a, xxxii

Social status, as prime variable, 231

Social stratification, theft in relationship to, 183

Social structure, as basis for homicide, 82

Society: and crime, xix, xxi, xxiv, xxviii, xxxii, 187–88, 229; mores of, xxvi; preliterate, sampling of the, 176; post-industrial, structural conditions in,

Index

44; urban industrial, and criminal adolescence, 33
Sociology, urban, tenets of, 85
Sorcery, belief in, 176, 187
Spain, on automobile ownership in, 21
Spearman-Brown correction formula, 176
Speculation, crimes of, 142
Statistics, crime, xxvii, 122, 150, 155, 156
Stealing, 53–54, 55, 108, 183
Stockholm, Sweden: convictions for theft in, 114; crime data similar to London pattern, 109–10; crime survey on petty and serious offenses, 108; population growth and crime decline in, 106–7, 119; on police force in, 114–15; free legal services in, 116; increase in crime rates for, 103
Stolen goods. See Stealing
Subcultures, 47, 83, 206–7, 211–13
Subsistence, level of, as related to crime, 137, 138
Suburbanization, 21, 139
Suburbs, victimized by urban offenders, 151
Suicide: altruistic, 54, 55; in Belgium, 224; cross-cultural study for, 176; by Japanese, 227; studies on, in America, 223
Suicide (Durkheim), 44
Supervision, parental, 63
Sutherland, E. H., work of, on youth crime, 55
Sweden: delinquency in, 25–26, 28; industrialization and the family in, 34; juvenile gangs in, 28–29; level of affluence in, 21; national control of police forces in, 114; purchasing power of adolescents in, 35; raggare gangs in, 29; ratio of criminal conviction rates for boys and completion of education, 38–39; study of narcotic offenders in, 233–34; thefts by adolescents in, 54; vocational training in correctional institutions, 228; youth crime in, 43
Switzerland: authority vested with families in, 61; basis for socioeconomic position of boys in, 58; comparative study of youth culture in, 49; on craftsmen and artisans of, 61; data on

boys in, 56–58; middle-class delinquency in, xxii–xxiii; ratio of youth enrolled in schools in, 61; study of crime patterns in, 223; youth offenders in, xxiii
Sydney, Australia, crime in, 103, 106–7, 110

Tarde, Gabriel, study of, on crime, 222
Tax evasion, 164
Teacher, multiplicity of roles of a, 59–60
Teenage culture. See Culture, youth
Teenagers, 59, 60–61, 67–70, 71
Terrorism, 164
Thailand, female arrest statistics for, 11, 12
Theft: automobile, 1, 27, 29, 72, 233; a capital offense, 196; changing laws of, in England, Sweden, and New South Wales, 113; correlates of, 134, 177, 179, 181–87; crime problem related to, 19; cross-cultural ratings for, 176–77; decrease in, 106, 157; fencing of stolen property from, 28; frequency of, 182, 187–88; high overall rates for years 1970–75, 161; increase in, 118, 119, 122, 158, 159, 163; rates serve as index of property crimes, 126; lack of identification of son with father as basis for, 188; by Lappen, 30; as the major German property crime, 125; petty, and grand, 76, 77; ratio data between London and Stockholm, 110; as related to the level of political integration, 183; reliable indices on, 123; social status and degree of, xxxii; in Stockholm, 109; study of, by adolescent as related to family, to school, 49; time series rates for, 81; from tourists, 172; study of, in Germany, 126–36; and women, 9
Thorp, Linton Theodore, 196
Tilly, C., study of, on crimes against the person, 86
Time-series indices, 135
Time-series studies, 136
Toby, J., study of, on delinquency, 52, 62
Tokyo, Japan, decline of homicide rates in, with city growth, 90, 92, 94
Törnudd, Patrick, 230–31

271